Corporate Communication
A Guide to Theory and Practice

3rd Edition

Joep Cornelissen

⑤SAGE

Los Angeles | London | New Delhi
Singapore | Washington DC

First edition published 2004
Second edition published 2008
Third edition first published 2011

SAGE Publications Ltd
1 Oliver's Yard
55 City Road
London EC1Y 1SP

SAGE Publications Inc.
2455 Teller Road
Thousand Oaks, California 91320

SAGE Publications India Pvt Ltd
B 1/I 1 Mohan Cooperative Industrial Area
Mathura Road
New Delhi 110 044

SAGE Publications Asia-Pacific Pte Ltd
33 Pekin Street #02-01
Far East Square
Singapore 048763

Library of Congress Control Number: 2010935164

British Library Cataloguing in Publication data

A catalogue record for this book is available from the British Library

ISBN 978-0-85702-242-4
ISBN 978-0-85702-243-1 (pbk)

Typeset by C&M Digitals (P) Ltd, Chennai, India
Printed in Great Britain by MPG Books Group, Bodmin, Cornwall
Printed on paper from sustainable resources

SUMMARY OF CONTENTS

CONTENTS

LIST OF FIGURES

LIST OF TABLES

LIST OF CASE STUDIES

PREFACE TO THE THIRD EDITION

The world of business is constantly changing. Since the previous editions of the book, there have been a number of high-profile scandals in the corporate world, including WorldCom, Enron and Martha Stewart Living. Besides such scandals, many multinational corporations have also had a rough time in communication and reputation terms. Consider, Wal-Mart, for example, which for many years was seen as a company that had grown from very humble beginnings and had excelled in a very effective market expansion and low-cost growth strategy. Wal-Mart has recently been heavily criticized for its aggressive competitive tactics and for the way in which it engages with, and cares for, important stakeholder groups, such as employees and members of the local communities in which the company operates. While such expectations for stakeholder engagement and collaboration are not new, current global issues, such as climate change and the credit crisis, have heightened these expectations. Stakeholders also increasingly demand insight and information from companies. The new media landscape has added further pressures, with everyone communicating about companies and with critical journalists zealously looking for gaps, contradictions and discrepancies in corporate messages. Decisions and actions of companies are increasingly put under the microscope.

While the environment for companies is constantly changing, the central message across these trends is clear: executives and practitioners within organizations need to be empowered with a way of thinking and with tools that can help them navigate the current corporate landscape in which reputations have become more fragile and stakeholders have become more demanding. The basic idea underlying the book, therefore, is to equip the reader with an understanding of the concepts and tools of corporate communication.

PURPOSE OF THE BOOK

This book is about corporate communication. Its chief aim is to provide a comprehensive and up-to-date treatment of the subject of corporate communication. The book incorporates current thinking and developments on the topic from both the academic and practitioner worlds, combining a comprehensive theoretical foundation with numerous practical guidelines and insights to assist managers in their day-to-day affairs and in their strategic and tactical communication decisions. Illustrative examples and case studies are based on companies in the USA, the UK, continental Europe, South-East Asia and Australia, and elsewhere.

Thus, in a comprehensive and practical manner, the book provides insights into the nature of corporate communication, the issues that define this critical area of practice, the strategies and activities that fall within its remit, and the ways in which it can be managed and organized in companies. Specifically, the reader will learn about the following:

- the nature of corporate communication, its historical emergence and its role in contemporary companies;
- the critical role of the corporate communication function in building and maintaining relationships with the stakeholders of a company;
- the key issues – corporate social responsibility, reputation management, corporate branding, corporate 'identity', integrated communication – that dominate the function, and how to deal with them;
- different approaches to developing corporate communication strategies and to implementing communication programmes and campaigns;
- different approaches to measuring and monitoring the impact of communication upon stakeholders' opinions and on the company's reputation;
- the key activities and skills in specific disciplines and emerging areas of practice, including media relations, issues management and public affairs, crisis communication, internal communication and community relations.

APPROACH OF THE BOOK

For the third edition of the book, the aim was to satisfy three key criteria by which any management text can be judged:

- *Depth*: the material in the book needed to be comprehensive in covering both the academic and practitioner literatures and knowledge base on corporate communication.
- *Breadth*: the book had to cover all the topics that define the field of corporate communication and that practising managers and students of corporate communication management find important or of interest.
- *Relevance*: the book had to be well grounded in practice and easily related to past and present practical examples and case studies.

Although a number of books have been written on corporate communication in recent years, no book has really maximized these three dimensions to the best possible extent. Accordingly, this book sets out to fill that gap by accomplishing three things.

First, instead of being solely based on practitioner experiences and anecdotes or case-based learning, the book also provides an evidence-based account of corporate communication by drawing upon theories, models and concepts from academic research.

Second, all the contemporary and important themes and topics within the remit of corporate communication, including 'corporate social responsibility' and 'stakeholder management', are discussed in detail. Particular attention is paid to central topics, such as the structuring of the communication function within organizations and the development of communication strategy and programmes – these have received little attention in other books.

Third, the book not only presents the latest academic thinking and research on the subject, but also features case studies and shorter case examples to illustrate the concepts and themes of the book and to meet the 'double hurdle' of rigour and relevance.

For the third edition, all the case studies and topics have been updated. The range of cases covered now also has a better spread around the world. New sections on specialist disciplines and new areas of interest within corporate communication, such as new media technologies and leadership and change communication, have been added. Based on feedback from lecturers and students, the book spells out in greater detail some of the key concepts and contemporary developments in corporate communication with more figures and tables throughout the text.

In summary, by combining theory and research with practical cases and examples, the third edition of the book provides a comprehensive, practically grounded and up-to-date overview of the state and playing field of this area of practice within organizations. Critical issues in managing corporate communication are discussed, providing practising managers with appropriate concepts, theories and tools to enable them to make better management and communication decisions. Readers will gain a greater appreciation and a better in-depth understanding of the range of topics covered in corporate communication as well as a means to organize their thoughts on those topics.

READERSHIP OF THE BOOK

A wide range of people can benefit from reading this book, including the following groups:

- Students at the graduate level enrolled on a business, management, marketing, corporate communication, public relations, or business communication course interested in increasing their understanding of the theory and practice of corporate communication.
- Managers and analysts with a professional interest in the area of corporate communication (and with responsibility for a slice of the corporate communications cake), who are concerned with making informed decisions that will maximize their day-to-day performance.
- Senior executives looking for an understanding of corporate communication and what it can do for their business.
- Academics researching and reading in the areas of corporate communication, public relations, marketing and strategic management looking for a resource guide that contains the themes and development of corporate communication in a single volume.

ORGANIZATION OF THE BOOK

As mentioned, the aim of this book is to present an overview of the theory and practice of corporate communication. The distinction made between the 'theory' and 'practice' of corporate communications is intentional and implies that the book aims to draw out and integrate theoretical accounts of the development of corporate communication with more hands-on, practice-based insights and skills from the profession. In the book, I also take the view that corporate communication is a field of management within organizations, and that not only our understanding of it but also the development of the field (as both a discipline and practice) is best served by a management spectre. This means that alternative perspectives on corporate communication, such as the critical, rhetorical and mass communication accounts that consider the role and effect of communication at the level of society, are included in the book's ruminations on the field, yet are considered of secondary importance in view of the core management perspective and theme of the book.

Adopting this management perspective, the book is laid out in five parts:

Part 1,   *Introduction to Corporate Communication* provides a characterization of the historical and practical roots of the field of corporate communication, and defines the role and use of corporate communication in contemporary organizations.

Part 2,   *Conceptual Foundations* includes two chapters on the key concepts of stakeholder, corporate identity and corporate reputation as well as communication models that provide the theoretical background to the practice of corporate communication.

Part 3,   *Corporate Communication in Practice* includes three chapters that focus on the development of communication strategy and planning, the development of corporate advertising and issue-specific campaigns, and on research and the measurement of communication effects.

Part 4,   *Specialist Areas in Corporate Communication* covers important specialist areas within the remit of corporate communication: media relations and public affairs, internal communication, issues management and crisis communication.

Part 5,   *New Developments in Corporate Communication* involves chapters on important and emerging areas of practice within corporate communication, including change and leadership communication and corporate social responsibility (CSR) programmes and community relations.

The chapters in each part include case studies and case examples and a list of sources for further reading. At the tail end of the book, the reader will find a glossary of key communication terminology that may be useful as a quick reference to the main concepts in corporate communication.

Joep Cornelissen
Leeds, August 2010

ABOUT THE AUTHOR

Joep Cornelissen is a Professor in Corporate Communication at VU University Amsterdam and Leeds University Business School, and previously taught at the Amsterdam School of Communications Research, the University of Amsterdam. He currently teaches corporate communication and organization theory on MA and MBA programmes in Leeds and Amsterdam. Besides his teaching commitments, he is also an active researcher within the fields of communication and management and a General Editor of the *Journal of Management Studies*, one of the leading academic journals on management. He frequently speaks at conferences and uses his management and communication expertise to work with entrepreneurs and managers in private and public organizations.

GUIDED TOUR

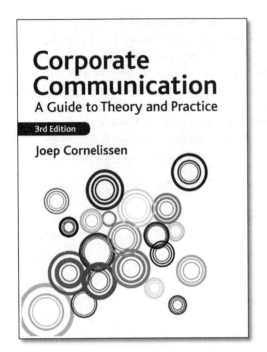

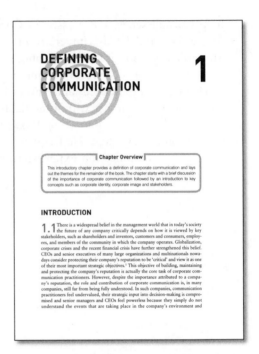

Chapter overview: A very brief synopsis of each chapter is provided.

Introduction: The introduction provides the overall framework of each chapter.

Example: Corporate communication topics are illustrated with full, real life examples.

Case study: Each chapter contains an international case study, accompanied by questions designed for reflective learning and the reinforcement of key concepts.

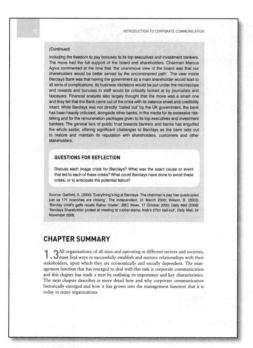

Chapter summary: We review the main concepts and issues to be sure that you are clear on what was covered, and why.

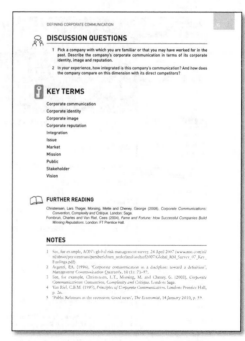

Discussion questions: Questions are provided at the end of each chapter to encourage you to explore what you have learnt.

Key terms: Each chapters' key terms are listed here and in the glossary at the back of the book, which covers all of the book's key concepts.

Further reading: Relevant articles and book chapters will enhance your understanding of each chapter.

COMPANION WEBSITE

Be sure to visit the companion website at http://www.sagepub.co.uk/cornelissen3e to find a range of teaching and learning materials for both lecturers and students, including the following:

For lecturers:

- **Instructor's manual**: Contains overviews of every chapter, along with materials to support lecturer's seminar and class teaching.
- **PowerPoint slides**: PowerPoint slides for each chapter for use in class are also provided.
- **Additional case studies**: These additional case studies will provide further teaching support.

For students:

- **Full-text journal articles**: Full access to selected SAGE journal articles provides students with a deeper understanding of the topics in each chapter.
- **Glossary**: A glossary of key terms and definitions is available online.
- **Links to relevant websites**: Direct links to relevant websites for each chapter are provided.
- **Video material**: Students can download a collection of videos relevant to the key themes and hot topics covered in the textbook directly from the site.
- **Study Skills**: This bank of downloadable chapters from existing SAGE books is packed with ideas to aid effective study.

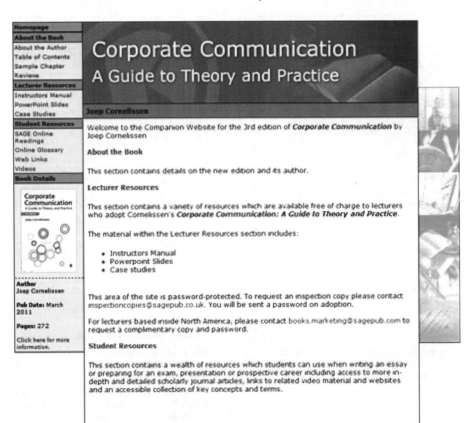

ACKNOWLEDGEMENTS

In writing this book, I have had a lot of help and encouragement from corporate communication colleagues and practitioners around Europe. I have also benefited from the wisdom of colleagues and graduate students at the various institutions with which I have been associated. I would also like to thank my reviewers:

Chris Aalberts, Erasmus University Rotterdam
Jane Crofts, University of Lincoln
Dale Cyphert, University of Northern Iowa
Nigel de Bussy, Curtin University of Technology
Sasha Grant, The University of Texas at Arlington
Kim Johnston, Queensland University of Technology
Gary Lunt, Edinburgh Napier University
Mohammed Mirza, University of Huddersfield
Irene Pollach, University of Aarhus
Peggy Simcic Bronn, Norwegian School of Management
Graham Spickett-Jones, University of Hull
Gyorgy Szondi, Leeds Metropolitan University
Kaja Tampere, University of Jyväskylä
Kati Tusinski Berg, Marquette University
Mary Welch, Lancashire Business School, University of Central Lancashire
Jennifer Ziegler, Valparaiso University

They, together with my students, have tested the ideas in their classrooms and companies and have given me feedback and inspiration to improve the current text. At Sage, Delia Alfonso has been a friend and supporter for years, and without her this book would have never been written. Finally, as always, I would like to thank Mirjam for allowing me to be a bit less social while I was writing the book and to work yet again on another project.

INTRODUCTION TO CORPORATE COMMUNICATION

1

In Part 1, we explore the historical development of communication within organizations, describe why corporate communication emerged and demonstrate the importance of corporate communication to contemporary organizations. The basic characteristics of corporate communication are described *vis-à-vis* related concepts such as marketing communication and public relations.

After reading Part 1, the reader should be familiar with the basic characteristics of corporate communication, its historical emergence and its relevance to contemporary organizations.

DEFINING CORPORATE COMMUNICATION

1

Chapter Overview

This introductory chapter provides a definition of corporate communication and lays out the themes for the remainder of the book. The chapter starts with a brief discussion of the importance of corporate communication followed by an introduction to key concepts such as corporate identity, corporate image and stakeholders.

INTRODUCTION

1.1 There is a widespread belief in the management world that in today's society the future of any company critically depends on how it is viewed by key stakeholders, such as shareholders and investors, customers and consumers, employees, and members of the community in which the company operates. Globalization, corporate crises and the recent financial crisis have further strengthened this belief. CEOs and senior executives of many large organizations and multinationals nowadays consider protecting their company's reputation to be 'critical' and view it as one of their most important strategic objectives.[1] This objective of building, maintaining and protecting the company's reputation is actually the core task of corporate communication practitioners. However, despite the importance attributed to a company's reputation, the role and contribution of corporate communication is, in many companies, still far from being fully understood. In such companies, communication practitioners feel undervalued, their strategic input into decision-making is compromised and senior managers and CEOs feel powerless because they simply do not understand the events that are taking place in the company's environment and how these events can affect the company's operations and profits. There is therefore a lot to gain when communication practitioners and senior managers are able to recognize and diagnose communication-related management problems and understand appropriate strategies and courses of action for dealing with these. Such an understanding is not only essential to the effective functioning of corporate communication, but it is also empowering. It allows communication practitioners and managers to understand and take charge of events that fall within the remit of corporate communication; to determine which events are outside their control, and to identify opportunities for communicating and engaging with stakeholders of the organization.

The primary goal of this book, therefore, is to give readers a sense of how corporate communication is used and managed *strategically* as a way of guiding how organizations can communicate with their stakeholders. The book combines reflections and insights from academic research and professional practice in order to provide a comprehensive overview of strategies and tactics in corporate communication. In doing so, the book aims to provide an armory of concepts, insights and tools that communication practitioners and senior managers can use in their day-to-day practice.

In this introductory chapter, I will start by describing corporate communication and will introduce the strategic management perspective that underlies the rest of the book. This perspective suggests a particular way of looking at corporate communication and indicates a number of management areas and concerns that will be covered in the remaining chapters. As the book progresses, each of these areas will be explained in detail and the strategic management perspective as a whole will become clearer. Good things will thus come to those who wait, and read.

SCOPE AND DEFINITIONS

1.2 Perhaps the best way to define corporate communication is to look at the way in which the function has developed in companies. Until the 1970s, practitioners had used the term 'public relations' to describe communication with stakeholders. This 'public relations' function, which was tactical in most companies, largely consisted of communication with the press. When other stakeholders, internal and external to the company, started to demand more information from the company, practitioners subsequently started to look at communication as being more than just 'public relations'. This is when the roots of the new corporate communication function started to take hold. This new function came to incorporate a whole range of specialized disciplines, including corporate design, corporate advertising, internal communication to employees, issues and crisis management, media relations, investor relations, change communication and public affairs.[2] An important characteristic of the new function is that it focuses on the organization as a whole and on the important task of how an organization presents itself to all its key stakeholders, both internal and external.

This broad focus is also reflected in the word 'corporate' in corporate communication. The word of course refers to the business setting in which corporate communication emerged as a separate function (alongside other functions such as human resources and finance). There is also an important second sense with which the word is being used. 'Corporate' originally stems from the Latin words for 'body' (*corpus*) and for 'forming into a body' (*corporare*), which emphasize a unified way of looking at 'internal' and 'external' communication disciplines. That is, instead of looking at specialized disciplines or stakeholder groups separately, the corporate communication function starts from the perspective of the 'bodily' organization as a whole when communicating with internal and external stakeholders.[3]

Corporate communication, in other words, can be characterized as a management function that is responsible for overseeing and coordinating the work done by communication practitioners in different specialist disciplines, such as media relations, public affairs and internal communication. Van Riel defines corporate communication as 'an instrument of management by means of which all consciously used forms of internal and external communication are harmonized as effectively and efficiently as possible', with the overall objective of creating 'a favourable basis for relationships with groups upon which the company is dependent'.[4] Defined in this way, corporate communication obviously involves a whole range of 'managerial' activities, such as planning, coordinating and counselling the CEO and senior managers in the organization as well as 'tactical' skills involved in producing and disseminating messages to relevant stakeholder groups. Overall, if a definition of corporate communication is required, these characteristics can provide a basis for one:

> Corporate communication is a management function that offers a framework for the effective coordination of all internal and external communication with the overall purpose of establishing and maintaining favourable reputations with stakeholder groups upon which the organization is dependent.

One consequence of these characteristics of corporate communication is that it is likely to be *complex in nature*. This is especially so in organizations with a wide geographical range, such as multinational corporations, or with a wide range of products or services, where the coordination of communication is often a balancing act between corporate headquarters and the various divisions and business units involved. However, there are other significant challenges in developing effective corporate communication strategies and programmes. Corporate communication demands an *integrated approach* to managing communication. Unlike a specialist frame of reference, corporate communication transcends the specialties of individual communication practitioners (e.g., branding, media relations, investor relations, public affairs, internal communication, etc.) and crosses these specialist boundaries to harness the *strategic interests of the organization at large*. Richard Edelman, CEO of Edelman, the world's largest independent PR agency, highlights the strategic role of corporate communication as follows: 'we used to be the tail on the dog, but now communication is the organizing principle behind many business decisions'.[5] The general idea is that the sustainability and success of a company depends on how it is viewed by key stakeholders, and communication is a critical part of building, maintaining and protecting such reputations. An illustration of this idea is the presence of Google in China (Case Example 1.1).

Case Example 1.1

Google and the People's Republic of China

From its founding in 1999, Google, the world's leading internet search provider, initially served Chinese internet users with a Chinese-language version of Google.com that could easily be reached by users in China. In 2002, the company learned that the site was frequently unavailable to Chinese users. Many search queries, including queries on politically sensitive issues and human rights, were also filtered out or censored. In 2006, Google then decided, after consultation with its stakeholders, to take a different strategy. The company launched a new country-specific website, Google.cn, which, while subject to Chinese self-censorship requirements, would nonetheless expand access to information for Chinese users. As Elliott Schrage, Google's Vice President for corporate communication and public affairs explained to the US government at the time, the thinking behind this was that the original strategy was largely ineffective because of lack of access and the active filtering and censorship. Besides the commercial benefits, the new site, he explained, would also contribute to Google's vision of making the world a better place.

Google's mantra is 'Don't be evil', which refers to ensuring that the company's decisions do not knowingly harm anyone. In more positive terms, the company tries to make the world a better, more informed and freer place by expanding access to information to anyone who wants it. In China, Google was also hoping to contribute to this kind of positive social change: users would be fully notified of blocked content, their privacy (including emails) would be fully protected, and they would generally be able to access all but a handful of politically sensitive subjects. The backdrop to Google's decision for launching Google.cn was the explosive growth of the internet in China. The company recognized that the internet was transforming China for the better, and as part of this development, Google.cn would help accelerate and deepen these positive trends towards social and political change. A few years later, however, in December 2009, Google announced that it would reconsider its presence in China, and that it may even pull out of the country altogether. Its server and private email accounts of users had been targeted and attacked from within China. One of the primary goals of these cyber attacks was to access the Gmail account of Chinese human rights activists. The attacks and the surveillance that they have uncovered, as well as the Chinese attempts to further limit free speech on the web, have led the company to reconsider its position. Google decided that the arrangement with Google.cn did not work and the company started to discuss with the Chinese government the possibility of operating an unfiltered search engine, if at all. Initially, the company had taken a pragmatic approach, accommodating its moral stance in the light of commercial opportunities. Despite its best communication efforts, Google got a lot of criticism for this at the time, with journalists, industry analysts, government officials and users questioning the company's ability to uphold its moral stance in the face of commercial opportunities in a fast-growing market. With the worsened situation for free speech and

(Continued)

(Continued)

the attacks on its servers, Google executives believe that its reputation with all of its stakeholders and its very identity are at stake if they continue with their current operations in China.

Source: http://googleblog.blogspot.com/2006/02/testimony-internet-in-china.html

A variety of concepts and terms are used in relation to corporate communication. Here, the chapter briefly introduces these concepts but they will be discussed in more detail in the remainder of the book. Table 1.1 lists the key concepts that readers will come across in this and other books on corporate communication and that form, so to speak, the vocabulary of the corporate communication practitioner. Table 1.1 briefly defines the concepts, and also shows how these relate to a specific organization – in this case, British Airways.

Not all of these concepts are always used in corporate communication books. Moreover, it may or may not be that mission, objectives, strategies, and so on are written down precisely and formally laid down within an organization. As will be shown in Chapter 4, a mission or corporate identity, for instance, might sometimes more sensibly be conceived as that which is implicit or can be deduced about an organization from what it is doing and communicating. However, as a general guideline, the concepts in Table 1.1 are often used in combination with one another.

TABLE 1.1   Key concepts in corporate communication

Concept	Definition	Example: British Airways*
Mission	Overriding purpose in line with the values or expectations of stakeholders	'British Airways is aiming to set new industry standards in customer service and innovation, deliver the best financial performance and evolve from being an airline to a world travel business with the flexibility to stretch its brand into new business areas'
Vision	Desired future state: the aspiration of the organization	'To become the undisputed leader in world travel by ensuring that BA is the customer's first choice through the delivery of an unbeatable travel experience'
Corporate objectives and goals	(Precise) statement of aims or purpose	'To be a good neighbour, concerned for the community and the environment', 'to provide overall superior service and good value for money in every market segment in which we compete', 'to excel in anticipating and quickly responding to customer needs and competitor activity'
Strategies	The ways or means in which the corporate objectives are to be achieved and put into effect	'Continuing emphasis on consistent quality of customer service and the delivery to the marketplace of value for money through customer-oriented initiatives (on-line booking service, strategic alliances) and to arrange all the elements of our service so that

(Continued)

TABLE 1.1   *(Continued)*

Concept	Definition	Example: British Airways*
		they collectively generate a particular experience'... 'building trust with our shareholders, employees, customers, neighbours and with our critics, through commitment to good practice and societal reporting'
Corporate identity	The profile and values communicated by an organization	'The world's favourite airline' (this corporate identity with its associated brand values of service, quality, innovation, cosmopolitanism and Britishness is carried through in positioning, design, livery, and communications)
Corporate image	The immediate set of associations of an individual in response to one or more signals or messages from or about a particular organization at a single point in time	'Very recently I got a ticket booked to London, and when reporting at the airport I was shown the door by BA staff. I was flatly told that the said flight in which I was to travel was already full so my ticket was not valid any further and the airline would try to arrange for a seat on some other flight. You can just imagine how embarrassed I felt at that moment of time. To make matters worse, the concerned official of BA had not even a single word of apology to say' (customer of BA)
Corporate reputation	An individual's collective representation of past images of an organization (induced through either communication or past experiences) established over time	'Through the Executive Club programme, British Airways has developed a reputation as an innovator in developing direct relationships with its customers and in tailoring its services to enhance these relationships' (long-standing supplier of BA)
Stakeholder	Any group or individual who can affect or is affected by the achievement of the organization's objectives	'Employees, consumers, investors and shareholders, community, aviation business and suppliers, government, trade unions, NGOs, and society at large'
Public	People who mobilize themselves against the organization on the basis of some common issue or concern to them	'Local residents of Heathrow Airport appealed in November 2002 against the Government and British Airways concerning the issue of night flights at Heathrow airport. The UK Government denied that night flights violated local residents' human rights. British Airways intervened in support of the UK Government claiming that there is a need to continue the present night flights regime'

(Continued)

TABLE 1.1 *(Continued)*

Concept	Definition	Example: British Airways*
Market	A defined group for whom a product is or may be in demand (and for whom an organization creates and maintains products and services)	'The market for British Airways flights consists of passengers who search for a superior service over and beyond the basic transportation involved'
Issue	An unsettled matter (which is ready for a decision) or a point of conflict between an organization and one or more publics	'Night flights at Heathrow Airport: noise and inconvenience for local residents and community'
Communication	The tactics and media that are used to communicate with internal and external groups	'Newsletters, promotion packages, consultation forums, advertising campaigns, corporate design and code of conduct, free publicity'
Integration	The act of coordinating all communication so that the corporate identity is effectively and consistently communicated to internal and external groups	'British Airways aims to communicate its brand values of service, quality, innovation, cosmopolitanism and Britishness through all its communications in a consistent and effective manner'

*Extracted from British Airways annual reports and the web.

A *mission* is a general expression of the overriding purpose of the organization, which, ideally, is in line with the values and expectations of major stakeholders and concerned with the scope and boundaries of the organization. It is often referred to with the simple question 'What business are we in?'. A *vision* is the desired future state of the organization. It is an aspirational view of the general direction that the organization wants to go in, as formulated by senior management, and that requires the energies and commitment of members of the organization. *Objectives and goals* are the more precise (short-term) statements of direction, in line with the formulated vision, and that are to be achieved by strategic initiatives or *strategies*. Strategies involve actions and communications that are linked to objectives, and are often specified in terms of specific organizational functions (e.g., finance, operations, human resources, etc.). Operations strategies for streamlining operations and human resource strategies for staff support and development initiatives are common to every organization as well as, increasingly, full-scale corporate communication strategies.

Key to having a corporate communication strategy is the notion of a *corporate identity*: the basic profile that an organization wants to project to all its important stakeholder groups and how it aims to be known by these various groups in terms of the *corporate images* and *reputations* that they have of the organization. To ensure that different stakeholders indeed conceive of an organization in a favourable and broadly consistent manner, and also in line with the projected corporate identity, organizations need to go to great lengths to *integrate* all their *communication* from brochures, advertising campaigns to websites in tone, themes, visuals and logos.

The *stakeholder* concept takes centre-stage within corporate communication at the expense of considering the organizational environment simply in terms of markets and publics. Organizations increasingly are recognizing the need for an 'inclusive' and 'balanced' stakeholder management approach that involves actively communicating with *all* stakeholder groups upon which the organization depends and not just shareholders or customers. Such awareness stems from high-profile cases where undue attention to certain stakeholder groups has led to crises and severe damage for the organizations concerned.

All these concepts will be discussed in detail in the remainder of the book, but it is worthwhile to emphasize already how some of them hang together. The essence of what matters in Table 1.1 is that corporate communication is geared towards establishing favourable corporate images and reputations with all of an organization's stakeholder groups, so that these groups act in a way that is conducive to the success of the organization. In other words, because of favourable images and reputations customers and prospects will purchase products and services, members of the community will appreciate the organization in its environment, investors will grant financial resources, and so on. It is the spectre of a damaged reputation – of having to make costly reversals in policies or practices as a result of stakeholder pressure, or, worse, as a consequence of self-inflicted wounds – that lies behind the urgency with which integrated stakeholder management now needs to be treated. The case study (1.1) of Barclays Bank illustrates the importance of managing communications with stakeholders in an integrated manner.

CASE STUDY 1.1

BARCLAYS BANK: HOW (NOT) TO COMMUNICATE WITH STAKEHOLDERS

In 2003, Barclays, a UK-based bank and financial services group, appointed a new advertising agency Bartle Bogle Hegarty (BBH). BBH was hired to spearhead a 'more humane' campaign, after the bank was lambasted for its 'Big Bank' adverts in 2000 that featured the slogan 'A big world needs a big bank'. Barclays had spent £15 million on its 'Big' campaign, which featured celebrities such as Sir Anthony Hopkins and Tim Roth. The adverts were slick and had received good pre-publicity, but they turned into a communication disaster when they coincided with the news that Barclays was closing about 170 branches in the UK, many in rural areas. One of the earlier adverts featured Welsh-born Sir Anthony Hopkins talking from the comfort

(Continued)

(Continued)

of a palatial home about the importance of chasing 'big' ideas and ambitions. The adverts provoked a national debate in the UK when a junior government minister, Chris Mullin, said that Barclays' customers should revolt and 'vote with their feet'. Barclays' image crisis worsened when it was revealed that the new Chief Executive, Matthew Barrett, had been paid £1.3 million for just three months' work. At the time, competitors, including NatWest, quickly capitalized on the fall-out from the Big Bank campaign and were running adverts which triumphed the fact that it has abolished branch closures.

Local communities that had lost their branch were particularly angry with the closures. The situation was further aggravated by the arrogance with which Barclays announced and justified the decision. Matthew Barrett had explained the branch closures by saying, 'We are an economic enterprise, not a government agency, and therefore have obligations to conduct our business in a way that provides a decent return to the owners of the business. We will continue to take value-maximizing decisions without sentimentality or excuses.' Barclays was openly admitting that their main focus was on shareholder returns and larger customers across their investment and retail businesses. Perhaps the most amusing story of the many that emerged during that period was of the fact that the village where Anthony Hopkins was born was one of the victims of the branch closures. He was seen as a traitor to his heritage, and the local Welsh Assembly Member wrote to him as part of her campaign about the closures. Hopkins was moved to write back to her, complaining about being used as a scapegoat when in fact he was just an actor and felt that he needed to set the record straight by pointing out that he did not run Barclays Bank. In an attempt to respond to the image crisis, Barclays extended opening hours at 84 per cent of its branches and recruited an extra 2,000 staff to service the extra hours.

Despite its best efforts, the bank very quickly found itself in another image crisis. In 2003, the CEO Matthew Barrett made a blunder by saying to a Treasury Select Committee that he did not borrow on credit cards because they were too expensive and that he has advised his four children not to pile up debts on their credit cards. The press jumped on his comments, saying that he would be dogged by what he said for the rest of his life. Journalists also said that he had 'done a Ratner', in memory of the famous blunder committed by jeweller Gerald Ratner in 1991 when he admitted selling 'crap' jewellery products in his high street shops. According to some analysts, the press jumped on the comment because the general public and, by proxy, the media had been waiting to land one on Matt Barrett and Barclays for three and a half years. The media openly linked Barrett's comments with what they saw as the other blunder of closing branches while launching an advertising campaign extolling the virtues of being a 'big' bank.

In 2008, at the height of the global financial crisis, many banks and financial services institutions (including the Royal Bank of Scotland and Lloyds TSB) turned to the UK government for cash injections. Barclays, however, decided not to turn to the government for aid. The Bank instead raised billions from investors in Qatar and Abu Dhabi, who together now own almost a third of the bank. The reason for this was that it would allow the bank to retain 'complete control' over running the business,

(Continued)

(Continued)

including the freedom to pay bonuses to its top executives and investment bankers. The move had the full support of the board and shareholders. Chairman Marcus Agius commented at the time that 'the unanimous view of the board was that our shareholders would be better served by the unconstrained path'. The view inside Barclays Bank was that having the government as a main shareholder would lead to all sorts of complications. Its business decisions would be put under the microscope and rewards and bonuses to staff would be critically looked at by journalists and taxpayers. Financial analysts also largely thought that the move was a smart one and they felt that the Bank came out of the crisis with its balance sheet and credibility intact. While Barclays was not directly 'bailed out' by the UK government, the bank has been heavily criticized, alongside other banks, in the media for its excessive risk-taking and for the remuneration packages given to its top executives and investment bankers. The general lack of public trust towards bankers and banks has engulfed the whole sector, offering significant challenges to Barclays as the bank sets out to restore and maintain its reputation with shareholders, customers and other stakeholders.

QUESTIONS FOR REFLECTION

Discuss each image crisis for Barclays? What was the exact cause or event that led to each of these crises? What could Barclays have done to avoid these crises, or to anticipate the potential fallout?

Source: Garfield, A. (2000) 'Everything's big at Barclays. The chairman's pay has quadrupled just as 171 branches are closing', *The Independent,* 31 March 2000; Wilson, B. (2003) 'Barclay chief's gaffe recalls Ratner howler', *BBC News,* 17 October 2003; Daily Mail (2008) 'Barclays Shareholder protest at meeting to rubber-stamp Arab's £7bn bail-out', *Daily Mail,* 24 November 2008.

CHAPTER SUMMARY

1.3 All organizations, of all sizes and operating in different sectors and societies, must find ways to successfully establish and nurture relationships with their stakeholders, upon which they are economically and socially dependent. The management function that has emerged to deal with this task is corporate communication and this chapter has made a start by outlining its importance and key characteristics. The next chapter describes in more detail how and why corporate communication historically emerged and how it has grown into the management function that it is today in many organizations.

DISCUSSION QUESTIONS

1 Pick a company with which you are familiar or that you may have worked for in the past. Describe the company's corporate communication in terms of its corporate identity, image and reputation.

2 In your experience, how integrated is this company's communication? And how does the company compare on this dimension with its direct competitors?

 # KEY TERMS

Corporate communication

Corporate identity

Corporate image

Corporate reputation

Integration

Issue

Market

Mission

Public

Stakeholder

Vision

 # FURTHER READING

Christensen, Lars Thøger, Morsing, Mette and Cheney, George (2008), *Corporate Communications: Convention, Complexity and Critique*. London: Sage.

Fombrun, Charles and Van Riel, Cees (2004), *Fame and Fortune: How Successful Companies Build Winning Reputations*. London: FT Prentice Hall.

NOTES

1 See, for example, AON's global risk management survey, 24 April 2007 (www.aon.com/nl/nl/about/perscentrum/persberichten_nederland/archief2007/Global_RM_Survey_07_Key_Findings.pdf).

2 Argenti, P.A. (1996), 'Corporate communication as a discipline: toward a definition', *Management Communication Quarterly*, 10 (1): 73–97.

3 See, for example, Christensen, L.T., Morsing, M. and Cheney, G. (2008), *Corporate Communications: Convention, Complexity and Critique*. London: Sage.

4 Van Riel, C.B.M. (1995), *Principles of Corporate Communication*. London: Prentice Hall, p. 26.

5 'Public Relations in the recession: Good news', *The Economist*, 14 January 2010, p. 59.

CORPORATE COMMUNICATION IN CONTEMPORARY ORGANIZATIONS

2

> ## Chapter Overview
>
> This chapter describes the historical development of communication within organizations and the emergence of corporate communication. It starts with a brief discussion of the historical development of separate communication disciplines, such as marketing communication and public relations, and moves on to explain why organizations have increasingly drawn these disciplines together under the umbrella of corporate communication. The chapter concludes with discussing the ways in which contemporary organizations organize communication activities in order to strategically plan and coordinate the release of messages to different stakeholder groups.

INTRODUCTION

2.1 The evolution of communication disciplines and techniques that are used by organizations to promote, publicize or generally inform relevant individuals and groups within society about their affairs began at least 150 years ago. From the Industrial Revolution until the 1930s, an era predominantly characterized by mass production and consumption, the type of communications that were employed by organizations largely consisted of publicity, promotions and selling activities to buoyant markets. The move towards less stable, more competitive markets, which coincided with greater government interference in many markets and harsher economic circumstances, resulted from the 1930s onwards in a constant redefining of the scope and practices of communication in many organizations in the Western world. Communication practitioners had to rethink their discipline and developed new practices and areas of expertise in response to changing circumstances in the markets and societies in which they were operating.

   This chapter is about the changing definition, scope and organization of communication in organizations, and about the societal and market dynamics that triggered its evolution. A brief sketch will be provided of the historical evolution of the two main individual communication disciplines in each organization: marketing and public relations. The chapter will describe the development of both disciplines and will then move on to discuss why organizations have increasingly started to see these disciplines not in isolation but as part of an integrated effort to communicate with stakeholders. This integrated effort is directed and coordinated by the management function of corporate communication. As a result of this development, managers in most corporate organizations have realized that the most effective way of organizing communication consists of 'integrating' most, if not all, of an organization's communication disciplines and related activities, such as media relations, issues management, advertising and direct marketing. The basic idea is that whereas communication had previously been organized and managed in a rather fragmented manner, a more effective organizational form is one that integrates or coordinates the work of various communication practitioners. At the same time, when communication practitioners are pulled together, the communication function as a whole is more likely to have an input into strategic decision-making at the highest corporate level of an organization. By the end of the chapter, the reader will have an overview of the historical development of communication, of the strategic role of corporate communication and of the various ways in which communication can be effectively organized.

HISTORICAL BACKGROUND

2.2
Communication management – any type of communication activity undertaken by an organization to inform, persuade or otherwise relate to individuals and groups in its outside environment – is, from a historical perspective, not new. But the modernization of society, first through farming and trade, and later through industrialization, created ever more complex organizations with more complicated communication needs.

   The large industrial corporations that emerged during the Industrial Revolution in the nineteenth century in the UK, in the USA and later on in the rest of the Western world required, in contrast to what had gone before, professional communication officers and a more *organized* form of handling publicity and promotions. These large and complex industrial firms sought the continued support of government, customers and the general public, which required them to invest in public relations and advertising campaigns.[1]

   In those early years and right up until the 1900s, industrial corporations hired publicists, press agents, promoters and propagandists for their communication campaigns. These individuals often played on the gullibility of the general public in its longing to be entertained, whether they were being deceived or not, and many advertisements and press releases in those days were in fact exaggerated to the point where they were outright lies. While such tactics can perhaps now be denounced from an ethical standpoint, this 'publicity-seeking' approach to the general public was taken at that time simply because organizations and their press agents could get away with it. At the turn of the nineteenth century, industrial magnates and large organizations in the Western world were answerable to no one and were largely immune to pressure from government or public opinion. This situation is aptly illustrated by a comment made at the time by William Henry Vanderbilt, head of the New York Central Railroad, when asked about the public rampage and uproar that his company's railroad extensions would cause. 'The public be damned,' he simply responded.

The age of unchecked industrial growth soon ended, however, and industrial organizations in the Western world faced new challenges to their established ways of doing business. The twentieth century began with a cry from 'muckrakers': investigative journalists who exposed scandals associated with power, capitalism and government corruption and raised public awareness of the unethical and sometimes harmful practices of business. To respond to these 'muckrakers', many large organizations hired writers and former journalists to be spokespeople for the organization and to disseminate general information to these 'muckraking' groups and the public at large so as to gain public approval for their decisions and behaviour.[2] At the same time, while demand still outweighed production, the growth of many markets stabilized and even declined, which led organizations to hire advertising agents to promote their products with existing and prospective customers in an effort to consolidate their overall sales.

In the following decade (1920–1930) economic reform in the USA and the UK and intensified public scepticism towards big business made it clear to organizations that these writers, publicists and advertising agents were needed on a more continuous basis, and should not just be hired 'on and off' as press agents had been in the past. These practitioners were therefore brought '*in-house*' and communication activities to both the general public and the markets served by the organization became more systematic and skilled.[3] This development effectively brought the first professional expertise to the area of communication within organizations and planted the seeds for the two professional disciplines that defined for the majority of the twentieth century how communication would be approached by organizations: marketing and public relations.

Both marketing and public relations emerged as separate 'external' communication disciplines when industrial organizations realized that in order to prosper they needed to concern themselves with issues of public concern (i.e., public relations) as well as with ways of effectively bringing products to markets (i.e., marketing). Both the marketing and public relations disciplines have since those early days gone through considerable professional development, yet largely in their own separate ways. Since the 1980s, however, organizations have increasingly started to bring these two disciplines together again under the umbrella of a new management function that we now know as corporate communication. This trend towards 'integrating' marketing and public relations was noted by many in the field, including Philip Kotler, one of the most influential marketing figures of modern times. Kotler commented in the early 1990s, 'there is a genuine need to develop a new paradigm in which these two subcultures [marketing and public relations] work most effectively in the best interest of the organization and the publics it serves'.[4]

In 1978, Kotler, together with William Mindak, had already highlighted the different ways of looking at the relationship between marketing and public relations. In their article, they had emphasized that the view of marketing and public relations as distinct disciplines had characterized much of the twentieth century, but they predicted that a view of an integrated paradigm would dominate the 1980s and beyond as 'new patterns of operation and interrelation can be expected to appear in these [marketing and public relations] functions'.[5] Figure 2.1 outlines the different models that Kotler and Mindak described to characterize the relationship between marketing and public relations, including the integrated paradigm (model (e)) where marketing and public relations have merged into a single external communication function.

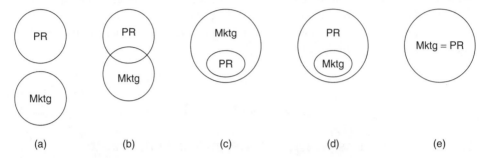

FIGURE 2.1 Models for the relationships between marketing and public relations.

Source: Reprinted with permission from the *Journal of Marketing*, published by the American Marketing Association, Kotler, P. and Mindak, W., 1978, 42(10), pp. 13–20.

INTEGRATED COMMUNICATION

2.3 Until the 1980s, marketing and public relations were considered as rather distinct in their objectives and activities, with each discipline going through its own trajectory of professional development.[6] Central to this traditional view (model (a) in Figure 2.1) was the simple point that marketing deals with markets, while public relations deals with all the publics (excluding customers and consumers) of an organization. Markets, from this perspective, are created by the identification of a segment of the population for which a product or service is or could be in demand, and involves product- or service-related communication. Publics, on the other hand, are seen as *actively* creating and mobilizing themselves whenever companies make decisions that affect a group of people adversely. These publics are also seen to concern themselves with more general news related to the entire organization, rather than specific product-related information. Kotler and Mindak articulated this traditional position (model (a)) by saying that 'marketing exists to sense, serve, and satisfy customer needs at a profit', while 'public relations exists to produce goodwill with the company's various publics so that these publics do not interfere in the firm's profit-making ability'.[7]

Over time, however, cracks appeared in this view of marketing and public relations as two disciplines that are completely distinct in their objectives and tactics. Rather than seeing them as separate, marketing and public relations, it was recognized, actually shared some common ground (model (b) in Figure 2.1). In the 1980s, for instance, concern over the rising costs and decreasing impact of mass media advertising encouraged many companies to examine different means of promoting customer loyalty and of building brand awareness to increase sales. Companies started to make greater use of 'marketing public relations': the publicizing of news and events related to the launching and promotion of products or services. 'Marketing public relations' (MPR) involves the use of public relations techniques for marketing purposes. It was found to be a cost-effective tool for generating awareness and brand favourability and to imbue communication about the organization's brands with credibility[8] (see Case Example 2.1 for a recent example). Companies such as Starbucks and the Body Shop have consistently used public relations techniques, such as free publicity, features in general interest magazines and grass-roots campaigning to attract attention and to establish a brand experience that is backed up by each of the Starbucks and the Body Shop stores.

Case Example 2.1

The use of marketing public relations to promote *The Passion of The Christ*

The movie, *The Passion of The Christ*, released in 2004, tells the story of the last 12 hours in the life of Jesus Christ. Directed and produced by Mel Gibson, the film tells in Aramaic (believed to have been Jesus' native language), Latin and Hebrew the moment of Christ's arrest, trial and crucifixion. Because of the subject, the graphic violence in the film and the fact that the movie-going public had to watch the movie with subtitles, Gibson reportedly had difficulty finding a company to distribute the movie. Newmarket and Icon Films eventually agreed to distribute the movie in the USA and around the world.

To promote the film, Gibson did not rely on traditional advertising but instead used public relations (pre-screenings and publicity in the media) and grass-roots marketing techniques. Gibson recognized that creating controversy was the key to building awareness of the film. He therefore invited prominent Christian and Jewish church leaders known for their political and social conservatism to watch the movie. An early version of the movie script was also leaked by an employee of the production company to a joint committee of the Secretariat for Ecumenical and Inter-Religious Affairs of the United States Conference of Catholic Bishops and the Department of Inter-religious Affairs of the Anti-defamation League. This committee concluded that the

> main storyline presented Jesus as having been relentlessly pursued by an evil cabal of Jews headed by the high priest Caiphas, who finally blackmailed a weak-kneed Pilate into putting Jesus to death. This is precisely the storyline that fueled centuries of anti-Semitism within Christian societies.

When the movie was released, although some Jews were supportive of Gibson and the movie, the overwhelming reaction from within the Jewish community was negative. Jewish religious groups expressed concern that the film blames the death of Jesus on the Jews as a group which, they claimed, could fuel anti-Semitism.

(Continued)

(Continued)

Through the pre-screening of the movie to church leaders and the leaking of the script, Gibson had created an enormous amount of media coverage focused on how incensed certain people were about the film and its message. This controversy in turn created so much buzz and word-of-mouth around the movie that it stimulated a core audience of Christian moviegoers, and also general moviegoers, into wanting to see the movie.

A further step that Gibson took to raise awareness, and to further increase the controversy surrounding his movie, was to claim that the late Pope John Paul II had seen the movie at a private viewing of the film shortly before its release. He claimed that the Pope had allegedly remarked to his good friend, Monsignor Stanislaw Dziwisz: 'It was as it was.' Dziwisz later denied that this ever happened, but it was widely reported by CNN and other news organizations that the Pope had said those words.

Finally, Gibson also undertook a grass-roots marketing effort with local church groups, who promoted the film with their constituents through free tickets and discounted ticket prices. In this way, he ensured that the core audience would not only watch the movie but would also spread favourable word-of-mouth about it to others.

In the end, many moviegoers went to see *The Passion of The Christ* and the movie went on to gross $611,899,420 worldwide ($370,782,930 in the USA alone) in 2004, putting it among the highest-grossing films of all time.

Source: Quelch, J.A., Elberse, A. and Harrington, A. (2004) 'The Passion of the Christ', *Harvard Business School*, Case 505-025.

'Marketing public relations' (MPR), because it is focused on the marketing of a company's products and services, is distinct from 'corporate' activities within public relations. These corporate activities, which are sometimes labelled as 'corporate public relations' (CPR), involve communication with investors, communities, employees, the media and government. Figure 2.2 displays a number of core activities of both the public relations and marketing disciplines, and outlines a set of activities (including specific tools and techniques) that are shared, indicating the overlap between the two functions.[9] Figure 2.2 also displays the difference between 'marketing public relations' (MPR) and 'corporate public relations' (CPR).

Starting on the left of the figure, marketing of course involves a range of activities such as distribution, logistics, pricing and new product development (area 'C' in Figure 2.2) besides marketing communications. Marketing communications, in the middle of the figure, involves corporate advertising ('A') and mass media advertising ('F'), direct marketing and sales promotions ('B'), and product publicity and sponsorship ('E'). Two of these activities, corporate advertising ('A') and product publicity and sponsorship ('E'), overlap with public relations. Corporate advertising involves the use of radio, TV, cinema, poster or internet advertising to create or maintain a favourable image of the company and its management. Although it is a form of advertising, it deals with the 'corporate' image of the company, and, as such, is distinct from mass media advertising ('F'), which is focused on the company's products

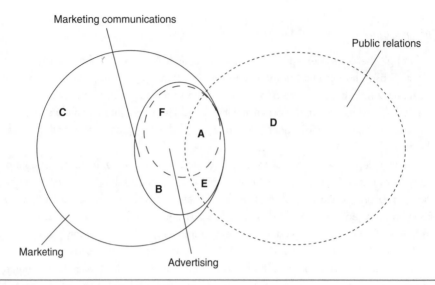

Key:
A = corporate advertising (advertising by a firm where the company, rather than its products or services, is emphasized)

B = direct marketing (direct communication via post, telephone or email to customers and prospects) and sales promotions (tactics to engage the customer, including discounting, coupons, guarantees, free gifts, competitions, vouchers, demonstrations and bonus commission)

C = distribution and logistics, pricing and development of products

D = 'corporate' public relations (public relations activities towards 'corporate' stakeholders, which excludes customers and prospects in a market); includes issues management, community relations, investor relations, media relations, internal communication and public affairs

E = 'marketing' public relations (the use of what are traditionally seen as public relations tools within marketing programmes); includes product publicity and sponsorship

F = mass media advertising (advertising aimed at increasing awareness, favour or sales of a company's products or services)

FIGURE 2.2   Marketing and public relations activities and their overlap

or services to increase awareness or sales. Product publicity and sponsorship involve activities that aim to promote and market the company's products and services. Both sets of activities draw upon techniques and expertise from public relations. Publicity in particular is often achieved through coverage in the news media. Sponsorship of a cause or event may also serve both marketing and corporate objectives. It can be tied into promotional programmes around products and services but can also be used to improve the company's image as a whole.

Besides the direct sharing of activities such as sponsorship, there are also a number of ways in which marketing and public relations activities can complement one another. For example, there is evidence that a company's image, created through public relations programmes, can positively reflect upon the product brands of a company, thereby increasing the awareness of the product brand as well as enhancing consumers' favourable impression of the brand.[10] Another complementary relationship that exists is the guardian role of public relations as a 'watchdog' or 'corrective' for marketing, in bringing other viewpoints and the expectations of stakeholders to bear upon strategic decision-making besides the need to boost sales with customers.[11]

This overlap and complementarity between marketing and public relations suggested to organizations that it is useful to align both disciplines more closely, or at least manage them in a more integrated manner. Not surprisingly, a lot of discussion and debate during the 1980s and 1990s took place on the importance of 'integration' and what such integration should look like within organizations. Back in 1978, Kotler and Mindak described three models of integration (models 'c', 'd' and 'e' in Figure 2.1). Each of these models articulates a different view of the most effective form of integration.

Model 'c' involves a view of marketing as the dominant function, which subsumes public relations. In this model, public relations becomes essentially part of a wider marketing function for satisfying customers. An example of this perspective involves the notion of Integrated Marketing Communications (IMC), which is defined as:

> a concept of marketing communication planning that recognizes the 'added value' of a comprehensive plan that evaluates the strategic role of a variety of disciplines (advertising, direct marketing, sales promotions and public relations) and combines these disciplines to provide clarity, consistency and maximum communication impact.[12]

Within IMC, public relations is reduced to activities of product publicity and sponsorship, ignoring its wider remit in communicating to employees, investors, communities, the media and government.

Model 'd' suggests the alternative view that 'marketing should be put under public relations to make sure that the goodwill of all key publics is maintained'.[13] In this model, marketing's role of satisfying customers is seen as only part of a wider public relations effort to satisfy the multiple publics and stakeholders of an organization. An example of this perspective involves the notion of 'strategic public relations', which assumes that all 'communication programs should be integrated or coordinated by a public relations department' including 'integrated marketing communication, advertising and marketing public relations' which should 'be coordinated through the broader public relations function'.[14]

Finally, model 'e' favours a view of marketing and public relations as merged into one and the same 'external communication' function. In the view of Kotler and Mindak: 'the two functions might be easily merged under a Vice President of Marketing and Public Relations' who 'is in charge of planning and managing the external affairs of the company'.[15] Despite Kotler and Mindak's preference for this model, it is not a form of integration that is much practised within organizations. Instead of merging the two disciplines into one and the same department, organizations want to keep them separate but actively coordinate public relations and marketing communication programmes. In hindsight, then, most organizations appear to practise model 'b', to coordinate marketing communications and public relations.

DRIVERS FOR INTEGRATED COMMUNICATION

2.4 In short, marketing and public relations disciplines are not merged or reduced within organizations to one and the same function. This may not be feasible in practice given the important differences in activities and audiences addressed by each (see Figure 2.1). However, both disciplines, while existing separately, are balanced against each other and managed together from within the overarching management framework of corporate communication. This management framework suggests a holistic way of viewing and practising communication management that cuts across the marketing and public relations disciplines (and activities such as advertising and media relations within them). According to Anders Gronstedt, a communication consultant, corporate communication 'inserts the various communication disciplines into a holistic perspective, drawing from the concepts, methodologies, crafts, experiences, and artistries of marketing communication and public relations'.[16]

The importance of 'integrating' marketing communications and public relations in this way has resulted from a variety of factors or 'drivers', as these can be more aptly called. Generally, these 'drivers' can be grouped into three main categories: those drivers that are market- and environment-based, those that arise from the communication mix and communication technologies, and those that are driven by opportunities, changes and needs from within the organization itself. All these drivers are set out in Table 2.1.

TABLE 2.1   Drivers for integration

Market- and environment-based drivers
Stakeholder roles – needs and overlap
Demand for corporate social responsibility (CSR) and greater transparency
Audience fragmentation
Communication-based drivers
Greater amounts of message clutter
Increased message effectiveness through consistency and reinforcement of core messages
Complementarity of media and media cost inflation
Media multiplication requires control of communication channels
Organizational drivers
Improved efficiency
Increased accountability
Provision of strategic direction and purpose through consolidation
Organizational positioning

Market- and environment-based drivers

The environment in which organizations operate has changed considerably over the past two decades. The *demands of different stakeholders*, such as customers, investors, employees and NGO and activist groups, have forced organizations to put considerable effort into integrating all their marketing and public relations efforts.

This integration is also important when one considers the multiple stakeholder roles that any one individual may have, and the potential pitfalls that may occur when conflicting messages are sent out.[17] Organizations are also facing increased demands for *corporate social responsibility* (CSR) and for *transparency* about their operations. In their efforts to respond to these social expectations and to present themselves as coherent, reliable and trustworthy institutions with nothing to hide, organizations across sectors increasingly embrace measures of integration. Organizations often adapt to the growing demand for information and stakeholder insight through *policies of consistency*, that is, by formalizing all communications and pursuing uniformity in everything they say and do. Stakeholder groups have also become more fragmented and less homogeneous than before. Customers, for example, have become much more individual in their consumption. Similarly, when organizations want to communicate to the news media, they are faced with a huge and diverse range of media organizations and outlets, including, these days, social media on the web. This greater *fragmentation* of stakeholder groups means that when organizations want to communicate with any one stakeholder group they have to use more channels and different media to reach them.

Communication-based drivers

In today's environment, it is more difficult for an organization to be heard and to stand out from its rivals. Media and communication experts have estimated that on average a person is hit by 13,000 commercial messages (including being exposed to company logos) a day. Integrated communication strategies are more likely to break through this *clutter* and make the company name or product brand heard and remembered than ill-coordinated attempts would. Through *consistent messages* an organization is more likely to be known and looked upon favourably by key stakeholder groups. Organizations have therefore increasingly put considerable effort into protecting their corporate image by rigorously aligning and controlling all communication campaigns and all other contact points with stakeholders.

Organizations also realized that *messages in various media can complement one another*, leading to a greater communication impact than any one single message can achieve. Because of the increasing costs of traditional mass media advertising and the opportunities afforded by the internet, many organizations have therefore re-examined their *media presence and how to control it*. As a result of these two developments, organizations now tend to look at media in a much broader sense and across the disciplines of marketing and public relations. Organizations have also become more creative in looking beyond corporate and product advertising to other media for communicating with stakeholders.[18] Many organizations today use a range of media, including corporate blogs and internet communication such as websites, banners and sponsored online communities.

Organizational drivers

One of the main organizational drivers for integration has been the need to *become more efficient*. By using management time more productively and by driving down the cost base (e.g., as research and communication materials are more widely shared and used for more than one communication campaign), organizations have been able to substantially improve the productivity of their communication practitioners.

The 1980s saw a powerful restructuring trend where every function was examined on its *accountability*. This led many organizations to restructure communication disciplines such as media relations, advertising, sales promotions and product publicity. This restructuring of communication, basically consisting of bringing various communication disciplines together into more integrated departments or into specific working practices, proved productive in that it offered direct organizational and managerial benefits. The consolidation of communication disciplines into one or a few departments enabled organizations to *provide strategic direction* to all of their communication with different stakeholder groups and to guide communication efforts from the strategic interests of the organization as a whole. Organizations recognized that fragmentation and the spreading out of communication responsibilities across the organization were counterproductive. Fragmentation is likely to lead to a situation where 'each department sub-optimizes its own performance, instead of working for the organization as a whole'.[19] Many organizations therefore developed procedures (e.g., communication guidelines, house-style manuals) and implemented coordination mechanisms (e.g., council meetings, networking platforms) to overcome fragmentation and coordinate their communication on an organization-wide basis.

A further driver for integration at the organizational level was the realization that communication had to be used more strategically *to position the organization* in the minds of important stakeholder groups. Since the early 1990s, organizations have started to become concerned with ideas such as 'corporate identity', 'corporate reputation' and 'corporate branding', which emphasize the importance of this positioning and of linking communication to the organization's corporate strategy. Figure 2.3 displays this development from a tactical orientation in communication to an orientation that emphasizes the strategic role of communication in 'positioning' the organization. Obviously, when organizations adopt a strategic perspective on communication and aim to build a distinctive reputation for their organization, the activities of marketing and public relations practitioners need to be actively coordinated so that messages to different stakeholders communicate the same corporate values and image for the organization.

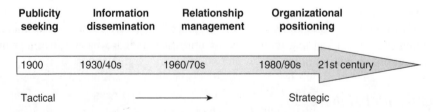

FIGURE 2.3   The shift from a tactical to strategic orientation to communication

ORGANIZING COMMUNICATION

2.5 This chapter began with a description of the historical context of communication in organizations and reviewed different perspectives on the relationship between two main disciplines of communication: marketing and public relations. These different perspectives on the relationship between marketing and public relations each present different views of how communication in organizations is managed and organized. The historical developments which led to a view of these two disciplines, first as distinct then as complementary, and finally to a view that sees them as integrated, provides a stepping stone for understanding the emergence of corporate communication. Corporate communication is a management framework to guide and coordinate marketing communication and public relations. Figure 2.4 displays this integrated framework of corporate communication.

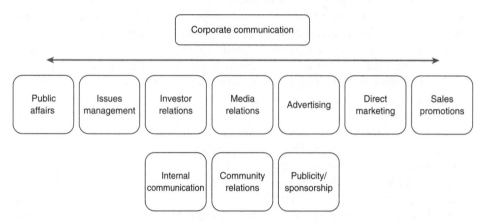

FIGURE 2.4 Corporate communication as an integrated framework for managing communication

Within this framework, coordination and decision-making take place between practitioners from various public relations and marketing communication disciplines. The public relations disciplines are displayed towards the left in Figure 2.4, whereas marketing communication disciplines are aligned towards the right. While each of these disciplines may be used separately and on their own for public relations or marketing purposes, organizations increasingly view and manage them together from a holistic organizational or corporate perspective with the company's reputation in mind. Many organizations have therefore promoted corporate communication practitioners to higher positions in the organization's hierarchical structure. In some organizations, senior communication practitioners are even members of their organization's management team (or support this management team in a direct reporting or advisory capacity). Marks & Spencer and Sony are two examples of companies that have recently promoted their most senior communication director to a seat on the executive board. These higher positions in the organization's hierarchy enable corporate communication practitioners to coordinate communication from a strategic level in the organization in order to build, maintain and protect the company's reputation with its stakeholders.

Many organizations have also started to bring the range of communications disciplines together into a single department so that knowledge and skills of practitioners are shared and corporate communication is seen as an autonomous and significant function within the organization. Some communication disciplines might still be organized as separate units or devolved to other functional areas (e.g., finance, human resources), but the general idea here is to consolidate most communication disciplines into a single department so that communication can be strategically managed from a central corporate perspective. Figure 2.5 illustrates this greater consolidation of communication disciplines in Siemens, one of the world's largest electrical engineering and electronics companies. Figure 2.5 highlights the different disciplines within the central corporate communication department, including media relations, corporate responsibility and employee communication. In addition, there are specific project teams for mergers and acquisitions (M&A) and crises, incorporating staff from these different areas within corporate communication. Interestingly, Siemens has organized market communications as part of the wider corporate communication function rather than as a separate department. The explanation for this may be that Siemens is mainly a business-to-business organization and does not market itself to end-consumers or end-users of its technology.

Larger organizations, such as multidivisional companies and multinational corporations, often locate the corporate communication department at a high level, vertically, within the organization. The *vertical structure* refers to the way in which tasks and activities (and the disciplines that they represent) are divided and arranged into departments (defined as the departmental arrangement) and located in the hierarchy of authority within an organization. The solid vertical lines that connect the boxes on an organization chart depict this vertical structure and the authority relationships involved (see Figure 2.5). Within such vertical lines, the occupant of the higher position has the authority to direct and control the activities of the occupant of the lower position. A major role of the vertical lines of authority on the organization chart is thus to depict the way in which the work and output of specialized departments or units are coordinated *vertically*, that is by authority in reporting relationships. The location of the communication department close to senior management also means that staff of this department directly report to the CEO and executive team. Most multidivisional and multinational corporations have a communication department linked to the CEO and executive team in an advisory capacity. In practice, this typically means that the communication department is a staff function at corporate headquarters, from where it can advise the senior decision-making team, and that the most senior communications practitioner has a direct reporting or advisory relationship to the Chief Executive Officer or even a seat on the executive board or senior management team.

The vertical structure divides each organization's primary tasks into smaller tasks and activities, with each box on an organization chart representing a position assigned to undertake a unique, detailed portion of the organization's overall mission. However, such vertical specialization, and the spreading out of tasks over

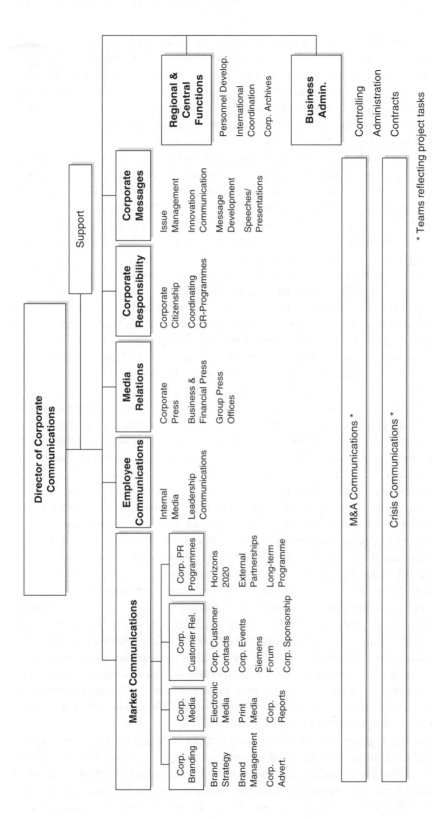

FIGURE 2.5 The organization of corporate communication within Siemens

different departments, requires some coordination or integration of work processes. This coordination or integration is achieved through so-called horizontal structures, which ensures that tasks and activities, while spread out over departments, are combined into the basic functions (i.e., human resources, finance, operations, marketing, and communication) that need to be fulfilled within the organization.

In the area of communication, horizontal structures are important as these enable companies to respond fast to emergent issues, provide control and ensure that consistent messages are being sent out through all the various communications channels. A final point, stressing the importance of horizontal structures, is that these may offset the potential disadvantages (functional silos, compartmentalization and 'turf wars') of the vertical structure and allow for cross-functional teamwork and flexibility. Horizontal structures can take various forms, including multidisciplinary task or project teams, standardized work processes and council meetings, and these are not normally displayed on an organization chart.

Multifunctional teams are an important mechanism in the coordination and integration of work of different communication disciplines.[20] Teams can be further distinguished in terms of the natural work team, permanent teams that work together on an ongoing basis (e.g., a cross-company investor relations team), and the task force team, created on an *ad hoc* basis for specific projects (e.g., around a crisis or a corporate restructuring). Task force teams are also assembled when an issue or crisis emerges in the company's environment (Chapter 11), and an adequate response needs to be formulated and communicated to key stakeholders.

Organizations can also use various tools to document work processes across disciplines and departments in visual and standardized formats, such as flow charts, process maps and checklists. Such process documentation creates a shared understanding among all communication practitioners about the processes of integration, institutionalizes processes of integration, thus making the organization less dependent on certain individuals, facilitates continuous improvements of the processes of integration, enables communication practitioners to benchmark their processes against other companies, and creates opportunities for cycle-time reduction.

In addition to documented work processes that are explicit and formal, integration also occurs through more informal channels. Much of the interaction among communication practitioners in fact takes place informally, in the email system, over the phone, and in the hallways. Companies can facilitate such informal communications by placing communication professionals physically close to one another (in the same building), by reducing symbolic differences such as separate car parks and cafeterias, by establishing an infrastructure of email, video conferences, and other electronic communication channels, and by establishing open access to senior management. In large organizations, it is also important that communication practitioners from different disciplines (e.g., marketing communications, internal communications) frequently meet at internal conferences and meetings, where they can get to know one another, network and share ideas.

Council meetings are another horizontal structure often used in multinational corporations.[21] A council meeting usually consists of representatives of different communication disciplines (e.g., media relations, internal communication, marketing communications), who meet to discuss the strategic issues concerning communication and review their past performance. Typically, ideas for improved coordination between communication disciplines bubble up at such council meetings, and the council appoints a subcommittee or team to carry them out. Generally, communication councils support coordination by providing opportunities for communicators worldwide to develop personal relationships, to coordinate communication projects, to share best practices, to learn from each other's mistakes, to learn about the company, to provide professional training, to improve the status of communication in the company, and to make communication professionals more committed to the organization as a whole. For all of this to happen, it is important that council meetings remain constructive and participative in their approach towards the coordination of communication (instead of becoming a control forum or review board that strictly evaluates communication campaigns), so that professionals can learn, debate and eventually decide on the strategic long-term view for communication that is in the interest of the organization as a whole.

A final mechanism for horizontally integrating work processes of communication practitioners involves the use of communication guidelines. Such guidelines may range from agreed upon work procedures (whom to contact, formatting of messages, etc.) to more general design regulations on how to apply logotypes and which colours to use. Many organizations have a 'house style' book that includes such design regulations, but also specifies the core values of the corporate identity. For example, Ericsson, the mobile phone manufacturer, has a 'global brand book' that distils the corporation's identity in a number of core values that communication practitioners are expected to adhere to and incorporate in all of their messages to stakeholders. Ericsson also convenes a number of workshops with communication practitioners across the organization to familiarize practitioners with the Ericsson identity and the brand book.

Case Study 2.1 illustrates how communication is organized in Philips, a large multinational corporation. It shows the choices that were made within Philips regarding the vertical and horizontal structuring of communication and how these relate to changes in the corporation's corporate strategy, the company's culture and the geographical complexity of its operations.

CASE STUDY 2.1

ORGANIZING COMMUNICATION IN PHILIPS

Philips, an international electronics corporation, started off as a manufacturer of light bulbs and electrical equipment in the Netherlands. Since its founding in 1891, the company has been at the vanguard of technological innovation and is credited with several inventions, such as the audio-cassette, the CD and the DVD. However, despite its strength in technological innovation, the company's financial health deteriorated in the 1990s because of a lack of focus, as the company operated in too many industries and markets, and because it was lagging behind its competitors in terms of marketing its products. Through the 1990s, Philips initiated several

(Continued)

(Continued)

restructuring exercises which included selling off several businesses. In 1992, a restructuring exercise called Operation Centurion (guided by C.K. Prahalad, a well-known management expert) involved reducing the workforce, effecting a change in the company's culture (which had become rather bureaucratic and resistant to change), and streamlining internal processes so that the time of bringing products to market could be reduced. In 1996, another intensive restructuring exercise included further job cuts, outsourcing component manufacturing, and selling off unprofitable as well as non-core businesses, including the computer, defence electronics and semi-conductor businesses. In addition, the restructuring in 1996 meant that responsibilities and activities became heavily decentralized, with each business unit having to work on its own to become profitable. In 2001, when Gerard Kleisterlee took over as CEO, he introduced a more cooperative approach through a programme termed 'Towards One Philips' (TOP). Kleisterlee's intention was to move away from promoting each division as a separate entity. In his view, Philips had, over the years, become rigidly compartmentalized with each division focusing only on its own activities and on its own bottom line. The TOP programme set out to promote a more cooperative approach, with divisions working together across the company and streamlining their operations. In doing so, the company would be able to cut costs and to become more focused on its customers and other stakeholders. In the words of Kleisterlee: 'The customer doesn't want to deal with individual product divisions, with individual product lines. He wants to have one treatment from a company called Philips and experience a brand called Philips in one and the same way.' In 2003, Kleisterlee also redefined the company's business domains and product portfolio as restricted to healthcare, lifestyle and enabling technologies. The company now includes three major divisions: lighting, healthcare and medical systems, and consumer electronics, including domestic appliances and personal care, with more focused business units within each division.

Brand positioning and communication

The Philips brand itself also underwent change as a result of these changes in the company's strategic focus, product portfolio and internal structure. In 1995, Philips launched the 'Let's make things better' campaign, which was meant to rejuvenate the Philips brand after a period of fragmented and ineffective product-led communication. The objective of the campaign was to project Philips as a company that delivers technology to improve people's lives. The campaign tried to convey that Philips technology, while improving people's lives, could also improve the world. In some ways, the campaign reflected the rich heritage of the company. This heritage goes back to the founders of Philips, Anton and Gerard Philips, who carried on a tradition begun by their father, Frederik, of providing housing, pension and free medical care, a sports centre (which led to the founding of PSV, the Philips sports association that is well known for its football team) and a foundation to finance the older children of Philips' employees through college. In true Dutch fashion, they even provided their early factories with full-time bicycle repair men. Anton and Gerard Philips set out to improve not just the lives of customers, through advanced technological products

(Continued)

(Continued)

such as the light bulb, but also those of their employees and of community members. Their founding belief was that by daring to make choices that improve the lives of people both inside and outside the company, they would be successful. Though the 'Let's make things better' campaign was successful in profiling the company as a single brand, senior managers of the company felt that it failed to convey the design excellence and technical superiority of Philips' products. Therefore, in 2004, the 'Sense and simplicity' campaign was launched.

The 'Sense and simplicity' brand positioning is rooted in Philips' traditional strengths of design and technology. In line with this positioning, the company set out to launch high-tech products that meet customers' needs but have simple designs and easy-to-use interfaces. By 'sense', Philips meant 'delivering meaningful and exciting benefits of technology that improve people's lives' while 'simplicity' referred to its ability to provide easy access to these benefits. Technological products had to be advanced but easy to operate and designed around the needs of the customer. In this way, the brand positioning is both a brand promise to customers as well as a potential differentiator from the company's competitors in the marketplace. While companies like Samsung and Apple are also working towards simplifying technology for customers, Philips is among the first to make it part of its brand positioning and as core to its product design. The emphasis on simplicity not only related to marketing and the design of products, but was internally also linked to the TOP programme in that both initiatives shared the objective of making Philips itself a more simple, lean and internally aligned company.

Reputation management

Corporate communication within Philips incorporates the new brand positioning in communications towards customers and the market. The company has set itself the target of becoming recognized as a market-driven company known for the simplicity of its products, processes and communication. Besides more market-focused communication around the theme of 'sense and simplicity', senior corporate communication managers of the company have also identified a further set of messages that they feel need to be consistently communicated to the company's core stakeholder groups.

These messages relate to its care and support for people inside and outside the business, the company's leadership in innovation, the company's vision, leadership and strategy, its track record in social and environmental responsibilities, and the company's ability to communicate effectively and engage with different stakeholder groups. Across the company, corporate communicators embed these messages in their ongoing communication with different stakeholders, an approach that Philips has termed 'themed messaging'. In essence, the idea behind this approach is that it allows Philips to 'manage' the drivers that contribute to its corporate reputation with different stakeholder groups. By using this approach, corporate communicators aim to change public perception of the company from a traditional consumer electronics group into a diversified healthcare and lifestyle company with a more unified voice and more consistent image being directed towards its stakeholders. The company

(Continued)

(Continued)

tracks the contribution of its themed messages and communication campaigns on its corporate reputation.

Vertical and horizontal structures

The themed messaging approach and the continuous measurement of Philips' corporate reputation reflect the company-wide importance that is now attributed to the company's reputation with different stakeholder groups. Reputation management is seen as wider than just the remit of corporate communication as it involves all of the business and many other functions (e.g., human resources, finance) that engage with stakeholders. The company has therefore formed a reputation committee with representatives from corporate communication and other key functions across the company and chaired by the CEO.

The committee is responsible for overseeing the deployment of improvements in the areas of the seven drivers of the company's reputation (leadership in innovation, performance management, care for employees, quality products and services, leadership in sustainability, market orientation and strong communication) in which action is thought to make sense. Corporate communication is organized as separate from marketing and is directed from the headquarters of the company in Amsterdam by Jules Prast, Global Director of Corporate Communication. Prast and his colleagues in the global corporate communication department are responsible for company-wide reputation issues, measurement and the formulation and planning of corporate communication and stakeholder engagement programmes. In the words of Prast, he and his colleagues had to 'select a communication model that fits and supports the culture, strategy and configuration' of Philips. The model that was adopted to organize communication involves an 'orchestration' model, whereby individual 'businesses participate in a global communications management system'. In other words, the global corporate communication department sets the themed messages for all corporate communication and supports local corporate communication functions in different regions (Europe–Middle East–Africa, North America, Latin America, and Asia Pacific) with their local communication to stakeholders. As Prast put it, 'we organized our internal and external communications around themes that served as a common reference point' for communication with stakeholders across global and at local levels of the company. Hence, like most multinational corporations, Philips has a combination of a centralized 'global' corporate communication department at the corporate centre and decentralized 'local' communication departments, teams and professionals in business units around the world. The themed messaging approach is one way in which the company tries to ensure consistency in its corporate communication across the organization.

Besides themed messaging, Philips has also introduced so-called process survey tools which document and standardize work processes across functions within the organization and allow professionals to improve upon their performance. Similarly, central processes in corporate communication, such as media relations, employee communication, editorial calendar management, crisis communication and speeches management, have also been documented and standardized. The decision to develop these process survey tools in corporate communication reflects the wider emphasis on standardization, optimization and measurement within the

(Continued)

(Continued)

engineering culture of Philips. The result of having these tools is that certain key processes are documented and standardized in flow charts and worksheets and specify a clear set of procedures and actions to professionals. For example, in media relations, the process survey tool tells a professional who else should be contacted in relation to a media enquiry and how to draft a press release. A further effect of these tools is that they allow professionals to adjust and optimize work processes and identify 'best practices' in corporate communication based upon their learning and feedback from stakeholders. In sum, these process survey tools have helped in making corporate communication processes more visible and consistent across the company and have strengthened the accountability of corporate communication in improving its performance and in delivering results.

QUESTIONS FOR REFLECTION

1   Describe the vertical and horizontal structuring of corporate communication within Philips. What can you say about the effectiveness of these structures in the light of the company's repositioning around 'sense and simplicity' and its increased focus on managing its corporate reputation with different stakeholder groups?

2   To what extent do you think that process survey tools can be effectively used within corporate communication in other multinational corporations? Are these tools applicable to any type of multinational or does their effectiveness depend on characteristics of the corporation, such as its size, strategy or culture?

Source: This case study is based upon Prast, J. (2005) 'The strategic importance of measuring corporate reputation: A Philips case study', *Critical Eye*, March–May, 4–9, documents from www.philips.com and Cornelissen, J.P., Van Ruler, B. and Van Bekkum, T. (2006) 'The Practice of corporate communication: Towards an extended and practice-based conceptualisation', *Corporate Reputation Review*, 9 (2), 114–133.

CHAPTER SUMMARY

2.6 This chapter has discussed the historical development of communication in organizations, the emergence and significance of corporate communication and the ways in which communication is organized in contemporary corporate organizations. This discussion provides a context for understanding why corporate communication emerged and how it is useful for today's organizations. The chapter also described the variety of factors or 'drivers' that triggered the emergence of corporate communication and continue to drive its widespread use within companies around the globe. Corporate communication has brought a more strategic and integrated perspective on managing communication for the benefit of the entire organization. To give this shape, many corporate organizations have consolidated communication activities into a single department with ready access to the executive decision-making team.

DISCUSSION QUESTIONS

1 What are the main benefits of integrating communication?

2 How is a strategic approach to communication different from a tactical approach? Can you give examples of companies that illustrate this difference?

3 How important is the organizational structure in ensuring integration and avoiding a fragmentation in communication?

KEY TERMS

Advertising

Audience fragmentation

(Communication) clutter

Corporate communication

Council meeting

Departmental arrangement

Direct marketing

Horizontal structure

Marketing

Marketing public relations

Market

Process documentation

Public relations

Publicity

Public

Reporting relationship

Sales promotions

Sponsorship

Team

Vertical structure

FURTHER READING

Grunig, Larissa A., Grunig, James E. and Dozier, David M. (2002), *Excellent Public Relations and Effective Organizations*. Hillsdale, NJ: Lawrence Erlbaum Associates.

Marchand, Ronald (1998), *Creating the Corporate Soul: The Rise of Public Relations and Corporate Imagery*. Berkeley, CA: University of California Press.

Ries, Al and Ries, Laura (2002), *The Fall of Advertising and the Rise of PR*. New York: Harper Collins, Collins Business.

NOTES

1   Marchand, R. (1998), *Creating the Corporate Soul: The Rise of Public Relations and Corporate Imagery*. Berkeley, CA: University of California Press.

2   Grunig, J.E. and Hunt, T. (1984), *Managing Public Relations*. New York: Holt, Rinehart & Winston.

3   See, for instance, Ewen, S. (1996), *PR! A Social History of Spin*. New York: Basic Books; Marchand (1998); Grunig and Hunt (1984); Cutlip, S.M., Center, A.H. and Broom, G.H. (2000), *Effective Public Relations* (7th edn). London: Prentice-Hall.

4   Kotler (1989), cited in Grunig, J.E. and Grunig, L.A. (1991), 'Conceptual differences in public relations and marketing: the case of health-care organizations', *Public Relations Review*, 17 (3): 257–278, quote on p. 261.

5   Kotler, P. and Mindak, W. (1978), 'Marketing and public relations: should they be partners or rivals?', *Journal of Marketing*, 42 (10): 13–20, quote on p. 20.

6   See, for example, Ehling, W.P., White, J. and Grunig, J.E. (1992), 'Public relations and marketing practices', in Grunig, J.E. (ed.), *Excellence in Public Relations and Communication Management*. Hillsdale, NJ: Lawrence Erlbaum Associates, pp. 357–383; Ehling, W.P. (1989), 'Public relations management and marketing management: different paradigms and different missions', paper presented at the meeting of the Public Relations Colloquium, San Diego.

7   Kotler and Mindak (1978), p. 17.

8   See, for example, Harris, T.L. (1991), *The Marketer's Guide to Public Relations: How Today's Top Companies Are Using the New PR to Gain a Competitive Edge*. New York: John Wiley & Sons; Harris, T.L. (1997), 'Integrated marketing public relations', in Caywood, C. (ed.), *The Handbook of Strategic Public Relations and Integrated Communications*. New York: McGraw-Hill, pp. 90–105; Ries, A. and Ries, L. (2002), *The Fall of Advertising and the Rise of PR*. New York: HarperCollins.

9   Based on Hutton, J.G. (1996), 'Integrated marketing communications and the evolution of marketing thought', *Journal of Business Research*, 37: 155–162.

10 See, for example, Brown, T.J. and Dacin, A. (1997), 'The company and the product: corporate associations and consumer product responses', *Journal of Marketing*, 61 (January): 68–84; Biehal, G.J. and Sheinin, D.A. (1998), 'Managing the brand in a corporate advertising environment: a decision-making framework for brand managers', *Journal of Advertising*, 27 (2): 99–111; Berens, G.A.J.M., Van Riel, C.B.M. and Van Bruggen, G.H. (2005), 'Corporate associations and consumer product responses: the moderating role of corporate brand dominance', *Journal of Marketing*, 69 (July): 35–48.

11 Grunig, L.A., Grunig, J.E. and Dozier, D.M. (2002), *Excellent Public Relations and Effective Organizations*. Hillsdale, NJ: Lawrence Erlbaum Associates.

12 Duncan, T. and Caywood, C. (1996), 'Concept, process, and evolution of IMC', in Thorson, E. and Moore, J. (eds), *Integrated Communication: Synergy of Persuasive Voices*. Mahwah, NJ: Lawrence Erlbaum Associates, pp. 13–34, quote on pp. 19–20.

13 Kotler and Mindak (1978), p. 18.

14 This perspective is associated with the IABC Excellence Study on strategic public relations. Work cited is Grunig, J.E. and Grunig, L.A. (1998), 'The relationship between public relations and marketing in excellent organizations: evidence from the IABC study', *Journal of Marketing Communications*, 4 (3): 141–162, quote on p. 141. See also Grunig, J.E. (1992), *Excellence in Public Relations and Communication Management*. Hillsdale, NJ: Lawrence Erlbaum Associates; and Grunig et al. (2002).

15 Kotler and Mindak (1978), p. 18.

16 Gronstedt, A. (1996), 'Integrating marketing communication and public relations: a stakeholder relations model', in Thorson, E. and Moore, J. (eds), *Integrated Communication: Synergy of Persuasive Voices*. Mahwah, NJ: Lawrence Erlbaum Associates, pp. 287–304, quote on p. 302.

17 See, for example, Scholes, E. and Clutterbuck, D. (1998), 'Communication with stakeholders: an integrated approach', *Long Range Planning*, 31 (2): 227–238; Fombrun, C. and Van Riel, C.B.M. (2004) *Fame and Fortune: How Successful Companies Build Winning Reputations*. London: FT Prentice Hall.

18 See, for example, Barwise, P. and Styler, A. (2003), *The MET Report 2003: Marketing Expenditure Trends 2001–04* (www.london.edu/assets/documents/PDF/MET_Report_Exec_Summary_2.pdf).

19 Gronstedt, A. (1996), 'Integrated communications at America's leading total quality management corporations', *Public Relations Review*, 22 (1): 25–42, quote on p. 26.

20 Gronstedt (1996).

21 See, for example, Gronstedt (1996); Fombrun and Van Riel (2004); Argenti, P., Howell, R.A. and Beck, K.A. (2005), 'The strategic communication imperative', *MIT Sloan Management Review*, Spring: 83–89.

CONCEPTUAL FOUNDATIONS

2

In Part 2, we explore the basic themes and concepts that are used in corporate communication, and provide the theoretical background to the management of corporate communication in practice. Subjects that are addressed include the notion of stakeholders, models for stakeholder communication and collaboration, the importance of an organization's corporate identity, image and reputation, and the rising interest in corporate branding.

After reading Part 2, the reader should be familiar with the basic vocabulary and theoretical concepts in corporate communication and understand the importance of stakeholder communication for contemporary organizations.

STAKEHOLDER MANAGEMENT AND COMMUNICATION

3

| Chapter Overview |

The need for companies to manage relationships with stakeholders is, both in theory and practice, one of the main purposes of corporate communication. The chapter starts with an introduction to the concept of stakeholders and is followed by an overview of different management and communication models that organizations use to communicate and collaborate with their stakeholders.

INTRODUCTION

3.1 Contemporary organizations increasingly realize that they need to communicate with their stakeholders to develop and protect their own reputations. The significance of stakeholder management partly came about because of pressures from governments and the international community promoting the stakeholder perspective. A range of stakeholder initiatives and schemes have sprung up in recent years at the industry, national and transnational levels, including the UN Global Compact Initiative, the Global Reporting Initiative, the World Bank's Business Partners for Development, and the OECD's Guidelines for Multinational Companies. These initiatives and schemes emphasize the wider responsibilities of organizations to *all* stakeholders and society at large. Stakeholder management, more than any other subject in business, has profound implications for corporate communication. It requires that managers think strategically about their business overall and about how they can effectively communicate with stakeholders, including customers, investors, employees and members of the communities in which the organization operates.

The chapter outlines how stakeholder management developed, as well as how that theory can be used to establish communication strategies in organizations. Managers of many corporate organizations realize that now, more than ever, they need to listen to and communicate with a whole range of stakeholder groups to build and maintain the reputation of their companies. We begin the chapter with an explanation of the basic theory behind stakeholder management, but then make a critical link with corporate communication and the use of stakeholder theory in practice.

STAKEHOLDER MANAGEMENT

3.2 Theoretically, the now widespread adoption of the stakeholder perspective in business marks a move away from a neo-classical economic theory of organizations to a socio-economic theory. The neo-classical economic theory suggests that the purpose of organizations is to make profits in their accountability to themselves and shareholders, and that only by doing so can business contribute to wealth for itself as well as society at large.[1] The socio-economic theory suggests, in contrast, that the notion of accountability in fact extends to other groups besides shareholders who are considered to be important for the continuity of the organization and the welfare of society. This distinction between a conventional neo-classical perspective and a socio-economic or stakeholder perspective on the management of organizations is highlighted by the contrasting models displayed in Figures 3.1 and 3.2.[2]

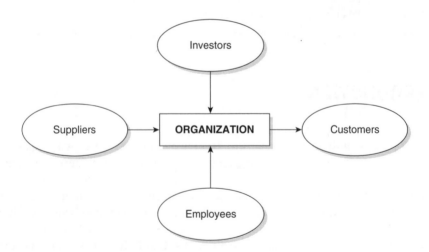

FIGURE 3.1   Input–output model of strategic management

In Figure 3.1, the organization is the centre of the economy, where investors, suppliers and employees are depicted as contributing inputs, which the 'black box' of the organization transforms into outputs for the benefit of customers. Each contributor of inputs is rewarded with appropriate compensation and, as a result of competition throughout the system, the bulk of the benefits will go to the customers. It is

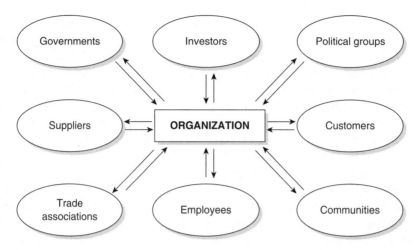

FIGURE 3.2 Stakeholder model of strategic management

important to note that in this 'input–output' model, power lies with the organization, upon which the other parties are dependent, and that the interest of these other
parties and their relationship to the organization are only financial.

The stakeholder model (Figure 3.2) contrasts with the input–output model.
Stakeholder management assumes that all persons or groups with legitimate interests
in an organization do so to obtain benefits and there is, in principle, no priority for
one set of interests and benefits over another. Hence, the arrows between the
organization and its stakeholders run in both directions. All those groups which have
a legitimate 'stake' in the organization, whether purely financial, market-based or
otherwise, are recognized, and the relationship of the organization with these groups
is not linear but one of interdependency. In other words, instead of considering
organizations as immune from government or public opinion, the stakeholder
management model recognizes the mutual dependencies between organizations and
various stakeholder groups – groups that are affected by the operations of the organization, but can equally affect the organization, its operations and performance.

The picture that emerges from the stakeholder perspective is far more complex
and dynamic than the input–output model of strategic management that preceded it.
More individuals and groups with legitimate interests in the organization are recognized and accounted for, and these individuals and groups all need to be considered,
communicated with and/or accommodated by the organization to sustain its financial performance and to secure continued acceptance for its operations. One significant feature of the stakeholder model is that it suggests that an organization needs to
be considered 'legitimate' by both 'market' and 'non-market' stakeholder groups.
This notion of legitimacy stretches beyond financial accountability to include
accountability for the firm's performance in social and environmental terms.

Framing accountability through this concept of legitimacy also means that organizations engage with stakeholders not just for *instrumental* reasons, but also for *normative* reasons. Instrumental reasons point to a connection between stakeholder
management and corporate performance. Stakeholder management may lead to
increases in revenues and reductions in costs and risks as it increases transactions

with stakeholders (e.g., more sales or more investments) or as a reputational buffer is created for crises or potentially damaging litigation. Normative reasons appeal to underlying concepts such as individual or group 'rights', 'social contracts', morality, and so on.[3] From a normative perspective, stakeholders are persons or groups with legitimate interests in aspects of corporate activity, and they are identified by this interest, whether the corporation has any direct economic interest in them or not. The interests of all stakeholders are in effect seen as of some intrinsic value to the organization, in this view. That is, each group of stakeholders merits consideration for its own sake and not merely because of its ability to further the interests of some other group, such as the shareholders.

Instrumental or normative reasons for engaging with stakeholders, however, often converge in practice, as social and economic objectives are not mutually exclusive[4] and as 'doing good' for one stakeholder group delivers reputational returns which are easily carried over and may impact the views of other stakeholder groups. So, while communication with a particular stakeholder group may have been started for normative, even altruistic reasons – to be a 'good corporate citizen' as an end in itself, so to speak – the gains that this delivers in terms of employee morale, reputation, and so on, are often considerable and clearly of instrumental value to the organization. The management gurus Kotter and Heskett observed that highly successful companies, such as Hewlett Packard and Wal-Mart, are deeply committed to their stakeholders: 'almost all [their] managers care strongly about people who have a stake in the business – customers, employees, stockholders, [and] suppliers'.[5]

THE NATURE OF STAKES AND STAKEHOLDERS

3.3 Having sketched some of the theoretical background to stakeholder management, it is helpful to devote a bit more space to discuss the concepts of 'stake' and 'stakeholder'. The standard definition of a stakeholder is the one provided by Edward Freeman:

> A stakeholder is any group or individual who can affect or is affected by the achievement of the organization's purpose and objectives.[6]

A stake, which is central to this definition and to the notion of stakeholder in general, can be described as 'an interest or a share in an undertaking, [that] can range from simply an interest in an undertaking at one extreme to a legal claim of ownership at the other extreme'.[7] The content of stakes that are held by different persons and groups is varied, and based on the specific interests of these individuals or groups in the organization. Special interest groups and non-governmental organizations (NGOs), for example, may demand ever higher levels of 'corporate social responsibility' from an organization. Investors, for their part, may apply relentless pressure on that same organization to maximize short-term profits. Stakes of different individuals and groups are thus varied and may be at odds with one another, putting pressure on the organization to balance stakeholder interests.

Edward Freeman was among the first to offer a classification of all those groups who hold a stake in the organization. In his classic book, *Strategic Management:*

A Stakeholder Approach, Freeman considered three types of stakes: equity stakes, economic or market stakes, and influencer stakes.[8] Equity stakes, in Freeman's terminology, are held by those who have some direct 'ownership' of the organization, such as shareholders, directors or minority interest owners. Economic or market stakes are held by those who have an economic interest, but not an ownership interest, in the organization, such as employees, customers, suppliers and competitors. Finally, influencer stakes are held by those who do not have either an ownership or economic interest in the actions of the organization, but who have interests as consumer advocates, environmental groups, trade organizations and government agencies. By considering these types of stake, Freeman specified the nature of stakes in terms of the interest of various groups in the organization – whether this interest is primarily economic or moral in nature – and whether this interest is bound in some form through a contract or (moral) obligation.

One standard way of looking at stakes is indeed to assess whether the interest of a person or group in an organization is primarily economic or moral in nature. Clarkson suggests, in this respect, that there are primary and secondary groups of stakeholders, with primary groups being those that are important for financial transactions and necessary for an organization to survive.[9] In short, in Clarkson's view, a primary stakeholder group is one without whose continuing participation the organization cannot survive. Secondary stakeholder groups are defined as those who generally influence or affect, or are influenced or affected by, the organization, but they are not engaged in financial transactions with the organization and are not essential for its survival in strictly economic terms. Media and a wide range of special interest groups fall within this secondary group of stakeholders. These secondary stakeholders do, however, have a moral or normative interest in the organization and have the capacity to mobilize public opinion in favour of, or against, a corporation's performance, as demonstrated in the cases of the recall of the Tylenol product by Johnson & Johnson (favourable) and the *Exxon Valdez* oil spill (unfavourable).

A second way of viewing stakes is to consider whether stakeholder ties with an organization are established through some form of contract or formal agreement, or not. Charkham talked about two broad classes of stakeholders in this respect: contractual and community stakeholders.[10] Contractual stakeholders are those groups that have some form of legal relationship with the organization for the exchange of goods or services. Community stakeholders involve those groups whose relationship with the organization is non-contractual and more diffuse, although their relationship is nonetheless real in terms of its impact. Contractual groups, including customers, employees and suppliers, are formally tied to an organization because they have entered into some form of contract; the nature of their interest is often economic in providing services or extracting resources from the organization (Table 3.1). Community stakeholders, on the other hand, are not contractually bound to an organization. This includes groups such as the government, regulatory agencies, trade associations and the media, which are nonetheless important in providing the authority for an organization to function, setting the general rules and regulations by which activities are carried out, and monitoring and publicly evaluating the conduct of business operations.

In summary, the notion of having a legitimate stake in an organization is 'inclusive' and ranges from economic to moral interests, and from formal, binding relationships

TABLE 3.1 Contractual and community stakeholders

Contractual stakeholders	Community stakeholders
Customers	Consumers
Employees	Regulators
Distributors	Government
Suppliers	Media
Shareholders	Local communities
Lenders	Pressure groups

as the basis of a stake to more diffuse and loose ties with the organization. This 'inclusiveness' implies that organizations ideally communicate and engage with all of their stakeholders. A particular way in which this 'inclusive' nature of the stakeholder concept is shown is in corporate social responsibility (CSR) initiatives that have been adopted by many organizations in recent years. These initiatives are a direct outcome of the shift from an 'input–output' model to a stakeholder model of strategic management (Figures 3.1 and 3.2). Corporate social responsibility includes philanthropy, community involvement, and ethical and environmentally-friendly business practices. The drive for CSR came with the recognition of the need for business to deliver wider societal value beyond shareholder and market value alone (see Chapter 13).

STAKEHOLDER COMMUNICATION

3.4 The stakeholder model of the organization suggests that the various stakeholders of the organization need to be identified and they must be addressed for the stake that they hold. In practice, this comes down to providing stakeholders with the type of information about the company's operations in which they have an interest. Financial investors and shareholders, for instance, will need to be provided with financial information concerning the organization's strategy and operations (e.g., through annual reports and shareholder meetings), while customers and prospects need to be supplied with information about products and services (e.g., through advertising, sales promotions and in-store communication). Each of these stakeholder groups, on the basis of the stake(s) that an individual holds in an organization, looks for and is interested in certain aspects of the company's operations. While the interests of stakeholders are intricately varied, and at times are even at odds with one another (e.g., staff redundancies are a blow to the workforce, but may be favoured by shareholders and investors who have an interest in the financial strength and continuity of the firm), it is important that an organization provides each stakeholder group with specific information and builds a strong reputation across exchanges with all of these stakeholders.

In order to do so, managers and communication practitioners typically start with identifying and analysing the organization's stakeholders, their influence and interest in the organization. In this way, they have a clearer idea what the information needs of stakeholders are, what specific positions they have on an issue or in relation to a corporate activity, and what kind of communication strategy can be used to maintain support or counter opposition. A basic form of stakeholder identification analysis involves answering the following questions, which capture the essential information for effective stakeholder communication:[11]

1   Who are the organization's stakeholders?
2   What are their stakes?
3   What opportunities and challenges are presented to the organization in relation to these stakeholders?
4   What responsibilities (economic, legal, ethical and philanthropic) does the organization have to all its stakeholders?
5   In what way can the organization best communicate with and respond to these stakeholders and address these stakeholder challenges and opportunities?

A similar approach is to use a mapping model to identify and position stakeholders in terms of their influence on the organization's operations or in terms of their stance on a particular issue related to the organization. There are two general mapping devices or tools that managers and communication practitioners can use for this task: the stakeholder salience model and the power–interest matrix. Both mapping devices enhance practitioners' knowledge of stakeholders and their influence, and enable them to plan appropriate communication strategies. Such mapping exercises should be carried out on an ongoing basis, but can also be performed in relation to issues or corporate decisions at a particular point in time.

Stakeholder salience model

In this model, stakeholders are identified and classified on the basis of their salience to the organization. Salience is defined as how visible or prominent a stakeholder is to an organization based upon the stakeholder possessing one or more of three attributes: power, legitimacy and urgency. The central idea behind the model is that the more salient or prominent stakeholders have priority and therefore need to be actively communicated with. Smaller or hardly salient stakeholders have less priority and it is less important for an organization to communicate with them on an ongoing basis.

The first step of the model is to classify and prioritize stakeholders according to the presence or absence of three key attributes: power (the power of the stakeholder group upon an organization); legitimacy (the legitimacy of the claim laid upon the organization by the stakeholder group); and urgency (the degree to which stakeholder claims call for immediate action).[12] Together, these three attributes form seven different types of stakeholder, as shown in Figure 3.3.

The three stakeholder groups on the edges of Figure 3.3 are classified as *latent* stakeholder groups, which are groups possessing only one attribute:

1   *Dormant stakeholders*: Those who have the power to impose their will on others but because they do not have a legitimate relationship or urgent claim, their power remains dormant. Examples of dormant stakeholders include those who wield power by having a loaded gun (coercive), by spending a lot of money (utilitarian), or by commanding the attention of the news media (symbolic). Dormant stakeholders, however, have little or no

interaction with the organization, but because of their potential to acquire a second attribute (urgency or legitimacy), practitioners should be aware of such stakeholders.

2 *Discretionary stakeholders*: Those who possess legitimate claims but have no power to influence the organization and no urgent claims. Recipients of corporate charity, for instance, fall within this group.

3 *Demanding stakeholders*: Those who have urgent claims, but neither the power nor legitimacy to enforce them. These groups can therefore be bothersome but do not warrant serious attention from communication practitioners. That is, where stakeholders are unable or unwilling to acquire either the power or the legitimacy necessary to move their claim into a more salient status, the 'noise' of urgency is insufficient to move a stakeholder claim beyond latency. For example, a lone demonstrator who camps near a company's site might be embarrassing to the company or a nuisance to employees and managers of an organization, but the claims of the demonstrator will typically remain unconsidered.

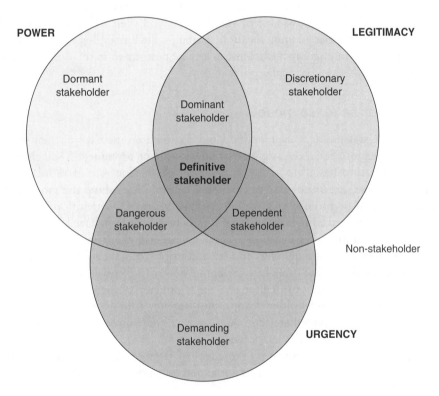

FIGURE 3.3 Stakeholder salience model

Three further groups are considered and classified as *expectant* stakeholders and are groups with two attributes present.

4 *Dominant stakeholders*: Those who have both powerful and legitimate claims, giving them a strong influence on the organization. Examples include employees, customers, owners and significant (institutional) investors in the organization.

5 *Dangerous stakeholders*: Those who have power and urgent claims, but lack legitimacy. They are seen as dangerous as they may resort to coercion and even violence. Examples of unlawful, yet common, attempts at using coercive means to advance stakeholder claims (which may or may not be legitimate) include wildcat strikes, employee sabotage and terrorism. The consumer electronics firm Philips, for example, was faced with such a dangerous stakeholder in March 2002, when an armed individual held several people hostage in the Rembrandt tower in Amsterdam (which is situated next to the company's main headquarters) to protest against the company's introduction of flat screen TVs which he thought communicated hidden codes.

6 *Dependent stakeholders*: Those who lack power, but who have urgent, legitimate claims. They rely on others for the power to carry out their will, at times through the advocacy of other stakeholders. Local residents of a community in which a plant of a large corporation is based, for instance, often rely on lobby groups, the media or another form of political representation to have their concerns voiced and considered by a company.

The seventh and final type of stakeholder group that can be identified is:

7 *Definitive stakeholder*: Those who have legitimacy, power and urgency. In other words, definitive stakeholders are powerful and legitimate stakeholders who, by definition, need to be communicated with. When the claim of a definitive stakeholder is urgent, communication practitioners and other managers have a responsibility to give it priority and attention. Shareholders, for example, who are normally classified as dominant stakeholders, can become active when they feel that their legitimate interests are not being served by the managers of the company in which they hold stock, and then they effectively act as definitive stakeholders. When the actions of such powerful shareholders may, for example, imply the removal of senior executives, communication practitioners and managers of the organization urgently need to attend to their concerns.

Once all the organization's stakeholders have been classified according to their salience, communication practitioners will have an overview of which stakeholder groups require attention and need to be communicated with. Based on the classification, they can develop communication strategies to most appropriately deal with each stakeholder. For example, dominant and definitive stakeholders of the organization, such as employees, customers and shareholders, need to be communicated with on an ongoing basis. Most organizations have ongoing communication programmes for these stakeholders, including newsletters, corporate events and an intranet for employees, advertising and promotional campaigns for customers and financial reports, investor briefings and the annual general meeting for shareholders. In addition, many organizations will often communicate directly with members of the local communities in which it operates (a dependent stakeholder), and will respond to dangerous stakeholders if the actions of those stakeholders affect others, including the company's employees. Organizations typically do not communicate on an ongoing basis with latent stakeholder groups, including dormant, demanding and discretionary stakeholders.

The power–interest matrix

A second mapping device is based on the same principles as the stakeholder salience model. The general objective is to categorize stakeholders on the basis of the power that they possess and the extent to which they are likely to have or show an interest in the organization's activities. Practitioners would estimate stakeholders on these two variables and plot the location of the stakeholders in the matrix. Figure 3.4 displays these variables and the four cells in which stakeholders can be located.[13]

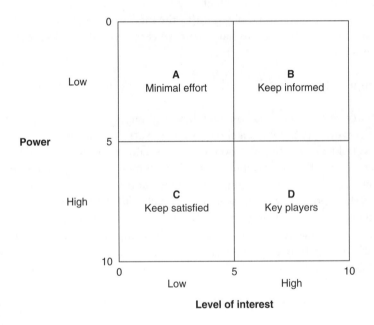

FIGURE 3.4   The power–interest matrix

Similar to the stakeholder salience model, the idea again is that communication practitioners can formulate appropriate communication strategies on the basis of identifying and categorizing stakeholders. In particular, the reaction or position of 'key players' (quadrant D) towards the organization's decisions and operations must be given key consideration. They need to be constantly communicated with. Similarly, those with a high level of interest in the organization but with a low level of power or influence (quadrant B) need to be kept informed of the organization, so that they remain committed to the organization and may spread positive word-of-mouth to others. Stakeholders in quadrant C are the most challenging to maintain relationships with as, despite their lack of interest in general, these stakeholders might exercise their power in reaction to a particular decision or corporate activity. Practitioners should also remain sensitive to the possible movement of stakeholders from one quadrant to another when, for example, levels of interest in the organization change.

Both mapping devices provide an overview and ordering of the importance and influence of particular stakeholders to an organization in general terms. Based upon this ordering, organizations know how intensely they need to communicate with particular groups and also what the key messages should be. In other words, these mappings give an insight into whether stakeholders should only be kept informed of decisions of the organization or its stance on a particular issue, or instead whether stakeholders should be actively listened to and communicated with on an ongoing basis. In broad terms, those stakeholders who are salient or have a powerful interest in the organization need to be communicated with so that they continue to support the organization. Important stakeholders, such as customers, employees, suppliers and shareholders, in any case need to be listened to and may also need to be actively involved in the decision-making of the organization. Figure 3.5 displays these differences between a strategy of simply providing information or disseminating information with stakeholders in order to raise their awareness, on the one hand, and a strategy of actively communicating with stakeholders and incorporating them in the organization's decision-making, on the other.

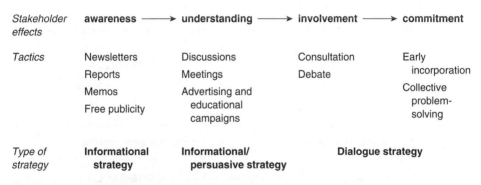

FIGURE 3.5 Stakeholder communication: from awareness to commitment

An *informational strategy* is simply a strategy of informing someone about something. Press releases, newsletters and reports on a company website are often simply meant to make information available about the organization to its stakeholders. Such a strategy may create awareness of organizational decisions and may also contribute towards a degree of understanding of the reasons for these decisions. A second strategy that organizations can use is a *persuasive strategy*, whereby an organization, through campaigns, meetings and discussions with stakeholders, tries to change and tune the knowledge, attitude, and behaviour of stakeholders in a way that is favourable to the organization. Corporate advertising and educational campaigns, for example, are often used to create a favourable image for the organization and to 'sell' a particular kind of understanding of the organization's decisions, its corporate values and its products and services. A third strategy that organizations may use is a *dialogue strategy*, in which both parties (organizations and stakeholders) mutually engage in an exchange of ideas and opinions. A dialogue strategy involves active consultation of stakeholders and incorporation of important stakeholders into the organization's decision-making. It involves working towards a process of mutual understanding and/or mutual decisions rather than strategic self-interest on the part of the organization.

The use of each of these strategies will depend on the salience and power–interest of a stakeholder group and the need for active engagement with stakeholders to build long-term relationships with them and to provide them with opportunities to connect with the organization. For example, when powerful institutional shareholders challenge a company's executive payment and reward scheme, they become definitive stakeholders who not only need to be actively communicated with but, ideally, would also at the very least be consulted in future decisions about such matters (a dialogue strategy).

Schematically, these three strategies have been described as a one-way symmetrical model of communication (informational strategy), a two-way asymmetrical model of communication (persuasive strategy) and a two-way symmetrical model of communication (a dialogue strategy), as shown in Figure 3.6. In the first model, communication is always one-way, from the organization to its stakeholders. There

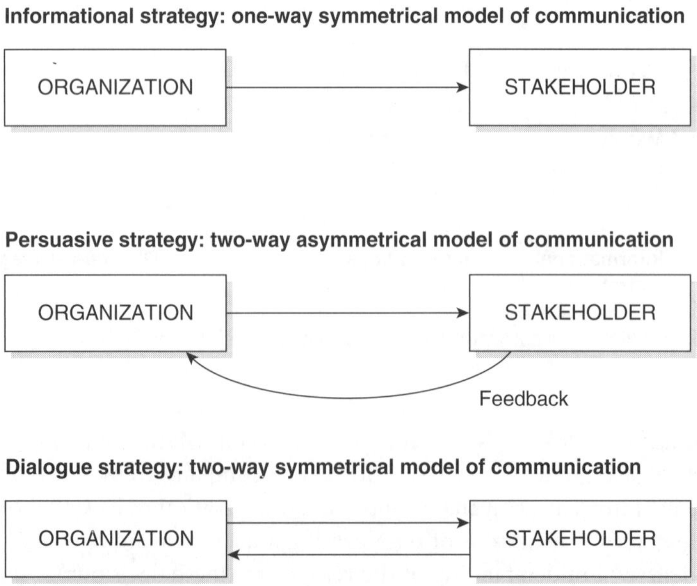

Informational strategy: one-way symmetrical model of communication

ORGANIZATION → STAKEHOLDER

Persuasive strategy: two-way asymmetrical model of communication

ORGANIZATION → STAKEHOLDER
Feedback

Dialogue strategy: two-way symmetrical model of communication

ORGANIZATION ⇄ STAKEHOLDER

FIGURE 3.6   Models of organization–stakeholder communication

is no listening to stakeholders or an attempt to gather feedback in this model. The aim is simply to make information available to stakeholders. However, the relationship between the organization and stakeholders is still 'symmetrical'. This means that communication practitioners aim to report objectively information about the organization to relevant stakeholders and do not try to persuade stakeholders regarding particular understandings, attitudes or behaviour. In other words, there is no explicit persuasive intent on the part of the practitioners, which is labelled an 'asymmetrical' relationship between an organization and its stakeholders, as that would involve a situation where the interests of the organization are emphasized at the expense of the interests of its stakeholders. In the second model, communication flows between an organization and its stakeholders and is thus labelled two-way communication. For example, an organization may gather feedback from stakeholders on how the organization is being perceived and understood. However, the two-way asymmetrical model is 'asymmetrical' because the effects of communication are unbalanced in favour of the organization. The organization does not change as a result of communicating with its stakeholders; instead, it only attempts to change stakeholders' attitudes and behaviours. The third model, the two-way symmetrical model, consists of a dialogue rather than a monologue. Communication again flows both ways between an organization and its stakeholders, but unlike the previous model, the goal is to exchange views and to reach mutual understanding between both parties. Both parties recognize the 'other' in the communication process and try to provide each other with equal opportunities for expression and for a free exchange of information.[14] British American Tobacco (Case Example 3.1) is an example of a company that has engaged with stakeholders on a whole range of social and environmental issues within its supply chain and in the marketing of its products.

Case Example 3.1

British American Tobacco (BAT) and stakeholder dialogue

British American Tobacco (BAT) is the world's most international tobacco group, with brands sold in more than 180 markets. The company is among the most profitable corporations in the world, delivering exceptional value to shareholders. Over the past ten years, for example, shareholders received a total return of 486 per cent on their investments, compared to 3 per cent for the 100 top listed corporations in London (the FTSE 100) as a whole. BAT's strategy is firmly focused on growing the business towards a strategic vision of regaining overall leadership in the global tobacco industry. The company recognizes that realizing its vision is, at least in part, dependent on effectively managing stakeholder relationships. BAT's products pose significant health risks for

(Continued)

(Continued)

individual consumers, which in turn affects the provision and costs of healthcare in countries around the world. The company has been criticized for this, with many advocacy groups calling for an outright prohibition of smoking. BAT itself takes a different ethical stance. The company recognizes that its products pose risks to health, but it constantly emphasizes that these products are legal, that calls for prohibition are exceptionally rare and that about a billion adults globally choose to smoke. In other words, their social responsibility does not extend to the responsible choices made by adults, or indeed the public costs associated with these choices. Instead, the company's corporate social responsibility efforts are aimed at improving its overall standards of business conduct. Fran Morrison, the Head of Corporate Communications, explains that the company has adopted 'a responsible approach to doing business from crop to consumer'. As part of this approach, the company is working on the elimination of child labour in the industry, provides support for leaf-growing communities, is tackling illicit trade and is curbing carbon emissions. While BAT does not actively campaign on the risks of smoking, its websites contain information on these risks. Corporate communication staff have also set up a dialogue forum with key stakeholders on social and environmental issues connected to the business. The feedback gained from stakeholders is used to set progressive targets on its social and environmental reporting. It also gives the company an insight into what stakeholders believe are the most contentious topics. In response, BAT has acted upon a number of these topics, resulting in the development of youth smoking prevention programmes and investments in the development of cigarettes with reduced toxicants that are less harmful to consumers.

Source: Material for this case study was sourced from Morrison, F. (2007), 'Corporate responsibility in a controversial industry', *European Communication Summit*, Brussels.

Each of these different strategies also requires different media or channels to communicate with stakeholders. Communication media or channels, such as reports, adverts and face-to-face communication, vary based on their capacity to process and channel 'rich' exchanges. A 'rich' exchange involves the ability to provide immediate feedback between the two parties, the ability to personalize and adapt messages based upon responses, and the ability to express and articulate the message in different ways.[15] Media that facilitate such 'rich' exchanges are central to a dialogue strategy and to some extent also feature in a persuasive strategy. These include face-to-face consultations and meetings and personalized documents such as letters or memos. Media which are less able to facilitate 'rich' exchanges, such as impersonal written documents (e.g., a financial report), are associated with an informational strategy where there is no direct need for the stakeholder to directly respond to the message. Face-to-face communication is the richest medium because it allows immediate feedback so that interpretations can be checked and subsequent communication can be adjusted. 'Rich' media are also useful for discussing ambiguous, sensitive, controversial or complex issues with stakeholders of the organization in order to overcome different frames of reference. Media of low 'richness' restrict immediate feedback and are therefore less appropriate for resolving ambiguous, sensitive, controversial or complex issues. However, an important point is that media of low richness are effective for reporting well-understood messages and standard data, such as, for example, reporting on financial performance.

STAKEHOLDER ENGAGEMENT AND COLLABORATION

3.5 In recent years, communication practitioners have developed a focus on the importance of engaging stakeholders in long-term relationships. Rather than focusing on a simple instance of communication or of exchanging goods, recent efforts focus on changing the relationship between the organization and its stakeholders from 'management' to 'collaboration' and from 'exchange' to 'long-term relationships'. The emphasis has moved from a focus on stakeholders as being managed by companies to a focus on the interaction that companies have with their stakeholders on a continuous and relational basis. 'Collaboration' implies a two-way symmetrical model of dialogue and consultation, through which communication practitioners build stakeholder relationships that are reciprocal, evolving and mutually defined, and that are a source of opportunity and competitive advantage.[16]

A summary of this change in focus is given in Table 3.2. The 'old' approach of stakeholder management consists of different practitioners and departments in the organization 'managing' interactions with stakeholders, often from the perspective of their own function or department. Another characteristic of the 'old' approach is the attempt to 'buffer' the claims and interests of stakeholders to prevent them from interfering with internal operations and instead trying to influence their attitudes and opinions. In this approach, in line with a persuasion strategy, an organization is trying either to insulate itself from external interference or to actively influence stakeholders in its environment through such means as contributions to political action committees, lobbying and advocacy advertising. The 'new' approach of stakeholder collaboration, in contrast, involves an emphasis on stakeholder relationships

TABLE 3.2 Characteristics of the 'old' and 'new' approaches to the organization–stakeholder relationships

Stakeholder management	Stakeholder collaboration
Fragmented among various departments	Integrated management approach
Focus on managing relationships	Focus on building relationships
Emphasis on 'buffering' the organization from stakeholders interfering with internal operations	Emphasis on 'bridging' and creating opportunities and mutual benefits
Linked to short-term business goals	Linked to long-term business goals
Idiosyncratic implementation dependent on department's interests and personal style of manager	Coherent approach driven by mission, values, and corporate strategies

across the organization. The aim here is to build long-term relationships and to seek out those stakeholders who are interested in collaboration. The 'new' approach is more in line with a dialogue strategy, with its emphasis on 'bridging' stakeholder claims and interests. Bridging occurs when organizations seek to adapt their activities so that they conform with the external expectations and claims of important stakeholder groups. It suggests that an organization actively tries to meet and exceed regulatory requirements in its industry or that it attempts to quickly identify changing social expectations in order to promote organizational conformance to those expectations.

There are many examples of this change in approach to organization–stakeholder relationships. For example, many leading brands, such as Saab, Lego and Harley Davidson, now involve their customers in long-term relationships by incorporating them in their internal research and development (R&D) processes and through participation in branded online communities. Another good example is the way in which Starbucks has moved form an arms' length relationship with key stakeholders to a direct dialogue that allows key stakeholders to influence the direction of the company (Case Study 3.1).

CASE STUDY 3.1

STARBUCKS COFFEE COMPANY AND STAKEHOLDER COLLABORATION

Starbucks, generally considered to be the most famous specialty coffee shop chain in the world, today has over 15,000 stores worldwide. Many analysts have credited Starbucks with having turned coffee from a commodity into an experience to savour. Starbucks has always felt that the key to its growth and its business success would lie in a rounded corporate brand identity, a better understanding of its customers and a store experience that would generate a pull effect through word-of-mouth. Howard Schultz, Starbucks' founder and chairman, had, early on in the company's history, envisioned a retail experience that revolved around high-quality coffee, personalized, knowledgeable services and sociability. So Starbucks put in place various measures to make this experience appealing to millions of people and to create a unique identity for Starbucks' products and stores.

Schultz felt that the equity of the Starbucks brand depended less on advertising and promotion and more on personal communications, on strong ties with customers and with members of the local community and on word-of-mouth. As Schultz put it:

> If we want to exceed the trust of our customers, then we first have to build trust with our people. A brand has to start with the [internal] culture and naturally extend to our customers. ... Our brand is based on the experience that we control in our stores. When a company can create a relevant, emotional and intimate experience, it builds trust with the customer. ... We have benefited by the fact that our stores are reliable, safe and consistent, where people can take a break.

Schultz regarded the baristas, the coffee makers in the stores, as his brand ambassadors and considered the company's employees as long-term 'partners' in making the company's strategic vision a reality. This commitment to employees is also anchored in Starbucks' mission statement, which, among other things, states

(Continued)

(Continued)

that the company aims to 'provide a great work environment and to treat each other with respect and dignity'.

From its founding onwards, Starbucks has looked upon each of its stores as a billboard for the company and as directly contributing to building the company's brand and reputation. Each detail has been scrutinized to enhance the mood and ambience of the store, to make sure everything signals 'best of class' and reflects the personality of the community and the neighbourhood. The company has gone to great lengths to make sure that the store fixtures, the merchandise displays, the colours, the artwork, the banners, the music, and the aromas all blend to create a consistent, inviting, stimulating environment that evokes the romance of coffee and signals the company's passion for coffee.

Just as treating employees as 'partners' is one of the pillars of Starbucks' culture and mission, so is contributing positively to the communities it serves and to the environment. Each Starbucks store supports a range of community initiatives and causes, and aims to be a long-term 'partner' to the communities in which it trades. At the community level, Starbucks store managers have discretion to make money donations to local causes and to provide coffee for local fundraisers.

Because of these initiatives, consumers and members of the community in which Starbucks operate associate the Starbucks brand with coffee, accessible elegance, community, individual expression, and 'a place away from home'. Besides engaging in long-term relationships with customers, employees and communities, Starbucks also collaborates with non-governmental organizations (NGOs), promoting the production and consumption of 'fair trade' coffee. In 2000, Global Exchange, an NGO dedicated to promoting environmental, political and social justice around the world, criticized the company for profiting at the expense of coffee farmers by paying low prices and not buying 'Fair Trade' coffee beans. While the company is at times still being criticized for its aggressive tactics in the coffee market, it has tried to collaborate with various organizations to promote the consumption of Fair Trade coffee. Starbucks has been an ongoing contributor to CARE, a worldwide relief and development foundation, specifying that its support should go to coffee-producing nations. The company also began a partnership in 1998 with Conservation International, a non-profit organization that promotes biodiversity in coffee-growing regions, to support producers of shade-grown coffee, which protects the environment. Finally, in order to appease Global Exchange, Starbucks agreed to sell Fair Trade coffee in all its stores. This decision has created a lot of goodwill from customers, industry analysts, communities and NGOs worldwide.

Despite its best efforts, however, Starbucks was criticized in March 2007 for attempting to block Ethiopia's desire to trademark some of its most famous coffees. Premium coffee is a growing market, and to benefit from the rising demand, the Ethiopian government set out to trademark three regions of the country associated with its finest beans: Sidamo, Harar and Yirgacheffe. With trademarks, the country could charge distributors a licensing fee for their use. The European Union, Japan and Canada all approved the trademark scheme. Starbucks, however, initially objected to the trademarks and was working with its industry lobbyists (a buffering tactic) to pressure the US Patent and Trademark Office to turn down Ethiopia's trademark applications. As a result, the Office refused to approve two of the three trademarks.

(Continued)

(Continued)

Oxfam took up Ethiopia's cause in a media campaign, generating some 70,000 complaints against Starbucks from consumers and the general public. In response, Starbucks launched a media counter-offensive, publicly rebuking Ethiopia's efforts. The company claimed that licensing would be more appropriate than trade-marking the three coffee regions, and argued that 'the trademark application is not based upon sound economic advice and that the proposal as it stands would hurt Ethiopian coffee farmers economically'. The active blocking of the Ethiopian government led to a public relations crisis for Starbucks, with the normally ethically-minded company accused of acting tough with one of the world's poorest countries. To defuse the situation, Starbucks agreed a wide-ranging accord with Ethiopia to support and promote its coffee, ending the dispute over the issue.

Starbucks also recently started to used social media to communicate directly with stakeholders and to strengthen the brand and community ties around the company. Starbucks V2V, for example, is a social networking site where people can connect on global relief causes and community issues. The networking site is closely connected to the company. Many people on the site either work for Starbucks or are loyal customers or members of the community. The company also directly facilitates the discussion and supports the identified causes and issues. On another site (www.mystarbucksidea.com), people can suggest ideas for products, store experiences and community involvement. Most of the people on the site are loyal customers, and in this way Starbucks is able to give them a direct voice in the company. Dedicated communication staff listen to the ideas being discussed, provide customers with information on what the company is doing, and may help develop these ideas into action.

QUESTIONS FOR REFLECTION

1   Consider the importance for Starbucks of developing long-term relationships and alliances with different stakeholders. Should the company develop relationships with all of its stakeholders or only a select few?
2   What strategies and models of communication should the company use for communicating with its different stakeholder groups? What opportunities are provided by social media for stakeholder communication?

Source: This case study is based upon Holt, D. (2007), 'Brand hypocrisy at Starbucks' and 'Starbucks coffee that cares?' (http://www.sbs.ox.ac.uk/faculty/Holt+Douglas/) and Argenti, P. A. (2004), 'collaborating with activists: How Starbucks works with NGOs', *California Management Review*, 47(1), 91–116.

CHAPTER SUMMARY

3.6 This chapter has described the importance of stakeholder management within contemporary organizations. It has provided the theoretical background to the concept of stakeholders and discussed different strategies and models which communication practitioners can use to identify and analyse the key stakeholders of the organization and communicate and collaborate with them.

DISCUSSION QUESTIONS

1   What is the difference between a stakeholder and a shareholder?

2   What are the main advantages for organizations when they adopt a stakeholder approach to their strategy and communication?

3   In your view, should an organization engage in dialogue with all of its stakeholders all of the time, or rather only with some of them or simply only on particular occasions such as crises?

KEY TERMS

Corporate social responsibility

Dialogue strategy

Economic/market stake

Equity stakes

Influencer stake

Informational strategy

Legitimacy

Neo-classical economic theory

Persuasive strategy

Power–interest matrix

Socio-economic theory

Stakeholder

Stakeholder collaboration

Stakeholder salience

FURTHER READING

Anderson, Rob, Baxter, Leslie A. and Cissna, Kenneth N. (2003), *Dialogue: Theorizing Difference in Communication Studies*. Thousand Oaks, CA: Sage Publications.

Carroll, Archie B. and Buchholtz, Ann K. (2009), *Business and Society: Ethics and Stakeholder Management* (7th edn). Cincinatti, OH: South-Western College Publishing.

Freeman, R. Edward, Harrison, Jeffrey S. and Wicks, Andrew C. (2007), *Managing for Stakeholders: Survival, Reputation, and Success*. New Haven, CT: Yale University Press.

NOTES

1   Friedman, M. (1970), 'The social responsibility of business is to increase its profits', *The New York Times*, 13 September.

2   See Donaldson, T. and Preston, L.E. (1995), 'The stakeholder theory of the corporation: concepts, evidence, and implications', *Academy of Management Review*, 20 (1): 65–91.

3   Berman, S.L., Wicks, A.C., Kotha, S. and Johnes, T.M. (1999), 'Does stakeholder orientation matter? The relationship between stakeholder management models and firm financial performance', *Academy of Management Journal*, 42 (5): 488–506; Jones, T. and Wicks, A. (1999), 'Convergent stakeholder theory', *Academy of Management Review*, 20: 404–437, quote on p. 206.

4   Jones and Wicks (1999), quote on p. 206; Porter, M.E. and Kramer, M.R. (2002), 'The competitive advantage of corporate philanthropy', *Harvard Business Review*, December: 5–16.

5   Kotter, J. and Heskett, J. (1992), *Corporate Culture and Performance*. New York: Free Press, p. 59.

6   Freeman, R.E. (1984), *Strategic Management: A Stakeholder Approach*. Boston: Pitman, p. 6.

7   Carroll, A.B. (1996), *Business and Society: Ethics and Stakeholder Management* (5th edn). Cincinatti, OH: South-Western College Publishing, p. 473.

8   Freeman, R.E. (1984), p. 8.

9   Clarkson, B.E. (1995), 'A stakeholder framework for analyzing and evaluating corporate social performance', *Academy of Management Review*, 20 (1): 92–117.

10 Charkham, J.P. (1992), *Keeping Good Company: A Study of Corporate Governance in Five Countries*. Oxford: Oxford University Press.

11 Carroll, A.B. (1989), *Business and Society: Ethics and Stakeholder Management*. Cincinnati, OH: South-Western Publishing, p. 62.

12 Agle, B.R., Mitchell, R.K. and Sonnenfeld, J.A. (1999), 'Who matters to CEOs? An investigation of stakeholder attributes and salience, corporate performance, and CEO values', *Academy of Management Journal*, 42 (5): 507–525; Mitchell, R.K., Agle, B.R. and Wood, D.J. (1997), 'Toward a theory of stakeholder identification and salience: defining the principle of who and what really counts', *Academy of Management Review*, 22 (4): 853–886.

13 Based upon Mendelow, A. (1991) *Proceedings of 2nd International Conference on Information Systems*, Cambridge, MA; also cited in Johnson, G. and Scholes, K. (1993), *Exploring Corporate Strategy: Text and Cases* (3rd edn). London: Prentice Hall International, pp. 176–177.

14 Based upon Grunig, J.E. and Hunt, T. (1984), *Managing Public Relations*. New York: Holt, Rinehart & Winston; Deetz, S. (2006), 'Dialogue, communication theory, and the hope of making quality decisions together: a commentary', *Management Communication Quarterly*, 19: 368–375; Morsing, M. and Schultz, M. (2006), 'Corporate social responsibility communication: stakeholder information, response and involvement strategies', *Business Ethics: A European Review*, 15: 323–338.

15 Based upon Daft, R.L. and Lengel, R.H. (1986), 'Organizational information requirements, media richness and structural design', *Management Science*, 32 (5): 554–571; and Kaplan, R.S. and Norton, D.P. (2001), *The Strategy-focused Organization: How Balanced Scorecard Companies Thrive in the New Business Environment*. Boston, MA: Harvard Business School Press.

16 Based on Svendsen, A. (1998), *The Stakeholder Strategy: Profiting from Collaborative Business Relationships*. San Francisco: Berrett-Koehler Publishers; Andriof, J., Waddock, S., Husted, B. and Rahman, S.S. (2002), *Unfolding Stakeholder Thinking: Theory, Responsibility and Engagement*. Sheffield: Greenleaf.

CORPORATE IDENTITY, CORPORATE BRANDING AND CORPORATE REPUTATION

4

Chapter Overview

One of the primary ways in which organizations manage relationships with stakeholders is by building and maintaining their corporate reputations. Reputations are established when organizations consistently communicate an authentic, unique and distinctive corporate identity towards stakeholders. Drawing on frameworks from theory and practice, the chapter discusses how organizations manage their corporate identity in order to establish, maintain and protect their corporate reputations with different stakeholder groups.

INTRODUCTION

4.1 In the previous chapter, we discussed the importance of organizations communicating with different stakeholders for both moral (legitimacy) and instrumental (profit) reasons. We also highlighted the challenges that organizations face in dealing with different expectations and demands of stakeholders. One way in which organizations have addressed these challenges is by strategically projecting a particular positive image of the organization, labelled as a corporate identity or corporate brand, to build, maintain and protect strong reputations with stakeholders. Such strong reputations in turn lead to acceptance of the organization by different stakeholders and to the organization being considered legitimate. Strong reputations also give organizations 'first-choice' status with investors, customers, employees and other stakeholder groups. For customers, for instance, a reputation serves as a signal of the underlying quality of an organization's products and services, and they therefore value associations and transactions with firms enjoying a good reputation.

Equally, employees prefer to work for organizations with a good reputation, and will therefore work harder, or even for lower remuneration.

The chapter focuses on how organizations manage the process by which they project a particular corporate image of themselves and come to be seen and evaluated in a particular way by their stakeholders. The chapter starts by outlining the traditional frameworks and principles of managing corporate identity and reputation and more recent models on corporate branding. After a discussion of the basic theory we turn to practice and demonstrate how these frameworks and principles can be used within corporate communication.

CORPORATE IDENTITY, IMAGE AND REPUTATION

4.2 The emphasis that organizations, both in theory and practice, place on managing their corporate image suggests a preoccupation with how they *symbolically* construct an image (as a 'caring citizen', for example) for themselves through their communication and how in turn that image leads them to be seen in particular symbolic terms by important stakeholders. In other words, corporate image management adds an important symbolic dimension to corporate communication and the process by which organizations communicate with their stakeholders. Corporate communication is not only seen as a matter of exchanging *information* with stakeholders (an informational or dialogue strategy, see Chapter 3) so that they can make informed decisions about the organization, but also as a case of *symbolically* crafting and projecting a particular image for the organization. In many actual instances of corporate communication, the two dimensions may blend together and may be hard to separate. For example, when Tesco, a UK retailer, announced its sponsorship of Cancer Research UK, it provided people with information regarding the decision about its sponsorship (to fund research into the prevention, treatment and cure of cancer) and tied the sponsorship into the promotion of its Healthy Living range of products to support a healthy lifestyle. At the same time, through the sponsorship, the company aimed to project an image of itself as a caring and responsible corporate citizen, contributing to the fight against a deadly disease.

Investing in the development of a corporate image for the organization has further strategic advantages for organizations. These can be summarized under the following headings:

- *Distinctiveness*: A corporate image may help stakeholders find or recognize an organization. When consistently communicated, a corporate image creates awareness, triggers recognition, and may also instil confidence among stakeholder groups because these groups will have a clearer picture of the organization.[1] Inside the organization, a clear and strong image of the organization can help raise motivation and morale among employees by establishing and perpetuating a 'we' feeling and by allowing people to identify with their organizations.

- *Impact*: A corporate image provides a basis for being favoured by stakeholders. This, in turn, may have a direct impact on the organization's performance when it leads to stakeholders supporting the organization in the form of buying its products and services, investing in the company or not opposing its decisions.
- *Stakeholders*: Any individual may have more than one stakeholder role in relation to an organization. When organizations project a consistent image of themselves, they avoid potential pitfalls that may occur when conflicting images and messages are sent out. Employees, for example, are often also consumers in the marketplace for the products of the company that they themselves work for. When companies fail to send out a consistent image (often by failing to match all their internal and external communication), it threatens employees' perceptions of the company's integrity: they are told one thing by management, but perceive something different in the marketplace.

For these reasons, corporate image management is seen as an important part of corporate communication. In theory and practice, the original set of concepts that were introduced to describe this particular aspect of corporate communication involves corporate identity, corporate image and corporate reputation. More recently, the term 'corporate branding' has gained traction in describing the way in which companies develop and build reputations with their stakeholders.

The original concept of corporate identity grew out of a preoccupation in the design and communication communities with the ways in which organizations present themselves to external audiences. Initially, the term was restricted to logos and other elements of visual design, but it gradually came to encompass all forms of communication (corporate advertising, sponsorship, etc.) and all forms of outward-facing behaviour in the marketplace. The German corporate design specialists Birkigt and Stadler proposed one of the first models of corporate image management (Figure 4.1).[2] Birkigt and Stadler's model put particular emphasis on the concept of corporate identity, which they defined as consisting of the following attributes:

- *Symbolism*: Corporate logos and the company house style (stationery, etc.) of an organization.
- *Communication*: All planned forms of communication, including corporate advertising, events, sponsorship, publicity and promotions.
- *Behaviour*: All behaviour of employees (ranging from managers and the receptionist to front-line staff such as salespeople and shop assistants) that leaves an impression on stakeholders.

Through these three attributes, organizations communicate and project an image of themselves to their stakeholders. Birkigt and Stadler also argued that the image that organizations project through symbolism, communication and behaviour is often also the way in which they are perceived by their stakeholders. The latter concept they called 'corporate image', which involves the image of an organization in the eyes of stakeholders.

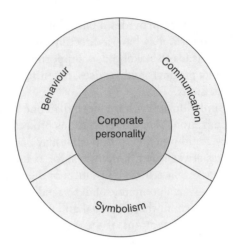

FIGURE 4.1 The Birkigt and Stadler model of corporate identity

Source: Birkigt, K., Stadler, M. and Funck, H.J. (1986) *Corporate Identity: Grundlagen, Funktionen und Beispielen.* Landsberg an Lech: Verlag Moderne Industrie.

One important implication of the Birkigt and Stadler model is that corporate identity has become quite a broad concept that encompasses more than corporate logos or corporate advertising campaigns. Because of its breadth, the concept also has a bearing upon different functional areas within the organization. Communication practitioners (including marketing communication professionals) often hold only the direct responsibility for corporate symbolism and communication, while product and brand managers are responsible for the positioning of products and services, and human resource staff and middle managers for the monitoring of employee behaviour.

A second important implication of the original Birkigt and Stadler model is that it suggests that corporate identity, as the outward presentation of an organization through symbolism, communication and behaviour, should emerge from an understanding of the organization's core mission, strategic vision and the more general corporate culture of an organization. The mission and vision represent the basic who and what of an organization, what business the organization is in and what it wants to be known and appreciated for. An organization's mission often already includes a statement on the beliefs that constitute the organization's culture, underpin its strategy and suggests how the organization wants to be known by stakeholder groups outside the organization. Birkigt and Stadler labelled the notion of core values in the organization's culture, mission and vision as the organization's corporate personality. Design guru Wally Olins articulates the difference between corporate personality and corporate identity as follows:

> Corporate personality embraces the subject at its most profound level. It is the soul, the persona, the spirit, the culture of the organization manifested in some way. A corporate personality is not necessarily something tangible that you can see, feel or touch – although it may be. The tangible manifestation of a corporate personality is a corporate identity. It is the identity that projects and reflects the reality of the corporate personality.[3]

In other words, corporate identity involves the construction of an image of the organization to differentiate a company's position in the eyes of important stakeholder groups. Corporate personality, on the other hand, is based on deeper patterns of meaning and sense-making of people within that same organization and includes the core values that define the organization.

The French sociologists Larçon and Reitter added a further dimension to the concept of corporate identity when they similarly argued that it not only involves the visible outward presentation of a company, but also the set of intrinsic characteristics or 'traits' that give the company its specificity, stability and coherence.[4] In their view, a corporate identity is not merely a projected image in the form of visual design and communication, but is also fundamentally concerned with 'what the organization is' – the core of the organization as it is laid down in its strategies and culture. This notion of corporate identity 'traits' has also been referred to as an 'organizational' identity as opposed to a 'corporate' identity, again to make the distinction between core values that people share within the organization ('organizational identity') and the outward presentation and communication of those values through symbolism, communication and behaviour ('corporate identity').

The management experts Albert and Whetten, who were among the first to define this notion of 'organizational' identity, similarly talked about specific characteristics or 'traits' of an organization in all its strategies, values and practices that give the company its specificity, stability and coherence. They argued that just as individuals express a sense of personal distinctiveness, a sense of personal continuity, and a sense of personal autonomy, equally organizations have their own individuality and uniqueness. And just as the identity of individuals may come to be anchored in some combination of gender, nationality, profession, social group, lifestyle, educational achievements or skills, so an organization's identity may be anchored in some combination of geographical place, nationality, strategy, founding, core business, technology, knowledge base, operating philosophy or organization design.

For each organization, according to Albert and Whetten, its particular combination of identity anchors imbues it with a set of distinctive values that are core, distinctive and enduring to it.[5] For example, many would argue that Sony's differentiation in the marketplace is quality consumer products, and they certainly do have ability in that area. But what makes Sony truly distinctive is the company's core value of 'miniaturization' – of producing ever smaller technology. This feature of miniaturization, which goes hand in hand with a drive for technological innovation, is at the heart of Sony's organizational identity or corporate personality. At the same time, this organizational identity has been carried through in all products, services and communications, that is, in Sony's corporate identity. Similarly, Virgin, a company that is active in very different markets (e.g., airlines, music stores, cola, and mobile phones) has meticulously cultivated the value of 'challenge' with all of its employees. Headed by its flamboyant CEO Richard Branson, Virgin has carried its core organizational identity of 'challenge' through in its distinctive market positioning of David versus Goliath: 'We are on your side against the fat cats'. This projected corporate identity has led to the widespread perception that Virgin is a company with a distinctive personality: innovative and challenging, but fun.

Figure 4.2 summarizes the process of corporate identity management as originally articulated by Birkigt and Stadler. The aim of corporate identity management is to establish a favourable reputation with the organization's stakeholders which, it is hoped, will be translated by such stakeholders into a propensity to buy that organization's

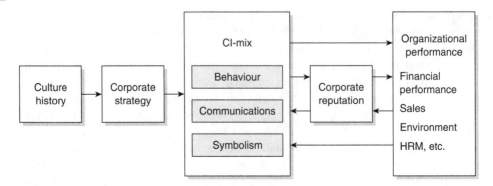

FIGURE 4.2 Corporate identity in relation to corporate reputation

Source: Based on C.B.M. Van Riel and J. Balmer (1997), 'Corporate identity: the concept, its measurement and management', *European Journal of Marketing*, 31: 342.

products and services, to work for that organization, or to invest in it (organizational performance). In other words, a good corporate reputation has a strategic value for the organization that possesses it. It ensures acceptance and legitimacy from stakeholder groups, generates returns, and may offer a competitive advantage as it forms an asset that is difficult to imitate. A good corporate reputation, or rather the corporate identity upon which it is based, is an intangible asset of the organization because of its potential for value creation, but also because its intangible character makes replication by competing firms more difficult.[6] Figure 4.2 shows the corporate identity mix (symbolism, communication and behaviour of members of the organization) as based on the organization's core values in its history and culture, and which inform every part of its strategy.

The general principle for corporate communication practitioners is that they need to link the corporate identity – the picture of the organization that is presented to external stakeholders – to the core values that members of the organization themselves associate with the organization (culture) and define the organization's mission and vision (organizational identity). Making sure that the corporate identity is rooted in the organizational identity not only offers a distinctive edge in the marketplace, but also ensures that the image that is projected is authentic rather than cosmetic, and is actually carried and shared by members of the organization. In this context, corporate identity and organizational identity or corporate personality rather should be seen as two sides of the same coin within corporate communication. Developing a corporate identity must start with a thorough analysis and understanding of the organization's core values in its mission, vision and culture, rather than rushing into communicating what might be thought to be the company's core values in a superficial manner. Equally, whatever picture is projected to external stakeholders has an effect upon the beliefs and values of employees, and thus on the organizational identity or corporate personality, as employees mirror themselves in whatever messages are being sent out to external stakeholder groups.[7]

The two sides to identity in organizations, organizational identity and corporate identity, therefore cannot and should not be seen as separate. This point is reinforced by studies into 'excellent' companies carried out over the past two decades. Writers such as Hamel and Prahalad, Peters and Waterman, and Collins and Porras, have found that what truly sets an 'excellent' company apart from its competitors in the marketplace in terms of the power of its image and products can be traced back to a set of values and related competencies that are authentic and unique to that organization and therefore difficult to imitate. Collins and Porras, in their analysis of companies that are industry leaders in the USA, argue that 'a visionary company almost religiously preserves its core ideology – changing it seldom, if ever'.[8] From this adherence to a fundamental set of beliefs or a deeply held sense of self-identity, as Collins and Porras point out, comes the discipline and drive that enable a company to succeed in the rapidly changing, volatile environments that characterize many contemporary markets.

CORPORATE BRANDING

4.3 Reputation scholars Fombrun and Van Riel carried out comparative analyses of corporate reputations of the most visible organizations across the world. Based upon stakeholder evaluations of the strongest corporate reputation within different countries, they suggest that organizations with the strongest reputations are on average characterized by high levels of *visibility* (the degree to which corporate themes are visible in all internal and external communication), *distinctiveness* (the degree to which the corporate identity or positioning of the organization is distinctive), *authenticity* (the degree to which an organization communicates values that are embedded in its culture), *transparency* (the degree to which an organization is open and transparent about its behaviour), and *consistency* (the degree to which organizations communicate consistent messages through all internal and external communication channels) in corporate communication.[9] In other words, a key driver for the strength of an organization's reputation is the degree to which the values that it communicates are not only authentic but also distinctive.

Many managers and communication practitioners indeed draw heavily on the idea of uniqueness or distinctiveness because it encapsulates the idea that the organization needs to express its uniqueness in the market and with other stakeholders. The idea is that this enables an organization to differentiate itself from its competitors and to attain a preferred 'position' in the consciousness of consumers and other stakeholders. While differentiated corporate values are seen as important in communicating a unique or distinct identity to stakeholders, recent research has also demonstrated that organizations in specific industry sectors may become more similar in the kinds of corporate identity that they project and that such convergence may be more or less appreciated by stakeholders dependent upon their expectations regarding appropriate corporate behaviour in a particular industry.[10] Communication scholars Deephouse and Carter have demonstrated that isomorphism (i.e., the similarity of an organization to others in its industry) improves the degree to which an organization is deemed legitimate (socially acceptable) by stakeholders, presumably because organizations converge on images and behaviours that are expected of them by stakeholders.[11] They also found that organizations with stronger corporate reputations were able to deviate from such pressures to communicate similar images and improve their distinct status without losing their legitimacy. Management scholars Lamertz, Heugens and Calmet similarly identified social pressures which stimulated organizations in the Canadian beer brewing industry to construct similar images (corporate identity) of themselves to meet stakeholder expectations. At the same time, they also found that alongside such similar images these beer brewing organizations also claimed distinctive attributes as part of their corporate identity.[12]

What this evidence suggests is that it is, first, important for organizations to claim the same generic values (e.g., technological innovation, customer care, ethical conduct) as its rivals in order to meet expectations of stakeholders that the organization is financially solid, socially engaging and ecologically sound in its business practices. At the same time, it remains crucial for organizations to claim some distinctive values in order to differentiate the organization from rival companies in the eyes of stakeholders. HSBC, for example, has claimed a distinctive value of being 'the world's local bank', whereby the company claims to tune its global scale to the local demands of individual customers. At the same time, HSBC has claimed very similar values as its competitors (Barclays, Citigroup, BNP and ING) regarding being a global or international institution that is focused on 'customer service', 'value creation', 'professionalism' and 'technological and financial innovation'.

In recent years, many analysts and writers have started to use the term 'corporate branding' to highlight the importance of distinctiveness. For many of them, the idea of an organization as a brand was a logical extension of the product branding approach, with its original focus on products and brand benefits and on individual consumers. The distinction between the two followed from Olins' framework on monolithic corporate, branded and endorsed identities. Figure 4.3 displays these three types of identity. The *monolithic corporate identity* refers to a corporate brand: a structure where all products and services, buildings, official communication and employee behaviour are labelled or branded with the same company name. Examples include Disney, Coca-Cola, Nike, McDonald's, Wal-Mart and BMW. The fully *branded identity* refers to a structure whereby products and services are brought to the market each with their own brand name and brand values. Companies such as Unilever and Procter & Gamble have traditionally followed this branded identity structure, where neither the company's name nor its core values figured in the positioning and communication of its products. This branded strategy traditionally made sense for Unilever and Procter & Gamble as they were addressing very different market segments through the different products in their product portfolio. An *endorsed identity* is one where different business and products have their own branded identity (including names and logos) but are at the same time endorsed or badged with the parent company name.

Many large organizations that were previously branded giants are changing their organizations into monolithic corporate brands. Kingfisher and Unilever are good examples of organizations that have moved towards endorsed and monolithic identities and aim to have their product brands more strongly associated with their company name (Case Example 4.1).

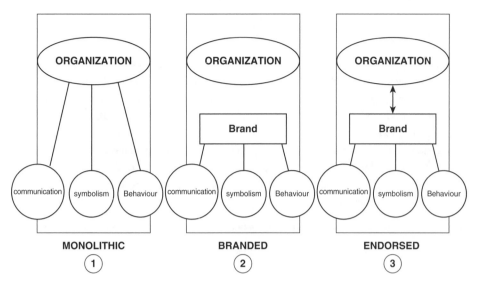

Identity structure	Definition	Example
Monolithic	Single all-embracing identity (products all carry the same corporate name)	Sony, BMW, Virgin, Philips
Branded	Individual businesses or product brands each carry their own name (and are seemingly unrelated to each other)	Procter & Gamble (Ariel, Ola) Electrolux (Zanussi), Unilever (Dove)
Endorsed	Businesses and product brands are endorsed or badged with the parent company name	General Motors, Kellogg, Nestlé, Cadbury

FIGURE 4.3 Monolithic, endorsed and branded identities

Case Example 4.1

Moves from branded identities to monolithic corporate brands

Kingfisher, a leading home improvement company in Europe and Asia, traditionally had a branded structure around retail brands such as B&Q and Castorama. Since 1998, the company has been strengthening its Kingfisher corporate brand, which originally was only a name for its financial holding and was used to communicate with the financial community and investors. One central part of its corporate branding strategy has been to sponsor the sailor Ellen MacArthur and her successful attempts to sail around the world in record-breaking times. MacArthur's boat was badged with the Kingfisher name and increased awareness of the corporate brand with consumers and other stakeholders across the world.

(Continued)

(Continued)

Similarly, Unilever announced in 2005 that the corporate brand will appear more prominently on all of its products. The announcement forms part of the company's 2010 strategy and is driven by the company's belief that many consumers are demanding more and more from the companies behind the brands, increasingly bringing their views as citizens into their buying decisions. The logo of the company has been redesigned and brings together 25 different icons representing Unilever and its brands. The redesigned logo and its more prominent place on products and in advertising are meant to highlight the company behind the products to consumers, employees, investors and other stakeholders.

Source: This case example is based on information drawn from http://www.kingfisher.com and http://www.unilever.com

One important reason for organizations to move from branded to endorsed and monolithic identities is that monolithic identities have become enormously valuable assets – companies with strong monolithic identities, and the reputations associated with it, can have market values that are more than twice their book values[13] – and can save money as marketing and communication campaigns can be leveraged across the company. Many brand rankings, such as the ones published by Interbrand and *Business Week*, confirm the impact of monolithic identities on companies' financial performance. Not surprisingly, therefore, many academic writers and communication professionals have started to emphasize the importance of branding the entire organization and of focusing communication and marketing on the organization rather than on individual products and services.

The idea of corporate branding is, however, in principle not that different from the idea of corporate image management, as discussed above. As Majken Schultz, one of the leading writers on corporate branding puts it, the focus in corporate branding is on how an organization can formulate an enduring identity that is relevant to all its stakeholders.[14] Similar to corporate image management, the approach in corporate branding is cross-disciplinary and includes input from communication, marketing and other functional areas within the organization. It is also aimed at all stakeholders of the organization, which contrasts the concept with product branding, which is exclusively focused on (prospective and current) customers and consumers.

Schultz emphasizes that the core of corporate branding is the alignment between the company's vision, culture and image. Central to this alignment is the idea of an organization's identity – who we are as an organization – and what that means to external stakeholders (image) and different cultures of employees within the organization (culture). The vision of senior managers then adds a strategic dimension to this process by setting directions for possible ways of further development or transforming who we are as an organization. For example, the vision of senior managers in Unilever of strengthening and highlighting the corporate brand behind its products is one that sets a strategic direction for the company. It fundamentally changes the identity of the organization and how it is seen by customers and stakeholders (image). Importantly, it also presents a break from the company's past strategy and internal culture where brand and product managers had executive responsibility to plan communication and marketing strategies (culture). The new identity would have to go hand in hand with a new culture that fosters collaboration between communication and marketing practitioners and a commitment to a monolithic Unilever identity.

As such, the role of all employees (not just communication and marketing staff) becomes much more important in corporate branding as employees are central as brand ambassadors. Ideally, the identity behind the corporate brand would thus pervade the entire organization, from top to bottom. Internal communication with employees is crucial in this respect (see Chapter 9) in order to make sure that employees know of upcoming communication and marketing campaigns. Many organizations provide additional support to employees in the form of brand manuals, intranet resources and brand briefings or workshops to ensure that employees do not just know about the corporate brand but also live and enact it as part of their day-to-day jobs, regardless of whether those jobs involve direct contact with stakeholders or not.[15]

ALIGNING IDENTITY, IMAGE AND REPUTATION

4.4 Generally speaking, in order to manage the company's reputation it is strategically important for organizations to achieve 'alignment' or 'transparency' between its internal identity and its external image. According to reputation experts Fombrun and Rindova, transparency is 'a state in which the internal identity of the firm reflects positively the expectations of key stakeholders and the beliefs of these stakeholders about the firm reflect accurately the internally held identity'.[16] Along these lines, many practitioners, consultants and scholars stress the importance of alignment between (a) the organizational culture as experienced by employees; (b) the corporate vision as articulated by senior managers; and (c) the corporate image or reputation in the minds of external stakeholders. Importantly, too, where these elements are misaligned (so that, for example, corporate rhetoric does not match the experienced reality), a range of suboptimal outcomes are anticipated, including employee disengagement, customer dissatisfaction and general organizational atrophy.

A useful way of analysing the alignment between an organization's vision, culture and image or reputation is the toolkit developed by Hatch and Schultz.[17] The toolkit (Figure 4.4) consists of a number of diagnostic questions based on three elements:

- *Vision*: Senior management's aspirations for the organization.
- *Culture*: The organization's values as felt and shared by all employees of the organization.
- *Image*: The image or impression that outside stakeholders have of the organization.

The questions each relate to a particular interface between the three elements and are meant to identify the alignment between them. The first set of questions involves

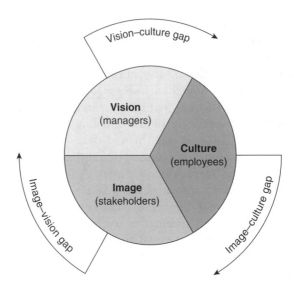

FIGURE 4.4 Toolkit to assess the alignment between vision, culture and image.

Source: The Regents of the University of California © 2003. Reprinted from the *California Management Review*, Vol. 46, No. 1. By permission of The Regents.

the interface between vision and culture, that is, how managers and employees are aligned. They are:

- Does the organization practise the values it promotes?
- Does the organization's vision inspire all its subcultures?
- Are the organization's vision and culture sufficiently differentiated from those of its competitors?

There is a potential for misalignment (*vision–culture gap*) here when senior management moves the organization in a strategic direction that employees do not understand or support. For example, senior managers may establish a vision that is too ambitious for the organization to implement and is not supported by its employees.

The second set of questions involves the interface between culture and image and is meant to identify potential gaps between the values of employees and the perceptions of stakeholders outside the organization. The questions are:

- What images do stakeholders associate with the organization?
- In what ways do its employees and stakeholders interact?
- Do employees care what stakeholders think of the organization?

Misalignment between an organization's image and organizational culture (*image–culture gap*) leads to confusion among stakeholders such as customers and investors about what a company stands for. For example, employees of the organization may not practise what the company preaches in its advertising, leaving a tarnished image with its stakeholders.

The final set of questions addresses the interface between vision and image. The key objective here is to find out whether management is taking the organization in a direction that its stakeholders support. The questions are:

- Who are the organization's stakeholders?
- What do the stakeholders want from the organization?
- Is the organization effectively communicating its vision to its stakeholders?

There is potential for misalignment (*image–vision gap*) here when organizations do not sufficiently listen to their stakeholders and create strategic visions that are not aligned with what stakeholders want or expect from the organization. These three sets of diagnostic questions help an organization meet the expectations of its stakeholders.

It is important for organizations to continuously monitor the alignment between their vision, culture and image so that they can make adjustments accordingly. All three interfaces are equally important to an organization in order to make sure that the identity or image that is projected to stakeholders is carried by both senior managers (vision) and employees (culture) and furthermore is understood and appreciated by stakeholders (image). A classic example of an organization that failed to sufficiently align its vision, culture and image involves British Airways' design of a new identity in the late 1990s that was not picked up nor appreciated by its staff and customers (Case Study 4.1).

Include.

CASE STUDY 4.1

BRITISH AIRWAYS AND ITS EFFORTS TO BUILD ITS REPUTATION AS THE WORLD'S FAVOURITE AIRLINE

British Airways (BA) was privatized in 1987. Over the years, BA has been one of the world's most profitable airlines. Strategically, BA has made concerted efforts to become not just a global player, but effectively a global company – senior executives of BA took the view that the airline industry was undergoing consolidation, and that the future industry would consist of a very small number of very large international airlines. Emphasis was therefore placed on globalizing the business, primarily through establishing alliances and partnerships in the USA, Australia and Europe, to overcome gaps in BA's coverage of routes as well as to access the lucrative but highly protected US domestic market. In line with this strategy, BA unveiled a new corporate identity in June 1997. Robert Ayling was CEO of British Airways at the time, and he and other senior managers articulated a vision for the company of becoming 'the undisputed leader in world travel'. This vision was coupled with a repositioning of the company in 1997 which involved blending the traditional British values of the company with new values of cosmopolitanism and global appeal.

To give this repositioning shape, BA unveiled a striking new visual identity scheme. The 50 ethnic designs commissioned from artists around the world were meant to adorn the tailfins of BA's entire fleet, as well as ticket jackets, cabin crew scarves and business cards. Over the next three years, the idea was that the new look would gradually replace the sober blue and red livery and crest along with the traditional motto 'to fly, to serve', which dated back to 1984. The decision to change was based on market research in the early 1990s which had suggested that passengers viewed

(Continued)

(Continued)

the airline as staid and stuffy. As Ayling commented at the time: 'We don't want to ram our Britishness down people's throats. ... There's no empire. We're just a small nation on an offshore island trying to make our way into the world.' The vision of senior managers within BA was that the repositioning presented the airline with an opportunity not just to tone down its national origins and project a more modern image, but also to reposition itself as a 'citizen of the world' in recognition of the fact that 60 per cent of BA's passengers came from outside the UK.

The colourful designs did attract tremendous free publicity at the time, with the front pages of most British newspapers featuring large colour photos. But they also generated more controversy than anticipated, many seeing the revamp as extravagant, confusing, or in the case of the then Prime Minister Margaret Thatcher, a national betrayal. At the launch of the new designs, Margaret Thatcher famously draped her handkerchief over one of the new designs. The backlash was disappointing, but Ayling hoped at the time that these emotionally charged reactions from the more conservative-minded sections of the British public would soon blow over.

However, the negative news coverage of the new designs endured and carried over to BA customers and the general public in the UK, who then voted with their feet (i.e., a vision–image gap). BA customers appreciated the company's traditional values and British heritage, which they felt were being lost with the new designs and repositioning. In addition to repainting the planes' tailfins, the company had also decided to remove the British flag from all its aircraft. This triggered a strike by cabin crew, who apparently did not agree with the new corporate values and also felt that they had not been included in consultations on the new vision (i.e., a vision–culture gap). Employees not only disagreed with the new vision, they also did not share and live the new values of a multicultural ethos as communicated in the new designs. Because they did not embody these values, there was thus a real potential for a gap between what the company communicated (cosmopolitanism) and employee behaviour, which was still firmly rooted in a sense of Britishness and stakeholder images (i.e., an image–culture gap). Before it came to that, Ayling and his senior management team acknowledged that they had made a wrong decision and abandoned the design programme. When Rodd Eddington took over from Ayling as CEO in 2000, one of his first actions was to announce a return to British livery and he reintroduced the Union Flag on each tailfin of the BA fleet.

QUESTIONS FOR REFLECTION

1   Describe the case using the vision–culture–image model. Where did it go wrong for British Airways?
2   What could senior management have done to avoid this and to essentially better align its vision, culture and image?

Source: This case study is based on Clark, A. (2006) 'British Airways warns staff of further job cuts', *The Guardian*, 10 March 2006 and INSEAD (2002) *Flying into a storm: British Airways* (1996–2000).

When the image or reputation of stakeholders is broadly consistent with the projected images in communication, symbolism and behaviour, it also ensures that the organization is respected and understood in the way in which it wants and aims to be understood. Alternatively, when there is a gap between the projected identity of an organization and the way in which it is regarded, an organization is not standing out on its own turf and may not have a strong enough reputation as a result. Its reputation is then based upon more general associations with the industry in which the organization is located or is informed by reports from the media. Shell, for instance, in the wake of the Brent Spar oil rig crisis, realized that its poor reputation in the 1990s had more often than not been based upon media reports and the tainted image of the oil industry than on its own identity and the values that were at the heart of its business and operations. Shell has since put considerable effort into rethinking its identity and values, redesigning systems for stakeholder management, and running a global identity campaign to close the gap between its identity and reputation. Case Study 4.2 describes how another company, BMW, went about aligning identity, brand and reputation.

CASE STUDY 4.2

BMW: AN EXERCISE IN ALIGNING IDENTITY, BRAND AND REPUTATION

BMW, the German car manufacturer, has been strategically focused on premium segments in the international car market. With its BMW, Mini and Rolls-Royce brands, the company has become one of the leading premium car companies in the world. BMW's strong identity and marketing campaigns are often credited as the building blocks of the company's continuing success. There are four values that define the BMW identity inside the organization and its corporate brand and communication to external stakeholders: dynamism, aesthetics, exclusivity and innovation. These values have been central to BMW's success in terms of the company's leadership in design and are consistently communicated across all its corporate communication, corporate design, consumer advertising as well as through the behaviour of managers, designers and retail staff. The brand consultancy Interbrand argues that these four brand values align customers' images and associations with the vision and culture of BMW.

BMW has long focused on innovation but made it the driving force for its product development process and its philosophy at the end of the 1990s. Since then, the company has put a lot of emphasis on its research and development (R&D), making it a core element of its corporate strategy. BMW's success has been its ability to nurture new ideas, short-list the potential ones and process them until the end stage through an integrated innovation process. The innovation process within BMW is aimed at systematically channelling potential innovations to the actual product development stage. The process focuses on three major areas: unique selling propositions for each car to be launched, breakthrough innovations, and concept cars to convey BMW's brand image at automobile shows. For this purpose, the company has implemented systems to search for and filter innovative ideas from across the world

(Continued)

(Continued)

(within and outside the company), which, after further development, can be carried over into actual product development and car vehicle manufacturing processes.

Besides its focus on innovation, the company has also been a powerhouse of creative and aesthetic designs of cars. According to Christopher Bangle, global chief of design for BMW, 'our fanaticism about design excellence is matched only by the company's driving desire to remain profitable'. Bangle sees the company's core value as being 'an engineering-driven company whose cars and motorcycles are born from passion'. In his words: 'We don't make "automobiles", which are utilitarian machines you use to get from point A to point B. We make "cars", moving works of art that express the driver's love of quality.'

The values of dynamism, aesthetics, innovation and exclusivity are carried through in all of the company's communication to consumers and to other stakeholders. They feature as brand promises in dealer and customer materials, including showroom interior designs, tradeshow materials, advertising and customer promotion packages. These values also featured as part of the company's branded entertainment strategy. This strategy consisted of product placement in movies (including a series of James Bond films) and an initial set of five short promotional films in 2000 that were made available online on the BMW website. The online films cleverly built BMW's brand image and were promoted using trailers on television, print and online advertisements that drove customers to visit the website. In 2002, BMW produced three more promotional films inspired by the success of the first five films.

Particularly because of its creative advertising, the BMW brand has come to be associated with the words 'driving' and 'performance'. The company's taglines in many adverts were 'The Ultimate Driving Machine' and 'Sheer Driving Pleasure'. According to marketing guru Al Ries, this association with 'driving' was a very powerful component of BMW's brand as it led consumers to associate BMW with high-performing cars.

However, a study commissioned by BMW in 2005 revealed that in the USA a large percentage of luxury car buyers did not consider BMW at the point of purchase. The management of BMW in the USA realized that some kind of change was needed in the company's communication. In the words of US Marketing Director Jack Pitney: 'We're entering new product segments all the time, and we can't afford to not be on the shopping lists of this many people. ... People think we have a cool persona as a brand, but say we lack humanity.' Pitney felt that BMW needed to draw upon its brand history and particularly its four identity values to add a sense of humanity to the brand.

Pitney and his colleagues in the USA felt that the situation faced by BMW was actually a direct result of the company's overemphasis on 'performance driving' over the past 33 years. He felt that consumers instead were looking for brands that stood for larger values. In the company's brief to ad agencies pitching for the account, the company said that: 'BMW wants to bring the excitement back to the brand and restore the equilibrium between its products and its marketing communications. Remember, your challenge is not to reinvent the brand but to evolve the marketing from its current one-dimensional focus on performance.'

A new agency was successfully recruited and in May 2006, the North American arm of BMW released a new advertising campaign promoting itself as a 'company of ideas'. The tone and tenor of the new campaign were different from previous adverts in the past. The series of new ads no longer stressed the BMW car's performance,

(Continued)

(Continued)

but were intended to project the company's competence in design and emphasized its corporate culture, which fostered innovation. In doing so, BMW wanted to build demand by reaching out to consumers who had until now not considered purchasing a BMW vehicle. At the same time, the company wanted to make the existing and loyal customers proud of the company's success story. The ad campaign was unveiled through various media, including adverts in magazines, on television, on outdoor billboards and on the internet. The campaign tried to communicate BMW's independence and freedom to pursue innovative ideas, as it was neither owned by nor part of a division of another company. The ads still featured the tagline 'The Ultimate Driving Machine', but placed little emphasis on its high-performance features. The focus instead was on the theme of BMW as a 'company of ideas', where radical design and ideas are encouraged as a way of supporting the tagline around performance. According to Pitney, the idea was to draw upon the company's distinctive identity based on aesthetics and innovation, and show consumers and the general public how a BMW car actually becomes an ultimate driving machine.

Recent campaigns have also emphasized a more caring side to the company. Marketing adverts emphasize the 'fun' and 'driving pleasure', as the main benefits associated with driving a stylish and high-performing car. BMW has also embarked on a series of ambitious sustainability initiatives, something which it has highlighted in corporate print adverts. The adverts highlight BMW's achievements in developing fuel-saving engines, clean production facilities and state-of-the-art recycling techniques. BMW also suggests in these adverts that it is:

> intent on playing our part in actively shaping the future – for the long term. We do so both for the common good and for the sake of the environment: in the interests of our customers – and, naturally, in the interests of our company, its employees and its shareholders. Because sustainability secures all our futures.

The company aims to integrate sustainability throughout the entire value chain, as it believes that sustainability will become a must in the premium segment of carmakers. As such, embracing sustainability issues and being at the forefront of development will give BMW a competitive edge. According to the Dow Jones Sustainability Index, BMW is the world's most sustainable carmaker, having been ranked at the top for the fifth consecutive year in 2009. The company has been driven to develop increasingly better solutions to sustainability issues on the basis of its strong innovation culture, but also to meet the growing expectations of its stakeholders. In this way, it aims to maintain the alignment between its internal culture and the company's external image or reputation.

QUESTIONS FOR REFLECTION

1 Describe the alignment between vision, culture and image for BMW and discuss the potential for gaps between them.
2 Consider the four values of the identity and brand positioning of BMW. Are these values, authentic, distinctive and unique from the perspective of consumers and other stakeholders in the premium car market?

(Continued)

(Continued)

Source: This case study is based upon Bangle, C. (2001) 'The ultimate creativity machine: how BMW turns art into profit', *Harvard Business Review*, January, 5–11; Ries, A. and Ries, L. (2000) *The 22 Immutable Laws of Branding*. New York: Harper Collins; Kiley, D. (2006) 'BMW targets new drivers', www.businessweek.com, 5 May.

CHAPTER SUMMARY

 4.5 The chapter has outlined the theoretical background to the frameworks and concepts that organizations use to build strong and distinctive reputations with their stakeholders. One important observation that was made is that communication practitioners need to look inside their organizations for the core values that define their organization and that can give them a competitive edge in communications with internal and external stakeholders. Indeed, many organizations which have not thought seriously about their corporate identity and whether their profile is appreciated by stakeholder groups, often appear to hire and fire outside agencies with regularity, trying to find the one with the ability to 'sell' a message that people do not seem to be 'buying'. In other words, such organizations have not given enough care to crafting an identity that is authentic and distinctive, and also meaningful to stakeholders.

DISCUSSION QUESTIONS

1   Pick a company with which you are familiar or that you have worked for in the past. Describe the alignment between the company's vision, culture and image. Are there any gaps between these elements?

2   Identify a company with a world-class reputation in its industry. What in your opinion has been the main driver of its reputation?

 ## KEY TERMS

Alignment

Brand(ed) identity

Corporate brand

Corporate identity

Corporate image

Corporate personality

Corporate reputation

Culture

Design

Organizational identity

Symbolism

Vision

 FURTHER READING

Hatch, Mary Jo and Schultz, Majken (2008), *Taking Brand Initiative: How Companies Can Align Their Strategy, Culture and Identity through Corporate Branding*. San Francisco: Jossey-Bass.
Ind, Nicholas (1997), *The Corporate Brand*. New York: New York University Press.
Olins, Wally (2008), *The Brand Handbook*. London: Thames and Hudson.

NOTES

1 Dowling, G.R. (2001), *Creating Corporate Reputations*. Oxford: Oxford University Press.

2 Birkigt, K. and Stadler, M. (1986), *Corporate Identity: Grundlagen, Funktionen und Beispielen*. Landsberg an Lech: Verlag Moderne Industrie.

3 Olins, W. (1978), *The Corporate Personality: An Inquiry into the Nature of Corporate Identity*. London: Design Council, p. 212.

4 Larçon, J.P. and Reitter, R. (1979), *Structures de pouvoir et identité de l'enterprise*. Paris: Nathan.

5 Albert, S. and Whetten, D.A. (1985), 'Organizational identity', in Cummings L.L. and Staw, B.M. (ed.), *Research in Organizational Behaviour*. Greenwich, CT: JAI Press, pp. 263–295.

6 Weigelt, K. and Camerer, C. (1988), 'Reputation and corporate strategy: a review of recent theory and applications', *Strategic Management Journal*, 9: 443–454.

7 Dutton, J.E. and Dukerich, J.M. (1991), 'Keeping an eye on the mirror: image and identity in organizational adaptation', *Academy of Management Journal*, 34: 517–554.

8 Hamel, G. and Prahalad, C.K. (1994), *Competing for the Future*. Boston, MA: Harvard Business School Press; Peters, T.J. and Waterman, R.H. (1982), *In Search of Excellence: Lessons from America's Best Run Companies*. New York: Harper & Row; Collins, J.C. and Porras, J.I. (1997), *Built to Last: Successful Habits of Visionary Companies*. New York: Harper Business, p. 8.

9 Fombrun, C. and Van Riel, C.B.M. (2004), *Fame and Fortune: How Successful Companies Build Winning Reputations*. London: FT Prentice Hall.

10 Brammer, S.J. and Pavelin, S. (2006), 'Corporate reputation and social performance: the importance of "fit"', *Journal of Management Studies*, 43: 435–455.

11 Deephouse, D.L. and Carter, S.M. (2005), 'An examination of differences between organizational legitimacy and organizational reputation', *Journal of Management Studies*, 42: 329–360.

12 Lamertz, K., Heugens, P.P.M.A.R. and Calmet, L. (2005), 'The configuration of organizational images among firms in the Canadian beer brewing industry', *Journal of Management Studies*, 42: 817–843.

13 Hatch, M.J. and Schultz, M. (2001), 'Are the strategic stars aligned for your corporate brand?', *Harvard Business Review*, February: 128–135.

14 Schultz, M. (2005), 'A cross-disciplinary perspective on corporate branding', in Schultz, M., Antorini, Y.M. and Csaba, F.F. (eds), *Corporate Branding: Purpose/People/Process*. Copenhagen: Copenhagen Business School Press, pp. 23–55.

15 Mitchell, C. (2002), 'Selling the brand inside', *Harvard Business Review*, January: 99–105.

16 Fombrun, C. and Rindova, V. (2007), 'The road to transparency: reputation management at the Royal Dutch/Shell', in Schultz, M., Hatch, M.J. and Larsen, M.H. (eds), *The Expressive Organization*. Oxford: Oxford University Press, pp. 76–96.

17 Hatch, M.J. and Schultz, M. (2001), 'Are the strategic stars aligned for your corporate brand?', *Harvard Business Review*, February: 128–135; and Schultz, M. and Hatch, M.J. (2003), 'Cycles of corporate branding: the case of the LEGO Company', *California Management Review*, 46: 6–26.

CORPORATE COMMUNICATION IN PRACTICE

3

Part 3 explores three practical issues in corporate communication: how overall communication strategies are developed; how specific communication programmes and campaigns are planned and executed; and how professionals can monitor and research the effects of their programmes and campaigns. These three issues are discussed in separate chapters, but are part of an integrated process of moving from strategy and planning to actions and outcomes.

After reading Part 3, the reader will be familiar with crucial steps in developing an overall communication strategy, in planning and producing creative and effective communication programmes and campaigns, and in researching the effects of those programmes and campaigns on the organization's stakeholders.

COMMUNICATION STRATEGY

5

Chapter Overview

The chapter describes the process and content of developing an overall communication strategy for an organization. The process refers to the steps in developing a communication strategy across communication disciplines and stakeholders and in line with the overall corporate strategy of an organization. The content refers to the overall positioning of the organization in the minds of stakeholders, the choice of themed messages to support that positioning and the use of specific message styles that creatively articulate those themes in communications to stakeholders.

INTRODUCTION

5.1 Managing corporate communication requires a communication strategy that describes the general reputational position that an organization aims to establish and maintain with its key stakeholders. A communication strategy also provides guidance to specific communication programmes and campaigns (e.g., a product launch or investor meeting). This chapter describes how communication strategies are developed in practice, as a stepping stone for the planning and execution of specific communication programmes and campaigns.

The first part of the chapter discusses the process of strategy-making in corporate communication. A comprehensive and fully-formed communication strategy is often developed in interactions between professionals from different communication disciplines and with the CEO and members of the executive team within an organization. The second part of the chapter elaborates on the content of a communication strategy in terms of what such strategies normally consist of and how they guide the design of particular communication programmes and campaigns. Specifically, the content involves a definition of the overall reputational position in the minds of stakeholders that an organization aims for, the choice of themed messages to support that positioning and the use of specific message styles that creatively articulate those themes in communication to stakeholders.

THE PROCESS OF COMMUNICATION STRATEGY

5.2 A communication strategy involves the formulation of a desired position for the organization in terms of how it wants to be seen by its different stakeholder groups. Based upon an assessment of the gap between how the company is currently seen (corporate reputation) and how it wants to be seen (vision) (Chapter 4), a communication strategy specifies a strategic intent, on which possible courses of action are formulated, evaluated and eventually chosen. Communication strategies typically involve a process of bringing stakeholder reputations in line with the vision of the organization in order to obtain the necessary support for the organization's strategy. In other cases, a communication strategy may be about reinforcing existing reputations of stakeholders if those are broadly in line with how the organization wants itself to be seen.

To illustrate, Wal-Mart wants to be known as a market-driven retailer that has the interests of its customers, employees, suppliers and local communities at heart. The company had for a long time been able to frame its low-cost market strategy in terms that not only fitted with its own customer-focused identity, but was also acceptable to consumers and the general US public. However, more recently, Wal-Mart has faced criticism for the way in which it engages with, and cares for, important stakeholder groups, such as employees and members of the local communities in which the company operates. The result is a gap between the company's vision of how it wants to be seen and the actual reputation that it currently has with employees, local communities, government and the general public in the USA. Because of this gap, Wal-Mart executives have realized that its poor reputation could eventually pose a threat to its growth in the USA and elsewhere. The company has therefore decided to recruit a senior director of stakeholder management to 'help pioneer a new model of how Wal-Mart works with outside stakeholders, resulting in fundamental changes in how the company does business'.[1] The company has started to formulate a communication strategy aimed at raising awareness of its environmental and social contributions and of its support for employees in the hope that stakeholder opinions will again become more favourable towards the company.

As in the case of Wal-Mart, the assessment of the gap between reputation and vision leads to the formulation of a *strategic intent* within the communication strategy. Based upon an analysis of the current reputation of the organization with its stakeholders, strategic intent sets a general direction for communication in terms of the change or consolidation of that reputation that is aimed for. The strategic intent also suggests a particular set of communication tactics and activities that aim to affect the awareness, knowledge, reputation and behaviour of important stakeholders. The next section outlines in detail the content of a communication strategy. The present section continues by discussing the process by which a communication strategy is developed.

A range of paradigms or different ways of thinking[2] exist on the *process of strategy-making*. How strategies are formed within organizations has become variously depicted in these different paradigms as following a rational planning mode, in which objectives are set out and methodically worked out into comprehensive action plans, as a more flexible intuitive or visionary process, or as rather incremental or emergent in nature, with the process of strategy formation being rather continuous and iterative. Each of these paradigms varies in whether the process of strategy formation is characterized and described as 'top-down' or 'bottom-up' in the organization, as deliberate and planned or as *ad hoc* and spontaneous and as analytical or visionary.

Besides the diversity and the distinct views presented by each of these different paradigms, there is also consensus on the following three points:

1 *Strategy formation consists of a combination of planned and emergent processes*: In practice, strategy formation involves a combination of a logical rational process in which visions and objectives are articulated and systematically worked out into programmes and actions, as well as more emergent processes in which behaviours and actions simply arise ('emerge') yet fall within the strategic scope of the organization. The same combination of planned and emergent processes of strategy formation can also be observed at the level of communication strategy. In practice, communication strategy typically consists of prestructured and annually planned programmes and campaigns as well as more *ad hoc*, reactive responses that 'emerge' in response to issues and stakeholder concerns in the environment.

2 *Strategy involves a general direction and not simply plans or tactics*: The term strategy is itself derived from the Greek '*strategos*' meaning a *general* set of manœuvres carried out to overcome an enemy. What is notable here is the emphasis on *general*, not *specific*, sets of manœuvres. Specific sets of manœuvres are seen as within the remit of those concerned with translating the strategy into programmes or tactics. In other words, strategy embodies more than plans and tactics, which often have a more immediate and short-term focus. Instead, strategy concerns the organization's direction and positioning in relation to stakeholders in its environment for a longer period of time.

3 *Strategy is about the organization and its environment*: Related to the previous point, the emphasis for managers is to make long-term, strategic choices that are feasible in the organization's environments. Managers who manage strategically do so by balancing the mission and vision of the organization – what it is, what it wants to be, and what it wants to do – with what the environment will allow or encourage it to do. Strategy is therefore often adaptive in that it needs to be responsive to external opportunities and threats that may confront an organization. A broad consensus exists in the strategy literature that strategy is essentially concerned with a process of managing the interaction between an organization and its external environment so as to ensure the best 'fit' between the two.

From a strategic perspective, corporate communication is an important 'boundary-spanning' function between the organization and the environment.[3] As a boundary-spanning function, corporate communication operates at the interface between the organization and its environment; to help gather, relay and interpret information from the environment as well as represent the organization to stakeholders in the outside world. Seeing corporate communication as a strategic boundary-spanning function requires that communication professionals are involved in decision-making on the corporate strategy itself. Such a view of communication means that communication strategy is not just seen as a set of goals and tactics at the functional or operational level – at the level of the corporate communication function – but that its scope and involvement in fact stretch to the corporate and business-unit levels of the organization as well.

At the corporate level, where strategy is concerned with the corporate mission and vision, communication practitioners can aid managers in developing strategies for interaction with the environment. In this sense, communication professionals are directly involved and support strategic decision-making through their 'environmental scanning' activities. Environmental scanning may assist corporate strategy-makers in analysing the organization's position and identifying emerging issues which may have significant implications for the organization and for future strategy development. Communication practitioners can at this corporate level also bring identity questions and a stakeholder perspective into the strategic management process, representing the likely reaction of stakeholders to alternative strategy options, and thereby giving senior management a more balanced consideration of the attractiveness and feasibility of the strategic options open to them. Finally, communication practitioners, of course, may also implement the corporate strategy by helping to communicate the organization's strategic intentions to both internal and external stakeholders, which can help avoid misunderstandings that might otherwise get in the way of the smooth implementation of the organization's strategy. With such involvement in the corporate strategy of an organization, the communication strategy itself will also be more substantial instead of being just a tactical ploy.[4] In other words, in an era of stakeholder management, a corporate communication strategy cannot be divorced from the organization's corporate strategy, to which it must contribute if it is to have a genuine strategic role.[5]

In summary, a corporate strategy is concerned with the overall purpose and scope of the organization to meet its various stakeholders' expectations and needs. A corporate strategy provides a strategic vision for the entire organization in terms of product, market or geographical scope or matters as fundamental as ownership of the organization. A vision often also articulates how the company wants to be seen by its various stakeholder groups. A communication strategy in turn is a functional or operational strategy concerned with how corporate communication can develop communication programmes towards different stakeholders to achieve that vision and to support the corporate objectives in the corporate strategy.

Figure 5.1 illustrates this dynamic between the corporate strategy and the corporate communication strategy. On the one hand, the decisions that are made at the level of the corporate strategy need to be translated into specific communication programmes for different stakeholders. In the words of Kevin Rollins, CEO of Dell: 'The job of a senior manager is to determine which elements of the overall strategy you want to communicate to each constituency.' Rollins, together with Dell's senior communication managers, decides how they 'break messages up into pieces and try to give the right piece to the right audience'.[6] At the same time, corporate communication and communication strategies need to be linked to the corporate strategy. This link consists of counselling and informing the CEO and senior executives on stakeholder and reputation issues so that these can be factored into the overall corporate strategy and the company's strategic vision. Michael Dell, the founder of Dell, articulates this link by saying that 'communications are an essential part of what you have to offer to customers and shareholders'. In his view, 'communications has to be in the centre to be optimally effective' and for it to support the corporate strategy.[7]

FIGURE 5.1   The link between corporate strategy and communication strategy

This nested model of strategy formation, in which a corporate strategy and communication strategy are seen as interrelated layers in the total strategy-making structure of the organization, depends on a number of conditions. For example, it goes against strict 'top-down' views of strategy formation where strategy is seen to cascade down from the corporate to the business unit and ultimately to the functional level of corporate communication, with each level of strategy providing the immediate context for the next, 'lower' level of strategy making. Strategy-making generally fares better when it does not strictly follow such a rigid, hierarchical top-down process. Instead, it should be more flexible and at least in part decentralized so that business unit and functions such as corporate communication are encouraged to initiate ideas that are then passed upward for approval at the appropriate senior management level. From this perspective, business units and functions may be responsible not only for developing strategic responses to the problems or opportunities encountered at their own level ('translating' in Figure 5.1), but may sometimes initiate ideas that then become the catalyst for changes in strategy throughout the organization ('informing' in Figure 5.1). Communication practitioners, for instance, may pass their ideas in relation to stakeholders at the functional level to the CEO and senior management level and may, as such, initiate a revision of corporate strategy in terms of how the organization needs to build and maintain relationships with those organizational stakeholders who have the power to influence the successful realization of its corporate goals.

   The input of corporate communication practitioners into corporate strategy and other operational areas of activity in the organization requires that these professionals have management expertise and skills. Specifically, it requires that professionals are able to formulate the importance and use of communication in the context of general organizational issues and objectives. In the words of a recent study in the USA: 'effective communicators are those who speak the same language as senior executives and have a deep understanding of the business and its strategy'.[8] Practitioners need to have knowledge of the industry or sector in which the organization operates and of the nature of the strategy-making process, and need to have a strategic view of how communication can contribute to corporate and market strategies and to different functional areas within the company.[9] Instead of a 'technical' approach to communication that is focused on the production of communications materials, a managerial role requires that a professional is able:

> to bring thoughtfully conceived agendas to the senior management table that address the strategic issues of business planning, resource allocation, priorities and direction of the firm. Instead of asking what events to sponsor and at what cost, [professionals] should be asking which customer segments to invest in and at what projected returns. ... Instead of asking how to improve the number of hits to the website, [professionals] should be asking who their key stakeholders are and how to get more interactive with them.[10]

Academic research into corporate communication has identified two main roles for communicators: that of a communication technician and a communication manager.[11] This distinction is helpful in capturing the activities, expertise and skills of practitioners, and also gives a sense of whether they are able to strategically work with senior executives and managers in other areas of the organization.

1 *Communication technician*: Communication practitioners are characterized as technicians if their work focuses on activities such as writing communication materials, editing and/or rewriting for grammar and spelling, handling the technical aspects, producing brochures or pamphlets, doing photography and graphics, and maintaining media contacts and placing press releases. Strictly speaking, a technician is defined as 'a creator and disseminator of messages, intimately involved in production, [and] operating independent of management decision making, strategic planning, issues management, environmental scanning and program evaluation'.[12] In other words, a technician tactically implements decisions made by others and is generally not involved in management decision-making and strategic decisions concerning communication strategy and programmes.

2 *Communication manager*: Practitioners enacting a manager role make strategy or policy decisions and are held accountable for programme success or failure. These professionals are primarily concerned with externally oriented, long-term decisions, rather than solving short-term, technical problems. Activities within the manager role include advising management at all levels in the organization with regard to strategic decisions and courses of action, taking into account their public ramifications and the organization's social or citizenship responsibilities, making communication programme decisions, evaluating programme results, supervising the work

of others, planning and managing budgets, planning communications programmes and campaigns, and meeting other executives. Communication managers also use research to monitor the organization's environment and the opinions of key stakeholders. And because they possess needed intelligence gained from research, managers are more likely to participate in the organization's decision-making and strategic planning.

Having practitioners in an organization who can enact a managerial role is crucial for communication to be involved in decision-making concerning the overall strategic direction of the organization. When communication professionals are involved at the decision-making table, information about relations with priority stakeholders are factored into the process of corporate decision-making and into corporate strategies and actions.[13] This would mean, among other things, that senior communication professionals are actively consulted regarding the effects of certain business actions (e.g., staff lay-offs, divestiture) on a company's reputation with stakeholders, and even have a say in the decision-making on it, instead of being called in after the decision has been made to draft a press release and to deal with any communication issues emerging from it.

Communication practitioners who are expected to adopt a managerial role, however, do not always meet these requirements for competencies and skills associated with the manager role. This may be partly the result of a lack of career development opportunities and professional support within their organizations. Many communication professionals lack knowledge and skills in financial management, the strategy-making process, and in the use of communication in organizational development and change. As a result, these professionals, and the communication disciplines that they represent, may be sidelined by companies and treated as a peripheral management discipline – one viewed as unimportant to the overall functioning of the corporation. The communication expert Pincus and his colleagues refer in this regard to a belief commonly held among some parts of senior management that communication adds little to corporate performance[14] as it is a 'fluffy' discipline that is insufficiently focused on the practicalities and demands of the business. A similar sentiment was expressed by CEOs in a recent survey in the UK. CEOs of leading corporations felt that corporate communication as an area of practice 'will be more valued when advice is offered by professionals who have the background, knowledge and standing that will enable them to contribute to decision-making at the highest levels'. CEOs felt that 'barriers to entry to the practice are, at the present time, too low and the practice fails to attract the most able candidates' as most CEOs 'felt there were too few high-caliber professionals and too few quality people coming into the industry'.[15] Professionals in senior positions who are expected to enact the manager role are thus under pressure to show and communicate the value of communication in terms of what it contributes to the organization:

> There is a lot of bemoaning in the hallways of marketing and communications offices of how CEOs 'don't understand communications', when the real problem is that marketing and communications professionals do not understand the intricacies of business management well enough to become part of the governing coalition.[16]

But practitioners can also actively look for ways in which they can develop themselves into managers and can learn about the organization, financial management and corporate strategy formation. When Lynn Tysen, Dell's vice-president of investor relations and corporate communication, first joined the company, she attended operations and other functional meetings so that she could learn about Dell inside and out.[17]

THE CONTENT OF COMMUNICATION STRATEGY

5.3 The content of a communication strategy is influenced by the process by which it is formed and by the different individuals and layers in the organization who have had a stake in it. Ideally, the content of the strategy starts from an organization-wide assessment of how the organization is seen by different stakeholders (reputation) in the light of the organization's vision (vision) at a particular point in time. The gap between the reputation and vision, as mentioned earlier, forms the basis for the formulation of a strategic intent: the change or consolidation in the company's reputation that is intended. The strategic intent, in turn, is translated into themed messages that are designed to change or reinforce perceptions in line with the vision of how the organization wants to be known (see, e.g., Case Example 5.1).

Case Example 5.1

Themed messages within Philips

Philips, the international electronics firm, in 2004 announced a new vision of wanting to become recognized as a market-driven company known for the simplicity of its products, processes and communication. This new vision was announced with its 'Sense and simplicity' slogan, which is both a brand promise to customers as well as a potential differentiator from the company's competitors in the marketplace. While companies like Samsung and Apple are also working towards simplifying technology for customers, Philips is among the first to make it part of its brand positioning and as core to its product design. The new vision also articulates a broad-based corporate reputation for Philips (as a monolithic corporate brand) instead of a product-based image based on particular products (such as Philishave) and one that is based on the company's strong leadership in innovation, the strengths of its management and strategy and the care that it shows for employees. Recent reputation research with stakeholders, however, demonstrated that the company still has a narrow consumer product-based image, that the company is seen as reliable but not as innovative, as lacking a clear strategy and vision, and with doubts surrounding its management capabilities.

Based upon these results, the strategic intent within Philips' communication strategy is defined as changing stakeholder reputations of the company from a product-based

(Continued)

(Continued)

image to an aspired positioning around a broad-based reputation that is rooted in a view of the company as a leader in innovation with a clear strategy and vision and capable management. To achieve its strategic intent and to claim the aspired reputational position in the minds of stakeholders, Philips has identified a number of themed messages that the company consistently communicates to different stakeholders. These include:

- leadership in innovation (on the ability of the company to develop new and exciting products),
- performance management (on the strong leadership and management within the organization),
- care for employees (on the care and support that the organization gives to its employees),
- quality products and services (on the reliable and high-quality products of the company),
- leadership in sustainability (the track record of the company in environmental and social performance),
- market orientation (the focus of the company on customer needs), and
- strong communication (the ability of the company to communicate and engage with its stakeholders).

The themed messages are specifically designed to address the company's reputation in a number of areas and in line with the company's vision.

Source: This case example is informed by Prast, J. (2005) The strategic importance of measuring corporate reputation: A philips case study, *Critical Eye*, March–May, 4–9, and documents from www.philips.com

Themed messages, in other words, are messages that relate to specific capabilities, strengths or values (as 'themes') of an organization. These messages are continuously and consistently communicated to stakeholders to achieve the strategic intent of changing or consolidating the company's reputation. A themed message may involve a company's specific capability, such as the ability of an organization to develop innovative products (e.g., Philips), its general strengths or achievements, such as the care that it has demonstrated in supporting its employees and the general community in which it operates (e.g., Co-operative Bank), or particular values associated with the company's identity, such as its claimed integrity or transparency (e.g., AstraZeneca). Themed messages are direct translations of the strategic intent: they emphasize an aspect (achievement, capability or value) that the organization wants to become associated with in the mind of important stakeholder groups. These messages, in turn, are translated into different message styles that communicate the claim about the company's capabilities, strengths or values in a convincing way (Figure 5.2). The case study of Lucent (Case Study 5.1) illustrates this link between strategic intent, themed messages and message styles.

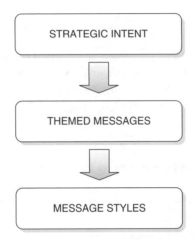

FIGURE 5.2   Stages in formulating the content of a communication strategy

CASE STUDY 5.1

DEVELOPING A COMMUNICATION STRATEGY FOR LUCENT

Lucent Technologies Inc. (Lucent) was created as a result of a divesture in 1995 by AT&T. The company designs, builds and delivers a wide range of network systems (public networking systems and software for telecommunications providers and cable companies), business communication systems (advanced communication products and solutions for business customers), consumer telephone and network systems, and microelectronics components (high-performance integrated circuits, optoelectronic components, circuit boards and power systems for application in the telecommunications and computing industries). When Lucent was launched as an independent company in 1995, it required the development of a communication strategy from scratch, including the choice for a new name, the formulation of a communication positioning platform and the development of specific communication programmes to launch the new company.

The search for a name and communication positioning platform

Landor Associates, a design agency, worked with marketing and communication professionals to identify what image the new name should convey. Before any naming or design work could commence, Landor advised the company to agree first on what they most wanted to communicate through the name and logo about their new company. Landor asked everyone what equity from the past had to be kept, what of the old image should be left behind and, finally, what new attributes should be added to the desired corporate image or reputation. The answers to these questions were not immediately clear and Landor decided to conduct research with managers, employees, customers and dealers, and the general public. This research

(Continued)

(Continued)

demonstrated that awareness of the new company was low to moderate with the general public. Senior management also wanted the company to be known for much more than the focus on telephony associated with AT&T. Thus they considered a name linked to the parent company to be limiting. Among dealers, awareness and knowledge of what the company did were much higher. Although the company was thought of as smart and innovative, it was also perceived by a significant proportion of this group as being slow to respond and as being slow in getting products to market. High-end business customers equally had a very strong awareness of the company, but considered the company not as fast to respond to their needs as they would like.

The result of this research and a follow-up debate among professionals in the organization was an agreement to create what they called a 'communication positioning' platform that would retain the attributes of quality, reliability, technological innovation and stature. At the same time, they wanted to lose the perceptions of slowness, arrogance and inflexibility, and to add the concepts of speed, energy and flexibility. In doing so, communication professionals formulated, with the help of Landor, the strategic intent (step 1) for the communication strategy: to change the company's image with customers and the general public from being a slow technology giant to a market-driven, flexible, competitive and innovative provider of network solutions. When the CEO, Chief Operations Officer and Executive Vice-President for corporate operations agreed to the new positioning, communication professionals and Landor Associates continued with identifying the set of themed messages (step 2) that were to be communicated about the new company. These themed messages followed on from the strategic intent and included the company's leadership in innovation, the breadth and competitively priced nature of its product portfolio, the company's culture of innovation and reliability built on customer needs, and its heritage of being part of the renowned Bell Labs, an innovation powerhouse within AT&T.

Desired image attributes

Keep	Lose	Add
Reliability	Slowness	Speed
Technology	Inflexibility	Energy
Stature	Arrogance	Flexibility
Integrity	High-priced	Competitive
Service reputation	Hard to do business with	Value-priced
Staying power		Customer-focused
Experience/capability		Global
		Vision for the business
		Focus 'can do'
		Innovative
		Enabling/user-friendly

In parallel with the development of a positioning platform, a visual audit was conducted of all materials that would carry the new name and/or logo of the company. Landor also audited competitors' brands and logos. After extensive work and research with

(Continued)

(Continued)

business decision-makers and the general public, the name Lucent emerged as the first choice. Landor made the point that 'together with the qualities and imagery it evoked [Lucent stands for 'glowing with light' and 'marked by clarity'], Lucent expressed the energy, innovation, entrepreneurial spirit, and clear vision of the company's purpose, principles and future'. At the same time, senior management and communication professionals felt the need to leverage the past by somehow linking the new company to Bell Labs. The team therefore added the descriptive endorsement of 'Bell Labs Innovations' to the Lucent name, a tactic that would not be contested by other companies connected to AT&T.

Communication at the launch

Communication professionals within the newly named company anticipated that employees would come to accept the new name and identity in time. However, because most were veteran AT&T employees, the sudden loss of the old identity was expected to cause serious emotional reactions from some. The new look and feel of the Lucent name and logo were also a clear break from the past logo. Initially, the objective towards employees was to raise awareness of the new name and identity and to communicate the themed messages about the new company's identity (step 2 – themed messages). An important message was to explain the new name and logo and its symbolic meaning in relation to the company's new purpose, principles and future. A symbolic association message style was adopted for this purpose (step 3 – message styles). This message was subsequently communicated through a live internal video conference which was viewed by more than 100,000 employees. Communication staff also set up remote two-way video in order to allow questioning from employees from different parts of the company. These events were followed up by meetings between (middle) managers and employees where, again, the new name and identity were explained to employees and incorporated into new initiatives and behaviours.

Communication with customers and the general public was all about raising awareness of the new name and about making a start with reshaping the image of the new company. Since the company needed to build its identity and image from scratch, communication professionals knew that it was important to 'establish a distinctive and memorable personality, along with very clear messages for the company'. The themed message that was highlighted in the communication campaign involved the company's long-standing leadership in developing innovative network and communication solutions (step 2 – themed messages). The key image attributes that professionals wanted to be reflected in the campaign were quality and reliability, speed and responsiveness, customer focus and innovation. A rational message style was adopted in the campaign (step 3 – message styles); the company's claim that it 'makes things that make communications work' featured as a central promise and was backed up by supporting evidence about the awards (including Nobel prizes) that it has won and its link to AT&T and Bell Labs. Communication professionals used mass media advertising to announce the new name and identity and to make a start with changing the company's image.

(Continued)

(Continued)

After the divesture, Lucent operated successfully for a number of years until it merged in 2006 with Alcatel, one of the leading global suppliers of high-tech equipment for telecommunications networks. The merger was meant to exploit the market opportunities for next-generation networks, services and applications by creating a global convergence leader. The combined company has struggled in recent years but has the broadest product portfolio in the industry of advanced network solutions.

QUESTIONS FOR REFLECTION

1 Describe the general communication strategy of Lucent and the specific programmes towards employees, customers and the general public. To what extent do you feel that the programmes are coherent with the overall strategy and are effectively planned and executed?
2 Lucent used a symbolic association message style in communication towards employees and a rational message style in advertising towards customers and the general public. Do you think that these message styles were wise choices? What other message styles would have been possible to communicate with these groups?

Source: This case study is based upon P.L. Philips and S.A. Greyser (1997) 'Creating a corporate identity for a $20 billion start-up: Lucent technologies', *Design Management Institute*, and on information retrieved from http://www.alcatel-lucent.com

There are various ways to communicate themed messages. Several relatively distinct message styles have developed over the years and represent various ways in which corporate messages are communicated to different stakeholder groups.[18] Table 5.1 summarizes five message styles and groups them into three categories: functional orientation, symbolic orientation and industry orientation. Functionally-oriented messages refer to tangible, physical or concrete capabilities or resources of an organization. Symbolically-oriented messages appeal to psychosocial needs, preferences and experiences of stakeholders. An industry-orientation message style does not necessarily use any particular type of functional or psychosocial appeal but is designed to achieve an advantage over competitors in the same industry. Finally, it is important to note that, as is the case with most categorization schemes, the message styles covered in the following section sometimes overlap in specific examples of corporate

TABLE 5.1 Alternative message styles

Functional orientation	Symbolic orientation	Industry orientation
Rational message style	Symbolic association message style	Generic message style
	Emotional message style	Pre-emptive message style

communication practice. In other words, distinctions are sometimes very fine rather than perfectly obvious, and a particular corporate communication strategy may simultaneously use multiple message styles in relation to themed messages.

1   *Rational message style*: In this approach, an organization makes a superiority claim about its products or achievements based upon a distinctive advantage in its capabilities, size or resources (including technology). The main feature of this message style is identifying an important difference that can be highlighted and then developing a claim that competitors either cannot make or have not chosen to make. The claim is seen as 'functional' because it addresses a basic need or expectation of stakeholders. The message style is labelled rational because it follows a basic argumentation structure where the grounds for the claim for superiority are supplied through supporting information. For example, when Lucent Technologies claims a superior ability to develop and deliver network solutions to clients, it is based upon its distinctive and proven track record in research and development in network technology (the company is associated with the world-renowned AT&T Bell Labs and the company's engineers have won many prizes for their ground-breaking technologies, including Nobel Prizes) (see Case Study 5.1). Similarly, BMW claims a superior ability in engineering aesthetically pleasing, high-performance cars that is backed up by the company's long-standing emphasis on innovation and aesthetics in the design process (see Case Study 4.2). The rational message style can be effective in cases where the organization can claim a distinctive advantage in its capabilities, size or resources. In cases where the organization cannot claim such an advantage, or where such an advantage is easily matched, alternative message styles are used. For example, organizations typically do not use a rational message style when they communicate about their corporate social responsibility (CSR) because standards for performance in such areas are not obvious and transparent (Chapter 13) and, as such, performance can often be easily matched by competitors. In addition, a hard-hitting rational message style may also be seen as socially unacceptable for communicating about CSR.

Rational message style

Definition: superiority claim based upon actual accomplishments or delivered benefits by the organization
Conditions: most useful when point of difference cannot be readily matched by competitors
Content: informational in the form of a claim that is supported with information as the grounds for the claim

---

2   *Symbolic association message style*: Whereas the rational message style is based on promoting physical and functional differences between an organization and its competitors, a symbolic association message style involves psychosocial, rather than physical differentiation. The aim with this

message style is to develop an image for the organization and to differentiate the organization psychologically from its competitors through symbolic association. In imbuing the organization with a symbolic image, communicators draw meaning from the culturally constituted world (that is, the world of symbols and values) and, through communication, transfer that meaning to the organization. The core of this message style consists of identifying a set of symbols and values that through repeated linkage with the organization may come to be associated with that organization. One example of this message style is the way in which organizations link themselves through sponsorship to values associated with a sport or certain cause. Kingfisher, for example, has associated itself with Ellen MacArthur's record-breaking sailing attempts around the world, which, through association, created a positive image of the organization with attributes of freedom, challenge, ambition and leadership. Similarly, Tesco's support of Cancer Research UK associates the company with caring for one of the deadliest diseases and with healthy living. Another example of this message style involves corporate value statements whereby an organization explicitly states values or moral attributes that guide its conduct. AstraZeneca, for instance, lists the values of integrity, honesty and trust as central to how the company engages with its different stakeholders. These values express the moral sentiments and social capital that make organizations legitimate in the eyes of stakeholders. AstraZeneca also gives examples of how the company tries to live up to its values in specific practices. Similar to sponsorship, these value statements are meant to link the company with general (culturally shared and recognized) moral values and sentiments which may then become associated with the organization.

A symbolic association message style may also be described as 'transformational' because it associates the organization with a set of culturally shared experiences and meanings which without corporate communication would not typically be associated with the organization to the same degree. Such communication is transforming (versus informing) by virtue of endowing the organization with a particular symbolic image that is different from any of its competitors.

Symbolic association message style

Definition: claims based on psychological differentiation through symbolic association

Conditions: best for homogeneous organizations where differences are difficult to develop or easily duplicated, or for messages around areas such as CSR or social capital that are difficult to communicate in concrete and rational terms

Content: transformational in the form of endowing the organization with a particular image through association with culturally shared and recognized values or symbols

3 *Emotional message style*: An emotional message style is another form of symbolically-oriented communication. By using this message style, organizations aim to reach stakeholders at a visceral level. One approach may be to use emotional appeals in corporate communication to regulate the emotional responses of stakeholders. The display of emotions may, for example, lead to greater levels of involvement and affiliation with an organization. Starbucks, for example, incorporates emotional appeals around love, joy and belonging into its in-store communication, which has led to consumers associating the Starbucks brand with community, individual expression, and 'a place away from home' (Case Study 3.1). Displays of positive emotions may also stimulate supportive, sharing and expansive behaviours of stakeholders while the display of negative emotions may lead to distancing and avoidance.[19] A good example of this message style involves the launch of Orange in 1994. At the time, the mobile phone market in the UK was a confusing place for customers. Digital networks had just been introduced, but few people yet understood the benefits and most members of the general public were worried about the safety of mobile technology. On top of this, Orange also faced an uphill task in differentiating itself in this market as the last entrant in a market which already included BT Cellnet and Vodafone. In response, Orange launched an advertising campaign which communicated the positive emotions afforded by using mobile phones (friendship, love, freedom) and assured people that the negative emotions (fear, safety) that they may have had concerning the introduction of this new technology were unfounded. In considering an emotional message style, it is important for organizations to make sure that the display of emotions is seen as authentic. If stakeholders perceive references to emotions to be inauthentic, an emotional message style may backfire. In the case of Starbucks, for example, the company's emotional message style has been verified as authentic by stakeholders because of the genuine enthusiasm, friendliness and professionalism conveyed by employees.

Emotional message style

Definition: attempts to provoke involvement and positive reactions through a reference to positive (or negative) emotions
Conditions: effective use depends on the perceived authenticity of the professed emotion and on the relevance of the emotion to stakeholders
Content: appeals to specific positive or negative emotions (e.g., romance, nostalgia, excitement, joy, fear, guilt, disgust, regret)

---

4 *Generic message style*: An organization employs a generic strategy when making a claim that could be made by any organization that operates in the same industry. With this message style, the organization makes no attempt to differentiate itself from competitors or to claim superiority.

This message style is most appropriate for an organization that dominates a particular industry. For example, Campbell's soup dominates the prepared-soup market in the USA, selling nearly two-thirds of all soup. Based upon its market dominance, the company has run advertising campaigns that stimulate demand for soup in general, rather than Campbell's soup in particular. The rationale behind this message style was that any advertising that increased overall soup sales would also naturally benefit Campbell's sales. Along similar lines, Novo Nordisk's 'changing diabetes' message emphasizes the company's long-standing leadership in developing products for the diagnosis and treatment of diabetes. Given Novo Nordisk's grasp on the worldwide diabetes market, the campaign communicated in the company's words 'a clearly differentiated corporate position in the global diabetes market'.

Generic message style

Definition: straight claim about industry or cause with no assertion of superiority
Conditions: monopoly or extreme dominance of industry
Content: general claim (stimulate demand for product category or raise awareness of cause)

---

5 *Pre-emptive message style*: A second message style that involves an industry-wide orientation is employed when an organization makes a generic-type claim but does so with a suggestion of superiority. Pre-emptive communication is a clever strategy when a meaningful superiority claim is made because it precludes competitors from saying the same thing. For example, many electronics firms can potentially claim to be about developing technological products that are advanced but easy to operate and designed around the needs of the customer, but no other firm could possibly make such a claim after Philips made it as part of its generic 'Sense and simplicity' campaign. This claim could potentially have been made by many other electronics firms, such as Sony and Samsung, but in appropriating this claim, with its implicit assertion of superiority, Philips has pre-empted competitors from using the simplicity tack in promoting their own organizations (Case Study 2.1). Another example of the pre-emptive message style involves BP's restyling of itself as being 'beyond petroleum' in its focus on renewable energies and on the reduction of carbon emissions within its business operations. When the company recognized the changing expectations of stakeholders towards the petroleum industry, BP was the first to take up an industry-wide position on climate change and on the industry's responsibilities in reducing carbon emissions. In doing so, the company came to be seen as an environmental leader in its industry ahead of Shell and Exxon-Mobil.

Pre-emptive message style

Definition: generic claim with suggestion of superiority
Conditions: changing industry allowing a company to take a position on an issue connected to that industry
Content: claim of industry-wide leadership on a relevant issue or capability

---

Five general message styles have been discussed and categorized as functional, symbolic or industry-oriented. These strategic alternatives to communicating corporate messages provide a useful aid to understanding the different approaches available to communicators and the factors influencing the choice for a particular message style. The message styles should, however, not be seen as mutually exclusive. In fact, organizations may use different message styles to communicate different messages to different stakeholders. The case study of Toyota (see Case Study 5.2) illustrates how organizations develop and plan particular communication programmes and campaigns as part of their communication strategy. These programmes and campaigns include different themed messages that may be communicated through multiple message styles. Both programmes and campaigns start from the basic model presented in Figure 5.2, but the planning and execution of programmes and campaigns requires added detail on communication objectives, the segmentation of target audiences, the media strategy and the budgeting of the programme or campaign. In the next chapter, we provide these details and present a framework for planning and executing communication programmes and campaigns.

CASE STUDY 5.2

TOYOTA: A ROCKY ROAD AHEAD

Toyota Motor Corporation (TMC) became the world's largest vehicle manufacturer in 2008, offering a full range of models from mini vehicles to large trucks. Toyota and its luxury line, Lexus, have been among the top automotive brands in terms of reliability, quality and long-term durability. Toyota had also, until recently, been one of the most profitable carmakers: in the financial year that ended in March 2007, for example, the company made a profit of $13.7 billion while General Motors (GM) and Ford reported losses of $1.97 billion and $12.61 billion respectively. But its fortune has recently turned. In January 2010 the company announced that it would temporarily shut down production at six assembly plants in North America and suspend sales of its most popular models, including the Camry, the best-selling car in the USA. The week before the company had already recalled 2.3 million vehicles with faults in the accelerator pedals. These announcements have come after a series of product recalls that have seriously damaged the carmaker's reputation for producing good quality, reliable cars at reasonable prices.

(Continued)

(Continued)

The company's pursuit of volume may have undermined its previously enviable record for reliability. In 2006, after another series of recalls, the company promised a 'customer first' strategy to restore its slipping reputation. But recalls continued and Toyota slid behind other carmakers in customer reliability polls. These troubles and the damage to its reputation have made customers wary of buying a Toyota. In addition, Toyota's initial leadership on sustainability, including the development of electric and hybrid cars, is quickly eroding as other big carmakers are launching their own green models and are integrating sustainability issues into their production and supply chains.

Toyota's vision

In 2002, Toyota had adopted a new strategic direction articulated in its 2010 Global Vision programme. In it, Toyota described how by 2010, the company expected society to encourage a pro-environmental stance and, specifically, to encourage the reuse and recycling of goods. In addition, the Global Vision suggested that nationalism will have declined by 2010 and given way to a mature society that respects all people regardless of nationalities and ethnic backgrounds – global corporations therefore need to respect their working environments and the different people and communities that they serve and with whom they interact. The Global Vision also articulated new marketing opportunities, including China, India and other emerging markets, that have yet to become fully car-oriented, and set the ambitious marketing aim of capturing around 15 per cent of the global vehicle market by tapping these emerging markets. The then President of Toyota, Fujio Cho, declared in 2002 that Toyota was pursuing growth more than anything else, aiming for 15 per cent of the global market by 2010.

The 2010 Global Vision also set out the corporate reputation (i.e., 'how each stakeholder views the organization') that Toyota should strive for, in line with the mentioned changes in society and societal expectations. The corporate identity that Toyota has since been seeking to project among its stakeholders is that of a leader in global regeneration and in the application of IT in automobiles for better and safer motoring. The company also wanted to be seen as one that is expanding the appeal of automobiles across the world, creating more 'fans' and achieving the largest global market share of all carmakers. Moreover, the company wanted to be considered as a truly global enterprise that transcends nationalities and ethnicities and is respected by all peoples around the world.

Toyota's track record in sustainability and environmental leadership in the industry goes back to 1992 when the company adopted a set of Guiding Principles, which among other things appealed to employees to dedicate themselves to 'providing clean and safe products and towards enhancing the quality of life everywhere through our activities'. In the same year (1992), the company adopted the Toyota Earth Charter. Based on this charter, the company began to produce cars that were friendlier to both people and the environment. In January 1998, Toyota created an Environmental Affairs Division under the direct supervision of its President.

(Continued)

(Continued)

Toyota also received the US Environmental Protection Agency's Global Climate Protection Award 1998 for developing Prius (the world's first passenger vehicle in mass production powered by a hybrid power train system). The introduction of Prius in 1997 allowed the company to make a clear statement on its commitment to environmental protection. Since 1998, Toyota has also been disclosing information on its environment-related activities through an Environmental Report. And in June 1999, Toyota became the first vehicle manufacturer to be awarded the United Nations Environmental Program (UNEP) Global 500 award for the leadership it demonstrated 'in the development of environmental technologies and measures'. In September 2003, it was reported that Toyota had earned the leading position on the 'Dow Jones Sustainability Index (DJSI)' in the automobile sector. DSJI analysts maintained that 'while VW [Volkswagen] scored significantly higher in the social dimension (i.e., standards for suppliers, human right issues in the value chain) than Toyota, Toyota seems to execute more systematically its strategies regarding environmental issues, including recycling, efficiency and technology'.

Toyota's environmental reputation

According to Toyota, cars have often been seen in a negative light because of air pollution, oil exhaustion and global warming. With more than 30 per cent of people worldwide using automobiles, Toyota felt that environmental issues would increasingly become a central issue for the car industry. The company has therefore given high priority to manufacturing cars that are safe and environmentally friendly. Viewing it as a strategic opportunity, Toyota has taken many initiatives to earn an environmentally-friendly image. Fujio Cho, a former president of Toyota, said 'Environmentally friendly cars will soon cease to be an option, they will become a necessity'. Toyota came out in 2005 with its Fourth Environmental Action Plan. Acting as a blueprint for Toyota's contribution to the environment, the plan outlines the activities that Toyota needs to undertake to sustain an environmentally-friendly corporate image. It includes enhancements in fuel efficiency and reduction in the carbon dioxide (CO_2) emission from vehicles. Through the adoption of superior environmental technologies, Toyota plans to reduce CO_2 emission from its own vehicles by 15 per cent. The company also believed that the introduction of the Prius has given it a 'green reputation'. Fujio Cho commented in 2002 that: 'Hybrids like the Prius are a starting point to address long-term environmental issues. Automakers that deliver practical, greener products will command the market in the 21st century.'

Toyota's stance with regards to technological development is to 'zeronize' and 'maximize'. 'Zeronize' symbolizes the company's efforts in minimizing the negative aspects of cars, such as environmental impact, traffic congestion and traffic accidents. 'Maximize' refers to efforts in maximizing the positive aspects of cars, such as comfort and convenience. Toyota is striving to combine the two by creating ecologically superior but safe and reliable cars. In 2007, Katsuaki Watanabe, Toyota's president at the time, articulated the challenge to the car industry in terms of 'the increasing demand for corporate social responsibility [and] to take on global

(Continued)

(Continued)

environmental problems such as global warming, depletion of natural resources and air pollution'. Watanabe also articulated the leadership position that Toyota had taken on environmental issues in the car industry. He specifically referred to hybrid technologies as an example of Toyota's environmental leadership: 'Toyota has positioned hybrid technologies as core technologies and will develop them with a commitment to leading the way in that field.'

In recent years, however, Toyota's edge and leadership on environmental issues has been challenged by other carmakers, notably VW and BMW. The current President of Toyota, Akio Toyoda, believes that the company needs to be more ruthless in exploiting its early leadership in commercializing hybrid systems and electric-vehicle technology. He is convinced that Toyota is still ahead of the pack. Although other carmakers are launching hybrids and electricity-powered vehicles, Toyota will be able to exploit its leadership on a much larger scale by bringing a hybrid version of every car Toyota makes on the market and by extending the Prius brand to cover a range of innovative low- and zero-emission vehicles.

Communication strategy

As a monolithic corporate brand, Toyota has been using both product-led communications around specific cars as well as corporate-led communications around themes identified in its Global Vision document. Specifically, the company has been trying to establish a reputation for itself associated with the 'environment' and the 'safety' and 'reliability' of its cars. From 2003, for example, Toyota has been running campaigns around its environmental technologies and achievements. As part of these campaigns, the company initially used a 'Leaf Car' logo to convey its 'commitment to reduce the environmental impact of products, plants and processes'. The 'Leaf Car' logo, a design that features a car in the shape of a green leaf of a tree, has featured in corporate advertising to symbolize the company-wide drive towards environmental awareness. Initially, then, the company adopted a symbolic association message style (with trees symbolizing the environment) to suggests its environmental credentials. Subsequent adverts highlighted the company's green credentials in more direct, rational terms with a claim being made about its overall environmental leadership, backed up by reference to the launch of Prius and the Lexus LS Hybrid, the company's global Earth Charter and guiding principles promoting environmental responsibility throughout the company and the reduction of carbon emissions at manufacturing plants.

At the marketing and consumer end, Toyota has been running specific products adverts that communicate the 'safety' and 'reliability' of its cars. In addition, the company has been participating in Formula One (F1). Toyota announced its participation in F1 in January 1999. Having made the announcement, Toyota made preparations on several fronts – it prepared its 'Toyota Panasonic Racing Team' for the F1 event, the F1 car was being developed, and on 23 March, 2001, Toyota unveiled its first ever F1 race car. Toyota's performance in the 2003 British Grand Prix has so far been the most memorable one in the company's brief F1 history. Toyota's

(Continued)

(Continued)

Cristiano da Matta and Olivier Panis led the race for some time before Barrichello scooped victory. Although the team's performance at F1 events has been patchy at best, Toyota's participation in the F1 World Championships is seen as 'the company's most successful communication tool yet. Internally and externally, the F1 program has had a significant impact' (Times Inc., 2003). Toyota's own communications to its employees suggests the same:

> It [the F1 project] helped to motivate Toyota's 260,000-strong workforce around the world. All the employees take great pride in the Toyota TF103, the racing car that competes in the F1 Grand Prix, which was built using the same technological basis as the production cars they build and sell.

Externally, the F1 participation enabled Toyota to invite stakeholders such as dealers, suppliers and sales personnel to the events, to watch the F1 spectacle and to talk business. The participation in F1 did help the company symbolically associate its cars with high performance, although it did not directly communicate the key themes of 'safety' and 'reliability'. In 2009, triggered by Toyota's first ever financial loss and the team's poor consistency in terms of results, the company decided to withdraw from F1 with immediate effect.

Challenges ahead

One of the main challenges ahead for Toyota is its faltering reputation in producing safe, reliable cars at affordable prices. Recent customer polls and market surveys put Toyota clearly behind its competitors. For example, Ford vehicles, long considered as also-rans, are now showing 'world-class reliability', beating the Toyota Camry in the segment of mid-size cars. If Toyota can no longer rely on its superior quality and reliability to appeal to customers, its vehicles will inevitably be judged increasingly on more emotional criteria, such as its design and styling, and the experience of driving a Toyota car. But this is not an area that has traditionally been Toyota's strength, nor has the company been consistently communicating such experiential or emotional benefits to its consumers. The company therefore finds itself in a bit of a dilemma. Mr Toyoda, the current President, believes that the company needs to return to its strengths (reliability) as well as add new spice to its cars. In October 2009, Toyoda addressed an audience of Japanese journalists and said that the company was in a spiral of decline, unless it would reinvent itself. Mr Toyoda had been reading *How the Mighty Fall*, a book on how previously mighty companies may step into a cycle of decline. The decline leads to a downward spiral triggered by an undisciplined pursuit of growth and by being out of touch with the changing values and expectations of customers and other stakeholders.

When Mr Toyoda took over in 2009, he immediately ordered a back-to-basics overhaul of product development across the firm's global operations. He also has been challenging his company's engineers to make less dull cars. At the Tokyo Motor Show in October 2009 he stated publicly: 'I want to see Toyota build cars that are fun and exciting to drive.' As Morizo, the *alter ego* under which he blogs, he even

(Continued)

(Continued)

went a step further. In his blog, he commented on the cars at the show: 'It was all green. But I wonder how many inspired people get excited. Eco-friendly cars are a prerequisite for the future, but there must be more than that.'

Mr Toyoda's challenge lies in rebuilding and extending Toyota's reputation from the initial dual focus on environmental leadership and the safety and reliability of its cars, to a reputation that stresses the emotional fun and enjoyment of driving Toyota cars. He may have to keep the company's traditional strengths – the dependability and affordability of its cars – while adding the emotional benefits that customers now appear to demand.

QUESTIONS FOR REFLECTION

1   Consider the vision articulated by Toyota and its alignment with the company's image with external stakeholders and the internal culture. Is there sufficient alignment between vision, culture and image? What gaps emerged and how can Toyota address these gaps?
2   Consider the overall communication strategy of Toyota, including its strategic intent and positioning, the themed messages and message styles in Toyota's communications. Given the challenges ahead for Toyota, how would you change the communication strategy in terms of strategic intent, themed messages and message styles?

Source: This case study is based on Baue, W. (2003), Dow lanes Sustainability Indexes Add Toyota, HP, Eject DaimlerChrysler, Bank of America, September 11, 2003 (www.sri-advisor.com); Chaudhuri, S., and Ramanathan, K. (2007), Global vision 2010: Toyota's strategic initiatives, IBSCDC; the Economist (2009) Struggling giants: Toyota slips up, 9th of December 2009; The Economist (2010), The machine that ran too hot, 25th of February 2010; The Economist (2010), Getting the cow out of the ditch, 11th of February 2010; The Economist (2010), no quick fix, 4th of February 2010 (other quotes throughout the text); Collins, J. (2009), *How the Mighty Fall: And Why Some Companies Never Give In*. New York: Random House.

CHAPTER SUMMARY

5.4 The chapter has described the process and content of corporate communication strategy. The process refers to the different individuals and groups that are involved in strategy formation and the way in which they work together to shape and formulate a communication strategy. The content refers to the themed messages within corporate communication and the message styles that are adopted to communicate those messages to different stakeholders. The next chapter takes the next step and focuses in more detail on the planning and execution of specific communication programmes and campaigns as part of a wider communication strategy.

DISCUSSION QUESTIONS

1   What is the difference between a themed message and a message style?

2   Select an industry or sector with which you are familiar or that you have worked for in the past. Identify the themed messages and message styles used in messages released by organizations in this industry or sector. Are their communication strategies comparable or different? What might explain this similarity or difference?

 # KEY TERMS

Boundary spanning

Communication strategy

Corporate strategy

Emotional message style

Environmental scanning

Generic message style

Manager

Pre-emptive message style

Rational message style

Strategic intent

Symbolic association message style

Technician

Themed message

Vision

 # FURTHER READING

Gronstedt, Anders (2000), *The Customer Century: Lessons from World-class Companies in Integrated Marketing and Communications*. London: Routledge.

Grunig, J.E. (2006), 'Furnishing the edifice: ongoing research on public relations as a strategic management function', *Journal of Public Relations Research*, 18: 151–176.

Haywood, Roger (2005), *Corporate Reputation, the Brand and the Bottom Line: Powerful, Proven Communication Strategies for Maximizing Value* (3rd edn). London: Kogan Page.

NOTES

1   *Financial Times*, 'Wal-Mart picks a shade of green', 7 February 2006.

2   Hamel, G. and Prahalad, C.K. (1989), 'Strategic intent', *Harvard Business Review*, May–June: 63–76, quote on p. 64.

3   See, for instance, Mintzberg, H. (1989), 'Strategy formation: schools of thought', in Frederickson, J. (ed.), *Perspectives on Strategic Management*. San Francisco: Ballinger; Mintzberg, H., Ahlstrand, B. and Lampel, J. (1998), *Strategy Safari: The Complete Guide through the Wilds of Strategic Management*. London: FT Prentice Hall; or Elfring, T. and Volberda, H.W. (2001), 'Schools of thought in strategic management: fragmentation, integration or synthesis', in Volberda, H.W. and Elfring, T. (eds), *Rethinking Strategy*. London: Sage, pp. 1–25.

4   Rumelt, R.P., Schendel, D.E. and Teece, D.J. (1994), 'Fundamental issues in strategy', in Rumelt, R.P., Schendel, D.E. and Teece, D.J. (eds), *Fundamental Issues in Strategy: A Research Agenda*. Boston, MA: HBS, p. 22.

5   Grunig, J.E. and Repper, F.C. (1992), 'Strategic management, publics and issues', in Grunig, J.E. (ed.), *Excellence in Public Relations and Communication Management*. Hillsdale, NJ: Lawrence Erlbaum Associates, pp. 122–123.

6   Argenti, P., Howell, R.A. and Beck, K.A. (2005), 'The strategic communication imperative', *MIT Sloan Management Review*, Spring, 83–89, quote on pp. 86–87.

7   Argenti et al. (2005), pp. 86–87.

8   Argenti et al. (2005), p. 89.

9   Moss, D., Warnaby, G. and Newman, A.J. (2000), 'Public relations practitioner role enactment at the senior management level within UK companies', *Journal of Public Relations Research*, 12: 277–307; Cropp, F. and Pincus, D.J. (2001), 'The mystery of public relations: unraveling its past, unmasking its future', in Heath, R.L (ed.), *Handbook of Public Relations*. Thousand Oaks, CA: Sage, pp. 189–204.

10 Gronstedt, A. (2000), *The Customer Century: Lessons from World-class Companies in Integrated Marketing and Communications*. London: Routledge, p. 203.

11 See, for example, Dozier, D.M. and Broom, G.M. (1995), 'Evolution of the manager role in public relations practice', *Journal of Public Relations Research*, 7: 3–26.

12 Dozier and Broom (1995), p. 22.

13 Moss, D., Newman, A. and DeSanto, B. (2005), 'What do communication managers do? Defining and refining the core elements of management in a public relations/corporate communication context', *Journalism and Mass Communication Quarterly*, 82: 873–890.

14 Pincus, J.D., Rayfield, B. and Ohl, C.M. (1994), 'Public relations education in MBA programs: Challenges and opportunities', *Public Relations Review*, 20(1), pages 55–71.

15 Murray, K. and White, J. (2004), *A Report on the Value of Public Relations, as perceived by Organizational Leaders* (www.chime.plc.uk/downloads/reputationkm.pdf).

16 Gronstedt (2000), p. 204.

17 Argenti et al. (2005), p. 89.

18 Based upon Shimp, T.A. (2003), *Advertising, Promotion and Supplemental Aspects of Integrated Marketing Communications*. Fort Worth, TX: Dryden Press; Rindova, V. (2007), 'Starbucks: constructing a multiplex identity in the specialty coffee industry', in Lerpold, L., Ravasi, D., Van Rekom, J. and Soenen, G. (eds), *Organizational Identity in Practice*. London: Routledge, pp. 157–173.

19 Rindova (2007), p. 167.

STRATEGIC PLANNING AND CAMPAIGN MANAGEMENT

6

| **Chapter Overview** |

The chapter describes the process of planning and managing strategic communication programmes and campaigns. It discusses specific steps in the development and planning of a comprehensive communication programme, and as part of an overall communication strategy. The chapter provides a practical model for planning programmes and campaigns and ends with a discussion of ways in which campaigns may persuade stakeholders into supportive behaviours towards the organization.

INTRODUCTION

6.1 A communication strategy involves the formulation of a desired position for the organization in terms of how it wants to be seen by its different stakeholder groups. Based upon an assessment of the gap between how the company is currently seen (corporate reputation) and how it wants to be seen (vision) (Chapter 5), a communication strategy specifies a strategic intent, on which possible courses of action are formulated, evaluated and eventually chosen. Communication strategies often involve a process of bringing stakeholder reputations in line with the vision of the organization in order to obtain the necessary support for the organization's strategy. In other cases, a communication strategy may be about reinforcing existing reputations of stakeholders if those are broadly in line with how the organization wants itself to be seen.

Once the content of a communication strategy has been roughly drawn out, communication practitioners translate that content into specific communication programmes and campaigns that are aimed at both internal and external stakeholder audiences. A communication programme is defined as a formulated set of activities directed towards targeted internal and external audiences, which may include outreach activities, community initiatives and other ways in which organizations and their employees communicate with stakeholder audiences. A communication programme is thus a broader concept than the idea of a communication campaign, which is restricted to the use of a mediated form of communication (e.g., mass media advertising) aimed at specific stakeholder audiences. Another way of distinguishing programmes and campaigns is in terms of the time-line. Campaigns are restricted to a single point in time in that they build to a decision point, such as garnering support for a particular company decision or in relation to a specific issue. A programme is like a campaign in that it may consist of different activities, but it differs in the sense that it does not have a pre-set endpoint. A programme is put in place to address ongoing needs for reputation building, as laid down in the overall communication strategy, and is reviewed periodically to determine whether its objectives have been met. All or parts of a programme will be continued as long as there is a need for communication with stakeholders, and in order to strengthen or maintain a company's corporate reputation.

In this chapter, we discuss practical steps to develop, plan and execute communication programmes and campaigns. While the chapter is largely practical in its scope and application, it concludes with a more theoretical discussion of ways in which programmes and campaigns may persuade stakeholders into changing their opinions and in demonstrating supportive behaviours towards the organization.

PLANNING AND EXECUTING PROGRAMMES AND CAMPAIGNS

6.2 Both programmes and campaigns start from the basic model presented in Figure 5.2 but with added detail on communication objectives, the segmentation of target audiences, the media strategy and the budgeting of the programme or campaign. Figure 6.1 presents communication practitioners with a framework for identifying the broad targets of their communication and for planning effective communication programmes and campaigns. The framework consists of seven steps, starting with the strategic intent.

Step 1: Strategic intent

At the onset of a communication programme or campaign, it is important to refer back to the organization's overall communication strategy and the identified strategic intent. Roughly speaking, the strategic intent formulates a change or consolidation of stakeholder reputations of the organization. It is based upon the gap between how the organization wants to be seen by important stakeholder groups and how it is currently seen by each of those groups.

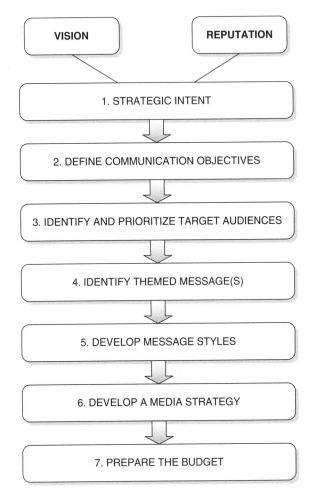

FIGURE 6.1   The process of planning communication programmes and campaigns

Step 2: Define communication objectives

Based upon the strategic intent, communication practitioners need to set specific communication objectives for each communication programme or campaign. Here, practitioners may decide to develop specific programmes or campaigns for particular stakeholder groups (e.g., employees, shareholders and investors, customers) or instead to develop a general corporate programme or campaign that addresses all of them. In both cases, however, practitioners need to define objectives in terms of whether they are seeking to change or consolidate a particular stakeholder's awareness, attitude, more general reputation, or behaviour. In line with the strategic intent, successful communication consists of appealing to stakeholders with a particular message so that they react favourably to it and change or consolidate a specific supportive behaviour towards the organization, such as investing in an organization or buying its products. Communication objectives should be as tightly defined as possible: specific, measurable, achievable (or, actionable), realistic and timely (SMART):

1   *Specific*: Objectives should specify what it is that the practitioner wants to achieve (e.g., knowledge change, change in reputation) of a particular stakeholder group.

2   *Measurable*: Practitioners should be able to measure whether they are meeting the objectives or not. This often consists of identifying clear indicators (e.g., a percentage change in supportive behaviours towards the organization) that can be measured and afterwards used to evaluate the success of the programme or campaign.

3   *Achievable*: Objectives should be achievable and attainable in the light of current stakeholder reputations of the organization and the competitive landscape.

4   *Realistic*: Objectives need to be realistic in the light of the resources and budget that is provided for a particular programme or campaign.

5   *Timely*: Objectives should also specify the time-frame in which they need to be achieved. Communication objectives often include a 'window' of 1–2 years after the programme or campaign to measure the direct impact of a programme or campaign.

Well-articulated objectives are measurable in that they specify a time-frame and the number of people that the programme or campaign sets out to reach and affect. It is then possible for communication practitioners to evaluate and determine whether objectives have been met.

Step 3: Identify and prioritize target audiences

Organizations have many stakeholder groups. Obviously, organizations cannot communicate with all of them, and practitioners therefore use the stakeholder salience model and the power–interest matrix (Chapter 3) to identify the most important stakeholder groups. Once important stakeholder groups have been identified, practitioners need to segment those groups into more specific target audiences that are prioritized for a particular programme or campaign. For example, the stakeholder group of 'employees' includes many segments of different groups (e.g., top management, middle management, front-line staff, back-office personnel, administrative staff, etc.) which may not all need to be addressed within a particular programme or campaign. A target audience is defined as the segment of individuals (from a particular stakeholder group) that is the focus ('target') of a particular programme or campaign.

Step 4: Identify themed message(s)

Based upon the identified communication objectives and selected target audiences, practitioners need to decide what the core message should be. The core message towards a particular target audience often evolves directly from how the organization wants to be seen. For example, Philips' vision of wanting to be seen as a leader in innovation provides a core message that can be translated into a specific campaign format and message style (Step 5 below). Themed messages may relate to the organization as a whole or to more specific areas, such as products and services, CSR or financial performance, in which case they may be primarily relevant to particular stakeholder groups.

Step 5: Develop message styles

A message can be told in different ways using one of the five message styles (see section 5.3). The message styles involve the creative concept that articulates the appeal of the message and brings it to life through the use of catchy slogans and visual stimuli (pictures, images, logos and the typographic setting of a message). As discussed in Chapter 5, the use of a particular message style depends on certain conditions and expectations of stakeholders. For example, an organization may adopt a rational message style when it communicates its financial growth and potential to investors at the annual general meeting by referring to its recent fiscal results and the growth of the market in which it operates. Simultaneously, an organization may adopt a symbolic association style by sponsoring a sports event or cause in an attempt to build a general corporate image that may lead to recognition and favour with all of its stakeholder groups. In short, an organization can use multiple message styles simultaneously to communicate with different target audiences. At the same time, organizations often use the same message style to communicate about certain specific areas, such as its products and services, its general corporate position, CSR or its financial performance. Philips, for example, has used the same pre-emptive message style around the core message of 'Sense and simplicity' in all its corporate advertising and market-focused communication (advertising, sales promotions, direct marketing) to consistently communicate its commitment to developing technology for people.

Step 6: Develop a media strategy

The sixth step in the process involves identifying the media that can best carry and execute the message, that is can reach the target audience in the most effective way. In developing the media strategy, the overriding aim is to identify the most effective and efficient means of reaching the target audiences within the given budgetary constraints. Practitioners need to consider criteria such as:

- the reach and coverage of the target audience (to what extent does a particular medium reach subjects within the target audience so that they are exposed to the message at least once?),
- the creative match of the medium with the message (to what extent does the medium support a particular message style and creative format?),
- competitors' use of the media (to what extent do competitors use the same medium?), and
- the ability of media to enable dialogue and interaction with the audience (does the medium simply supply information or does it also allow interaction with the organization?).[1]

Media selection is ideally 'zero-based',[2] meaning that the most appropriate medium in the light of these criteria is chosen rather than a pre-fixed and stand-ard choice for a medium that may have worked in the past. In other words, prac-titioners need to stay open to the wide range of media options available to them (e.g., free publicity, video-conferencing, promotions, meetings with stakeholders, sponsoring events, people or causes) rather than heading straight for, for example, (corporate) advertising. Practitioners also need to decide upon the right mix of media for a particular communication programme or campaign. For example, when an organization launches a new product, it will need to use a range of media, including mass media advertising to generate awareness, marketing public rela-tions to generate excitement and interest in the product and sales promotions to stimulate people to try the product. Within the constraints of the budget, practi-tioners will aim to select multiple media, and need to specify how these media complement each other in the achievement of the communication objectives, and when each medium is put to use within the time-frame of the programme or campaign.

Step 7: Prepare the budget

Finally, it is important to budget for the communication programme or cam-paign. Most of the budget will be spent on media buying, with the remaining amount going towards the production of the programme or campaign (including the hiring of communication consultants, advertising professionals and copy-editors) and the evaluation of results. Based upon the budget that is available for a particular programme or campaign, practitioners may have to revise the previous steps and select a different mix of media and/or adjust their communication objectives.

When the entire programme or campaign is planned and executed, it will be evaluated for its results – specifically in terms of whether it has achieved the com-munication objectives. Effectiveness of the programme or campaign can be evalu-ated on the basis of process and communications effects. *Process effects* concern the quality of the communication programme or campaign (in terms of intelligence gathered, the detail that has gone into the planning, the appropriateness of message content and overall organizational support) and whether the programme has been executed in a cost-effective manner. *Communication effects* include the range of cognitive and behavioural effects with targeted stakeholder audiences that the pro-gramme or campaign aimed to achieve. Here it is important to identify suitable impact measures (i.e., changes in awareness, attitude and reputation, or behaviour) rather than relying on interim measures of communication effects, such as media coverage or simple exposure,[3] and to evaluate the effects, achieved against the tar-gets or benchmarks set within the objectives of the communication programme or campaign.

The entire process of developing a communication strategy and of planning spe-cific communication programmes and campaigns is illustrated in the classic case example of Orange (Case Study 6.1).

CASE STUDY 6.1

DEVELOPING A CAMPAIGN TO SUPPORT THE LAUNCH OF ORANGE

The story of Orange is one of the most exciting corporate brand-building successes in recent years, with the company's market value having gone from nothing in 1994 to £28 billion ($46.6 billion, €39.7 billion) in 2000. Apart from great deal-making, service innovations and technological developments, the lion's share of this achievement can be attributed to the power of the Orange corporate brand and the integrated approach towards communication that enabled the company to reach the corporate objectives that it had set at its launch.

The enormity of the task facing Orange at its launch is perhaps difficult to grasp and appreciate today, given the current popularity of mobile phones. In 1994, the mobile phone market in the UK was a confusing place for customers. Digital networks had just been introduced, but few people yet understood the benefits. On top of this, Orange faced an uphill task in differentiating itself in this market as the last entrant in a field of four. Cellnet and Vodafone, two of its competitors, already had ten years of market dominance at that time, with full national coverage for their mobile phones and millions of captive subscribers on their analogue networks. Both Cellnet and Vodafone had also successfully developed low-user tariffs as part of a pre-emptive strategy to block entry into the consumer market and had continuously strengthened their dominance of the business market through the development of their digital (GSM) networks.

Orange faced a daunting task in 1994 if it was to reach the ambitious corporate objective that it had set 'to become the first choice in mobile communications' (step 1 – strategic intent). Before the Orange name was launched in 1994, the company's trading name was Microtel. Executives of Hutchison Group, Microtel's mother corporation, met at that time to discuss strategies of overcoming, or minimizing, the huge disadvantage of being last in the market. They soon realized that effective communication would be an integral part of this and crucial in achieving the company's ambitious aim of market leadership.

In May 1993, a team of senior managers and communications specialists from Microtel, corporate identity specialists Wolff Olins and advertising agency WCRS was set up and was charged with developing a clear and strong communication strategy and positioning. This team quickly realized that the new corporate brand could not be built on a 'low-cost' strategy, emphasizing price benefits, as this would have pitched the brand directly against one of Cellnet and Vodafone's greatest strengths, namely exceptionally low entry costs. Instead, there was room to develop a fully rounded corporate brand identity built upon the market high ground, which had been left conspicuously unoccupied by the competition and would be a better alternative for capturing market share. The objectives that were set were not only to raise awareness, but also to build a strong favourability towards the Orange brand with external stakeholders, including customers and consumers, industry analysts and prospective investors (steps 2 and 3 – define communication objectives and identify target audiences). As part of this, the team needed to flesh out a strong value-based branded identity for Orange that would set it apart from its low-cost competitors.

The team brainstormed names and propositions and finally arrived at the word Orange as best representing their ideas, with its connotations of hope, fun and

(Continued)

(Continued)

freedom (step 4 – identify themed messages). Market research at the time indicated that people found the name Orange distinctive and friendly, extrovert, modern and powerful. The name Orange, along with the term 'wire-free' (as one of the communicable values), was subsequently registered as a trademark. Advertising and the design of a logo followed and were all based on the positioning for Orange as formulated by the team:

> There will come a time when all people will have their own personal number that goes with them wherever they are so that there are no barriers to communication; a wire-free future in which you call people, not places, and where everyone will benefit from the advances of technology. The Future is Bright. The Future is Orange.

The launch campaign that was developed communicated the positive emotions afforded by using mobile phones (friendship, love, freedom) and assured people that the negative emotions (fear, safety) that they may have had around the introduction of this new technology were unfounded (step 5 – develop message style). The team also realized that given the doubts which surrounded Orange as a late entrant at its launch, the most important task for media was to imbue the brand with as much confidence as possible (step 6 – media strategy). A multi-media schedule was therefore adopted: a dominating presence for the Orange brand with advertising posters heralding each new campaign theme, TV adverts communicating core brand benefits, and public relations and press providing detailed messages in the information-led environment of newspapers.

This launch campaign proved enormously successful for Orange. The launch campaign itself received many media awards and accolades, but more importantly it helped Orange quickly gain market share and a market capitalization that enabled it to expand into other international markets. In 1996, barely two years after its launch, Orange PLC underwent its first public offering with shares being listed on the London and Nasdaq markets on 2 April. With a valuation of £2.4 billion, Orange PLC became the youngest company to enter the FTSE 100. In August 2000, France Télécom acquired Orange. Despite the changes in ownership, Orange has continued to concentrate on its brand-led communication strategy, rather than on hard-hitting competitive strategies, including price cuts and distribution growths, as this strategy has propelled the company to the corporate success and position that it now enjoys. France Télécom announced in 2006 its intention to make Orange its flagship commercial brand and has extended the brand beyond mobile telecommunications to internet, fixed-line and TV offers. In 2007, Millward Brown and the *Financial Times* listed Orange at number 67 in the worldwide BRANDZ Ranking with an estimated brand value of US$9,922,000.

QUESTION FOR REFLECTION

Reflect upon the launch campaign for the Orange brand. What in your opinion explains the great success that the campaign achieved?

Source: For further details on this case, see Olins, W. (2008) *The Brand Handbook*. London: Thames and Hudson.

THEORIES ON EFFECTIVE MESSAGES AND PERSUASION

6.3 A key success factor in any communication programme or campaign is the formulation of the overall message and the way in which it is tuned towards a target audience. The choice of a message style (Chapter 5) is often paramount in this respect as well as the overall presentation and clarity of the message. Historically, communication scholars have thought in different ways about the effectiveness of messages. At the start of the twentieth century, the mass media were assumed as omnipotent in their effect – messages, once communicated, were directly consumed and acted upon by willing audiences. In the 1950s and 1960s, mass communication experts changed quite radically in their assessment as they noticed that on a closer look mass media campaigns were having little effect. One belief at that time was that campaigns often simply reinforced existing beliefs or attitudes, rather than changing an audience's attitudes or behaviours. In the early 1970s, Mendelsohn stepped into the fray with a more realistic diagnosis of effects and a more optimistic prognosis for communication practitioners.[4] He simply believed that both sides had some truth to them; campaigns often failed simply because communicators overpromised, assumed audiences would automatically receive and accept messages, and blanketed audiences with messages that were not properly targeted and therefore likely to be ignored or misinterpreted. Mendelsohn's claims still appear to hold today. Most campaigns fail these days because they overpromise or because they are insufficiently tuned to a particular target audience. Mendelsohn also offered a very helpful prescription for communicators: target your messages and set reasonable goals and objectives that are not only achievable but demonstrate a sound knowledge of the current levels of awareness, beliefs and behaviours of your target audience.

Essentially, at the heart of Mendelsohn's recommendations is a critique of traditional linear models of communication and communication effects. McGuire, another communication scholar, suggested a receiver-oriented view as an alternative, commonly known as the hierarchy of effects theory of persuasion.[5] The model is based on the assumption that campaign messages have to achieve several intermediate steps before a member of a target audience moves from exposure to a message to actual desired behavioural changes (Figure 6.2).

Exposure is of course a necessary step for any effect on a target audience, but exposure may not automatically assume attention to the message. A message must attract at least a basic level of attention to succeed, and this implies that communicators need to be clear about the messages and the message style, and need to design messages in such a way that they attract attention. This may involve particular visuals, such as colours and positive images, which may draw in the audience, as well as simple, catchy or counter-intuitive phrases. At the same time, although people will orient themselves to messages with appealing sounds and visual effects, research has shown that they may stop paying attention if a message seems irrelevant or uninteresting to them. Messages that come across as relevant will sustain attention and will trigger an interest or involvement of the target audience. Any change in attitude or behaviour towards a company, in turn, then requires a sustained number of reinforcing

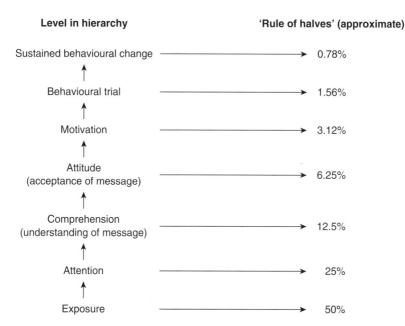

FIGURE 6.2 The hierarchy of effects model

messages. In particular, being motivated to take certain supportive behaviours towards an organization, say of buying products or shares, often requires a series of messages or a specific set of convincing reasons to follow through. The benefits offered in a message, whether functional or emotional, essentially need to outweigh the cost, and must seem realistic and easy to obtain.

McGuire's greatest insight was to suggest that the effectiveness of messages depends on audience factors and on different stages leading up to any change in behaviour, as the ultimate effect. With this *hierarchy of effects*, he also suggested a way for communicators to calculate the attrition rate, moving from exposure effects to attention, interest and attitude to behavioural effects. This brings a certain sense of realism to the process of understanding and measuring effects. Communication practitioners and public relations agencies often want to assume that exposure will produce success in terms of reputation, and often focus on exposure or output measures such as the advertising value equivalent (i.e., amount of press coverage received in relation to a campaign or event, measured in terms of equivalent advertising spending). However, the likelihood of continued success along each step is probably far less than they assume. McGuire estimated a drop of 50 per cent with each step from sending a message out to exposure to, in turn, the desired behavioural effects, making the final outcome only a fraction of the number of the target audience that was originally exposed to the campaign (see Figure 6.2). The theory has found its uses as a campaign planning tool among communication professionals and agencies. Ketchum, a public relations agency, for example, uses a communication effectiveness yardstick, fashioned in the image of the hierarchy of effects model.

The hierarchy of effects model has, however, a basic limitation: it incorporates the assumption that recipients of a campaign will process messages in a logical way, carefully considering the message in a rational manner to decide whether they wish to perform the proposed behaviour. Of course, people do not always act rationally, and indeed some messages and message styles appeal to emotions or symbolic values and associations. Two alternative theoretical models have therefore since gained ground as another way of looking at communication effects. Both models allow for other kinds of appeals beyond logical or rational appeals, and both also recognize the importance of prior beliefs and involvement with an issue or topic as a critical factor that determines success.

The first alternative to the hierarchy of effects theory is the *elaboration likelihood model* (ELM).[6] According to ELM, people process messages differently depending on their involvement with an issue. Those people who are interested, will be more involved and will elaborate a message in detail, whereas those with less interest will not process messages deeply. The result is that persuasion may be designed as following one of two possible routes:

1 The central route emphasizes logical and careful consideration, or systematic processing. This route is desirable if a target audience can be reached easily and when the audience has a moderate to high degree of involvement with an issue, or with the organization in question. The effect may also be more sustained, providing that audience members agree with the conclusions once they have systematically processed the message.
2 The peripheral route, on the other hand, forgoes logical arguments in favour of more emotionally or heuristically based strategies of processing. With this route, an audience simply short-circuits the processing of the message to their own beliefs or interests, which may range from logical elements of the content of the message, to the presentation and other factors associated with a message, such as attractiveness or likeability of the message or the credibility of the media source. The effect of the peripheral route may be less pronounced in the long term, although it may achieve changes more quickly because it requires less thoughtful consideration.

The second alternative effects model, that of *framing*, comes from research in anthropology and linguistics, which found its way into communication science.[7] The earliest work on framing traces back six decades to Gregory Bateson, an anthropologist, and also to the sociologist Erving Goffman, who both described words and non-verbal interactions as intimating larger culturally-rooted frames which help individuals interpret messages through the lens of existing cultural beliefs and worldviews. In the 1970s, cognitive psychologists Daniel Kahneman and Amos Tversky continued this line of thinking and studied framing in experimental designs to understand risk judgements and consumer choices.[8] They found that the different ways in which a message is presented or framed – apart from the content itself – can result in very different responses, depending on the terminology used to describe the problem or the visual context provided in the message. In a nutshell, models of framing assume that messages consist of three parts:

1 The activation of an overall frame in terms of certain keywords of formulations.
2 The manifest or latent reasoning or arguments as part of that frame.
3 The connection with deeper and culturally shared categories of understanding that supports and legitimizes the framing as a whole.

A good example of the way in which framing works is how climate change has been framed within public and policy debates. Some politicians and corporate executives have referred to climate change as scientifically uncertain, and hence as not warranting any drastic or immediate policy actions. Others have framed the topic as essentially conflicting with the goal of economic growth and progress; any actions to curtail current levels of consumption, for example, would hurt economic activity, including jobs. Scientists and environmental advocates, on the other hand, have framed climate change as a real immediate crisis and about doing the right thing (morality). In other words, even if the science cannot fully predict how the effects of global warming will work out, we need to do something collectively and sooner rather than later to anticipate or avoid leaving the world in a poorer state for future generations. Essentially, the same issue is framed in different ways, and in doing so, these messages attempt to appeal to underlying cultural associations and beliefs. For communicators who wish to break through the communication barriers of partisan identity and cultural beliefs, messages need to be tailored to a specific medium and audience, using carefully researched metaphors, allusions and examples that trigger a new way of thinking about the personal relevance of issues such as climate change.

Framing, in other words, is about selecting and highlighting certain dimensions of an issue, and as such giving it higher salience and relevance than alternative readings. To make sense of issues, audiences use frames provided by organizations and the media as interpretative shortcuts but integrate these framed presentations with pre-existing interpretations forged through personal experience, ideology and beliefs, and their social identity. Framing is therefore about convincing an audience through a particular highlighted interpretation and arguments as well as by appealing to underlying cultural values or beliefs (see Case Study 6.2).

CASE STUDY 6.2

HSBC: ESTABLISHING THE WORLD'S LOCAL BANK

HSBC was officially formed in 1991 as a holding company. The acronym stands for the company's founding member, the Hong Kong and Shanghai Banking Corporation. In 1992, HSBC acquired Midland Bank in the UK, and continued expanding through strategic acquisitions in developed and emerging markets. The competitive advantage of HSBC lies in its global presence, monolithic brand

(Continued)

(Continued)

name, its unmatched scale and efficiency, as well as product breadth. The company is also well positioned in China, which reflects its historical roots in Asia, having moved into the country long before other foreign players. To signal its long-term commitment to China, HSBC moved its China head office from Hong Kong to Shanghai in 2000. Partly as a result of shrewd acquisitions, HSBC now ranks as one of the largest banks in the world: its network, for example, comprises more than 10,000 branches and offices in 82 countries. Through this international network linked by advanced technology (including an e-commerce capability), HSBC is able to provide in each local market a comprehensive range of commercial banking services to businesses and individual consumers alike. From a marketing perspective, the company's main capability is the way in which it incorporates local banks into the network, which effectively allows for the provision of local currency banking services while tapping into a global network and a global pool of expertise.

The move towards a corporate brand

While initially set up as a holding company, management decided in the late 1990s to adopt a monolithic corporate brand for the entire corporation, using HSBC as the brand name and the hexagonal symbol for all its operations. The symbol (a white rectangle divided diagonally to produce a red hourglass shape) had originally been adopted by the Hong Kong and Shanghai Banking Corporation, and like many other company logos in Hong Kong was based on the cross of Saint Andrew. Before this change to a single monolithic brand, subsidiary companies and franchisees had carried their own name within an umbrella branding structure that signified their part of the overall HSBC corporation. The change towards a single corporate brand was seen as an important part of the company's strategy for growth and internationalization. The chairman at the time, Sir John Bond, articulated the strategic intent as follows:

> We want the HSBC brand to be known in every country and in every sector in which we operate as synonymous with integrity, trust and excellent customer service. I am confident that a unified brand and the strong recognition it will bring for HSBC's exceptional strengths is an important step forward as we work to maximize shareholder value.

He also emphasized that the central use of a single brand would help in 'making HSBC one of the world's leading brands for customer experience'.

The corporate brand name and symbol were adopted in 1998, with the initial tagline of 'Your world of financial services'. The tagline referred to the diverse range of products and services that HSBC offered as well as to the company's global presence. In 2002, the tagline was changed to 'The world's local bank', which is still in use today. The emphasis within the tagline shifted to the company's experience and understanding of a great variety of markets and countries.

(Continued)

(Continued)

Internal alignment around the corporate brand

From that point onwards, companies that were acquired by HSBC also adopted the new corporate brand, phasing out their own names and the earlier umbrella structure. The global HSBC brand is defined around five brand values:

1 Being perceptive – anticipating and meeting the needs of diverse customers around the world by using the ability to combine global reach across markets and segments with local knowledge and expertise.
2 Being progressive – a commitment to continuous improvement in quality, effectiveness and efficiency through team work.
3 Being responsive – acting quickly to ensure meeting and exceeding customers' changing expectations.
4 Being respectful – exercising corporate responsibility, valuing long-term ethical client relationships and a commitment to the welfare and development of local communities.
5 Being fair – demonstrating high levels of integrity.

Brain Caplen, editor of *The Banker*, suggests that the successful corporate branding of HSBC shows that this 'cannot be a short-term project. Successful banks such as HSBC and Santander work at getting all the parts of the operation to work in favour of the branding'.

HSBC has worked hard to cultivate its brand internally within the corporation, aligning local operations around its global brand presence. To illustrate this point, when Crédit Commercial de France (CCF) was acquired by HSBC, Charles-Henri Filippi had become the Chairman presiding over the integration of CCF into HSBC. He was responsible for the introduction of the HSBC name and designs and the overall brand promise. He initially framed the importance of changing to the HSBC brand to his staff by creating a booklet about the HSBC Group, which presented a map with the flags of all the nations in which HSBC operated. He spoke about how various countries had joined the Group and he also spoke of unity: 'We are not the first nor the last to join the group … we are joining a global federation.' He stressed that the company would remain an active voice within the global set-up, and that it was actually not an acquisition as such. 'It is not a take-over; we are joining a club.' He also instigated a consultation and research process, which confirmed that the move towards adopting the HSBC name would actually be beneficial to the French network of branches. In this way, he did not force through the name change but, through subtle acts of framing, staff realized that the change would be in their best interests.

A global communication programme with changing campaigns

On a worldwide level, a global corporate communication programme has consistently emphasized the above-mentioned brand values and, in particular, the perceptive commitment to combine global reach with local knowledge to

(Continued)

(Continued)

meet the personal banking needs of customers. Specific advertising campaigns have, since 2002, illustrated how the bank celebrates the diverse cultures and customs of people around the world, and that 'Every individual has their own priorities and values, and that these form the basis of many important decisions', as HSBC puts it.

Besides a commitment towards personal needs, which requires a deep cultural awareness and understanding, HSBC also suggests in its advertising campaigns that this provides a learning experience which may benefit other clients around the world. 'Through our campaigns, HSBC challenges people to address their own values and discover what drives and motivates them in their daily lives', HSBC says on its website 'and through this journey it is our belief that what we learn from one customer will help us to better serve another'. In other words, there are advantages associated with a global banking corporation which learns from its practices and clients around the world to constantly update and optimize its services to customers.

In 2008, HSBC ran a similar series of ads which playfully suggested that cultural context matters. The same human act or gesture (e.g., showing your bare feet) in one country or cultural setting may mean something completely different in another. The ads were meant to demonstrate the company's wider understanding of its customers and the world they live in by recognizing their different customs and values. In fact, since 2002 most corporate advertising campaigns have been part of the same communication programme to develop and consolidate the bank's reputation as a global player. Each campaign has played on the same themed message of being the world's local bank, reiterating and re-emphasizing through symbolic association and emotional message styles the bank's culturally local understanding and commitment to personally relevant banking services.

The programme has been so successful that HSBC has been named for three years running as the most valuable banking brand in the world by *The Banker* magazine and Brand Finance. HSBC increased its brand value in 2010 by 12 per cent to US$28.5 billion (£18 billion). In terms of communication effects, the programme as a whole has been hugely successful. 'The world's local bank' themed message is now firmly associated with HSBC, and has been a reputational driver for customer loyalty and new customer acquisitions across its range of businesses.

In the wake of the financial crisis, HSBC has now gone one step further in emphasizing how personal responsibility and integrity comes with their focus on local markets. The latest advertising campaigns in 2009 emphasize the overall brand values of integrity and responsibility. As such, they are a slight turn away from the earlier emphasis on perceptiveness. Brian Caplen said: 'In the wake of the financial crisis, banks are approaching the issue of branding with renewed vigour.' Two HSBC ads, entitled 'Responsibility' and 'Integrity', focus on people's personal values in terms of how they choose to make money. The bank aims to suggest with these ads the importance of responsibility and integrity in the lives of its customers and their financial decisions, and how, similarly, it cherishes these same values in the context of what, it subtly suggests, is an at times ethically tainted business (i.e., a symbolic association message style).

(Continued)

(Continued)

QUESTIONS FOR REFLECTION

1   Discuss the effectiveness of the HBSC corporate brand communication programme and its positioning as 'the world's local bank' from the perspective of (a) the hierarchy of effects, (b) elaboration likelihood and (c) framing models of persuasion.

2   Which of these models do you believe is best able to explain the effectiveness of the company's campaigns and messaging?

Source: This case study is based on O'Conner, A. and Waiter, I. (2009) HSBC Holding: Building a global wholesale banking capability. INSEAD case study; www.brandfinance.com; www.HSBC.com; and Szulanski, G. and Raver J. (2009); HSBC France: Rebranding CCF. INSEAD case study.

CHAPTER SUMMARY

 6.4 The chapter has described the process of planning and managing strategic communication programmes that aim to build and maintain strong reputations with an organization's stakeholders. Practically, it outlined specific steps for designing communication programmes and specific campaigns as part of such programmes. The chapter concluded with a more theoretical discussion of ways in which campaigns may persuade stakeholders into changing their opinions and in demonstrating supportive behaviours towards the organization.

DISCUSSION QUESTIONS

1   Discuss how the model for planning communication programmes and campaigns may help in developing more effective communication.

2   How and on what basis should a communication professional select the media for a particular communication campaign?

3   Pick a number of corporate brands with strong reputations. Which one of the presented communication effects models (hierarchy of effects, elaboration likelihood model, and framing) best describes your responses to the campaigns and messages around each of these brands?

 # KEY TERMS

Attention

Attitude

Budgeting

Campaign

Communication effects

Communication programme

Communication strategy

Elaboration likelihood model

Exposure

Framing

Hierarchy of effects

Persuasion

Planning

Strategic intent

Supportive behaviour

'Zero-based' media planning

 FURTHER READING

Smith, Ronald D. (2009), *Strategic Planning for Public Relations* (3rd edn). New York: Routledge.
Austin, Erica W. and Pinkleton, Bruce E. (2006), *Strategic Public Relations Management: Planning and Managing Effective Communication Programs* (2nd edn). Mahwah, NJ/London: Lawrence Erlbaum Associates.

NOTES

1   Jones, J.P. (1992), *How Much Is Enough?* New York: Lexington Books; Rossiter, J.R. and Danaher, P.J. (1998), *Advanced Media Planning*. Boston, MA: Kluwer.

2   See, for example, Deighton, J. (1996), 'Features of good integration: two cases and some generalizations', in Thorson, E. and Moore, J. (eds), *Integrated Communication: Synergy of Persuasive Voices*. Mahwah, NJ: Lawrence Erlbaum Associates, pp. 243–256; Deighton, J. (1999), 'Integrated marketing communications in practice', in Jones, J.P. (ed.), *The Advertising Business: Operations, Creativity, Media Planning, Integrated Communications*. London: Sage, pp. 339–355; Schultz, D.E. (1999), 'Integrated marketing communications and how it relates to traditional media advertising', in Jones (ed.), *The Advertising Business*, pp. 325–338.

3   Cutlip, S.M., Center, A.H. and Broom, G.H. (2000), *Effective Public Relations* (7th edn). London: Prentice-Hall.

4   Mendelsohn, H. (1973), 'Some reasons why information campaigns can succeed', *Public Opinion Quarterly*, 37: 50–61.

5   McGuire, W. (1981), 'Theoretical foundations of campaigns', in Rice, R. and Paisley, W. (eds), *Public Communication Campaign*. Beverly Hills, CA: Sage, pp. 41–70.

6   Petty, R.E. and Cacioppo, J.T. (1986), *Communication and Persuasion: Central and Peripheral Routes to Attitude Change*. New York: Springer-Verlag.

7   See, for example, Hallahan, K. (1999), 'Seven models of framing: implications for public relations', *Journal of Public Relations Research*, 11: 205–242; Entman, R.M. (1993), 'Framing: toward clarification of a fractured paradigm', *Journal of Communication*, 43 (4): 51–58.

8   Kahneman, D. and Tversky, A. (1979), 'Prospect theory: an analysis of decision under risk', *Econometrica*, 47: 263–291.

RESEARCH AND MEASUREMENT

7

Chapter Overview

Research and measurement is a cornerstone of professional corporate communication. Research helps in establishing the effects of communication campaigns and to document the organization's reputation in the eyes of its stakeholders. As such, it also has an important formative role in suggesting the extent to which communication strategies and campaigns are working, or whether indeed they may need to be revised. The chapter outlines practical issues and principles around research and measurement within corporate communication, including methods associated with campaign-based research and evaluation as well as standardized methods for measuring corporate reputations and corporate identity.

INTRODUCTION

7.1 Previous chapters have discussed the strategic role of corporate communication in developing and maintaining strong and favourable reputations with stakeholders, upon which the organization depends for its performance and survival. At the heart of this role lies an understanding of the fundamentals of reputation, and of measuring any changes in reputation to drive through business strategy and communication campaigns. In strategically focused communication departments, senior communication managers use research as the bedrock for the formulation of communications objectives for the organization and to help design specific communication programmes and campaigns. Over the years, many communication experts and scholars have recognized the importance of research for corporate communication, both in a direct and indirect sense. Research is, of course, important for gathering feedback on communication campaigns and, more generally, for getting a sense of the overall profile and reputation that is attributed to an organization. In this way, research gives a direct assessment, which will indicate whether objectives have been achieved, and it may also, in a more formative manner, guide communication professionals to either reinforce or revamp their communications to stakeholders. Indirectly, research is important as it may improve the perception of the value of corporate communication in the eyes of Chief Executive Officers (CEOs) and other senior managers in an organization. When corporate communication objectives and campaigns are directly informed by research, it suggests that the function is, like other functions in an organization, similarly focused on results and on the practicalities and demands of the business. Such perceptions, as an indirect effect of doing research – rather than relying on intuition or informal feedback alone – are important for corporate communication to secure a seat at the decision-making table and to make sure that research evidence and information about relations with priority stakeholders are factored into the decision-making process and into any corporate strategies and actions.[1]

The purpose of this chapter is to discuss practical issues around research, including methods associated with campaign-based research and evaluation, and to provide an overview of standardized methods for measuring corporate reputations and corporate identity. The first section deals with research methods around campaigns, and is focused on the direct outcomes of a specific, planned set of messages. The subsequent sections focus on measuring the general identity and reputation of an organization in the minds of stakeholders. Thus, these sections focus on the general profile and reputation of an organization, and suggest issues to consider when planning and carrying out research. These issues consist of asking specific questions before starting a research project, and the advantages and disadvantages of using qualitative and quantitative research methods.

RESEARCH AND EVALUATION

7.2 Communication professionals use research throughout the campaign planning, execution and evaluation stages, as demonstrated in Figure 7.1. The way they use research changes as the programme or campaign evolves. Professionals may use pre-campaign, or formative, surveys, for example, to better understand the problems or issues and to help segment stakeholder audiences. Professionals may also use focus groups to explore any detailed effects of a campaign in terms of changing people's opinions regarding key issues or to help them pre-test or refine message strategies. Research often provides important benchmarks against which results achieved by the programme or campaign can be measured. Using research throughout the campaign planning process helps in delivering results and in improving on past performance, but, as mentioned above, it also gives much needed credibility with other senior managers in the organization. Organizations, of course, are looking for a concrete return on investment and research gives them an indication of what communication is contributing to the organization and its objectives, and in light of the budget and resources invested in corporate communication.

At its most basic level, research is simply about collecting information, and professionals can use a number of methods to gather information, each with its own strengths and weaknesses. One basic form of research that is often used, even unwittingly, is informal research, which consists of casual interactions with key stakeholders or experts to define issues and to get a better understanding of any problems informing a communication programme or activity. The main disadvantage of informal research is that it may not be a systematic effort across stakeholder groups and is unlikely to be representative. Any information may therefore be subject to biases, in terms of who was asked (and who was not), which may seriously undermine the ability to draw strong conclusions from the information gathered.

Formal research methods include more systematic data-gathering methods that are set up for the purpose at hand (e.g., finding out about a problem or issue) and are sensitive to issues of representativeness in sampling stakeholders. These methods include, for example, focus groups, surveys and content analyses. A focus group is a semi-structured group discussion, facilitated by a researcher, which tries to dig deep into the underlying motivations around an issue or problem. Focus group sessions are taped or recorded, and the recorded data (i.e., verbal transcripts or audio-visual recordings) are analysed using qualitative methods, which means that researchers interpret responses instead of trying to count them.

Surveys are structured questionnaires which are sent to a representatively sampled part of a population, such as a customers or employees. Survey methods are quantitative in nature; they attempt to record in numbers the level of awareness, attitudes or behaviours of the population in relation to certain issues or circumstances. Such methods may also be analytical in nature when there is an attempt to explain why certain circumstances, attitudes and behaviours exist among members of a specific population. Advanced forms of statistical analyses (e.g., statistical regressions) are then used to test hypotheses concerning relationships among a group of variables under study. In many cases, surveys serve both descriptive and analytical purposes.

Content analysis, as another formal research method, is a scientific research method used for describing communication content in a quantitative, or numerical, form. Many professionals use content analysis to monitor and track media coverage of issues and of organizations. Such analyses are often carried out with the use of statistical software packages for the coding and tabulation of news coverage in terms of frequency of coverage and the overall tone (favourable versus unfavourable) of the reporting.

As already mentioned, a key suggestion is that research and evaluation should be an integral part of the planning process for communication programmes or campaigns. The entire sequence, with research and evaluation at the heart of it, is broken down into five stages. Figure 7.1 displays the planning cycle. The stages of the cycle are as follows:

1 *Audit*: This stage consists of taking stock of and analysing existing data, with research being used to identify issues as well as to create benchmarks. This stage is often also called formative research. It provides the data on which professionals will build their communication programme or campaign.

2 *Objectives*: This stage involves setting objectives, which follow from the audit and are in line with the organization's general business aims. Objectives are broken down by stakeholder audience and time-frame, and

are specified in measurable terms. Objectives are often set in terms of the required changes in awareness, attitude and behaviour of stakeholders.

3 *Planning and execution*: This stage involves deciding on the design and execution of the campaign, which may involve a pre-testing of messages and communication tactics.

4 *Measurement and evaluation*: This stage is the first of several possible types of campaign measurement, or continuous measurement. During the campaign, communication professionals can ask themselves whether they are getting the desired results, or whether the campaign needs to be adjusted. This may involve monitoring the execution and any costs associated with it as well as taking stock of the initial results achieved.

5 *Results*: The final stage involves an assessment of the overall post-campaign results, and identifying any potential issues or learning points that may again inform the audit stage and a new cycle of activity.

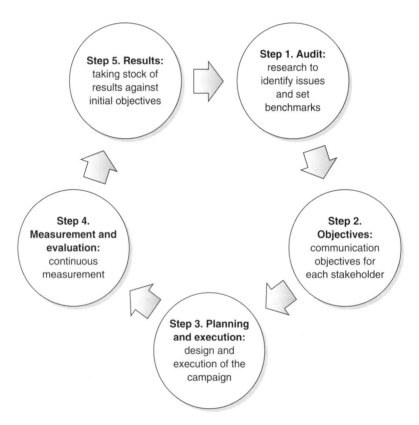

FIGURE 7.1   Research and evaluation within communication campaigns

A good example of this cycle, with research and measurement providing a valuable input into communication campaigns, is the example of FedEx (Case Study 7.1). The company extensively surveyed stakeholder opinion on a realignment of the company's operations and a new branded structure, with the survey results informing communications towards specific stakeholder groups.

CASE STUDY 7.1

FEDEX: FROM A PORTFOLIO OF BRANDS TO A SINGLE COMPANY

FedEx was founded in 1973 as an overnight delivery company. It has since established itself as a leading company in global air transportation, securing a strong reputation for service and reliability. The company faced some stiff competition from rival UPS and novel ventures in the express carrier market during the 1990s. In addition, FedEx acquired Caliber Systems, which included a suite of logistics and express companies, in the late 1990s. Both these developments triggered the need within the FedEx Corporation to rethink its corporate brand and communication. In particular, there was the belief that rather than slowly assimilating these companies, while keeping marketing activities separate, customers increasingly requested a 'one-stop' transportation interface – a single point of contact with the same company.

In January 2000, FedEx responded by rolling out a single corporate brand across all its operating companies. The company name was badged on all its services and operations, with sub-brands such as FedEx Express for express services and FedEx Freight for less-than-truckload services. While the structural alignment within FedEx and the choice for a monolithic brand made a lot of sense, strategically, stakeholders were initially not convinced. Media journalists were not persuaded by the new structure and questioned its viability; employees continued to identify with their own operational units; and financial analysts felt that the new structure did not provide additional synergies over the model of having a portfolio of separate brands and companies.

Bill Margaritis, the Vice President for Corporate Communication, aimed to address these stakeholder opinions through a campaign that set out to gain recognition for the new business model. The campaign would also help in creating acceptance and support across stakeholder groups. Before the campaign was developed, Margaritis and his team carried out extensive research on the current awareness of, and attitude towards, the new FedEx structure (step 1: audit). They surveyed employees, journalists and financial analysts, who each expressed a lack of understanding and even scepticism towards the new model. Margaritis used these research findings to develop change communication programmes internally that would create an understanding of the new structure (steps 2 and 3: objectives, planning and execution). The research also led them to intensify their efforts to convince journalists and financial analysts of the advantages of the new structure and to demonstrate to them some early successes.

The themes for the change campaign, which was labelled as 'The Change Ahead', and for the exchanges with journalists and analysts came directly out of the initial research study. For the media, for example, Margaritis felt that it would be key to demonstrate the positives of the new structure and to nip any negative rumours in the bud – a point that had been drawn out in the initial survey. He therefore set up a systematic system for educating the media. Margaritis and his team identified an inner circle of media contacts and conducted personal briefings with these journalists to forge and strengthen relationships with them and to reinforce messages and reduce any gaps in understanding. They also set up a 'FedEx Truth Squad', a move analogous to political campaign tactics. This squad monitored media coverage of FedEx in real-time and kicked into action when inaccuracies or negative news was reported, which was then immediately corrected and challenged.

(Continued)

(Continued)

Continuous measurement during and after the initial communication efforts (step 4: measurement and evaluation) demonstrates that media coverage was increasingly supportive of the new business model. The Truth Squad had done its job effectively; few inaccuracies about the new structure had been reported. Employees also demonstrated an improved understanding of how the new structure worked. In addition, customer successes proved the merits of the business model and the power of an integrated brand.

The FedEx brand has since gone from strength to strength, jumping from 74th position in the 2001 *Fortune* reputational rankings to seventh in 2002 (step 5: results). In turn, when the company had positive news to tell, this informed a new cycle of activity. For example, FedEx released a series of global ads in 2002 that celebrated the company's achievements and reputational accolades and which recognized the importance of FedEx employees.

QUESTIONS FOR REFLECTION

1   What was the role of research in the development of the corporate branding campaign for FedEx?
2   What are the advantage of a single corporate brand for FedEx as opposed to a branded or endorsed arrangement?

Source: This case study draws on presentations delivered by Bill Margaritis at the Institute for Public Relations' 2010 Annual Distinguished Lecture & Awards dinner, New York City, November 2010; and the 2006 Reputation Institute Conference, Madrid.

The advantage of seeing research and evaluation as part of a cycle of interrelated activities is of course that each cycle of activity can be more effective than the preceding cycle, especially if the results of evaluation are used to make adjustments to a programme or campaign, or to improve future communication efforts. Evaluating each stage of the cycle is also key to maximizing the effects of the programme or compaign. Evaluation is here broadly defined as the use of research for informing and assessing the conceptualization, design, execution and effects of communication programmes or campaigns.

In the audit stage, research consists of gathering data on an issue in order to inform the development of a programme or campaign. Such research may involve gathering data through informal contacts with stakeholders, colleagues or experts, and examining any available secondary data (e.g., past surveys) to get a sense of the issues. If necessary, professionals may decide to conduct primary research, as in the example of FedEx (see Case Study 7.1 above), to get to a more detailed understanding of the issues with each stakeholder group. During the planning and preparation of the programme or campaign, communication professionals may pre-test the appropriateness of the messages and activities, and the way in which the messages and activities are presented.

The execution or implementation of the programme or campaign, in turn, is associated with continuous measurement and evaluation of the outputs in terms of, for example, the amount of media coverage received or the number of stakeholders who have received or attended to the messages and activities. In this stage, the monitoring of such output effects may lead to real-time adjustments in the course of the programme or campaign.

Finally, in the results stage, research and evaluation attempt to establish the actual outcomes in terms of awareness, attitude and behavioural changes achieved by a programme or activity. Here, research and evaluation go one step further in moving from outputs (e.g., the amount of media coverage as established through newspaper clippings) to outcomes (e.g., the number of people who have changed their opinions and who behave towards the organization as desired). Researching outcomes requires formal methods, such as focus groups, content analysis and surveys, to determine with a higher degree of accuracy the strengths of the effects achieved with a programme or campaign. The entire sequence of effects is displayed in Figure 7.2.[2]

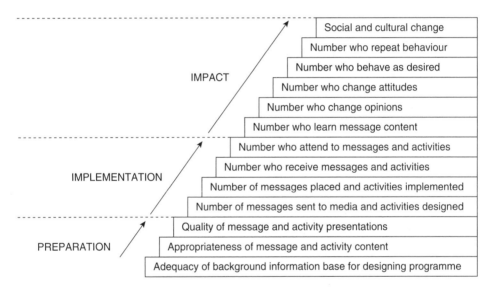

FIGURE 7.2   Stages and levels of evaluation

Source: Cutlip, S. M., Center, A. H., Broom, G.M. (2000) *Effective Public Relations*, 8th Edition, p. 437. Upper Saddle River, NJ: Pearson Education, Inc. Reprinted by permission.

MEASURING CORPORATE REPUTATION

7.3 Research and evaluation can be used to inform specific communication programmes or campaigns. Although they may be used throughout the cycle of planning a programme or campaign, as we have seen, the scope of research is often confined to a particular programme of activity or campaign. It is often focused on, and limited to, a particular communication activity at a particular point in time.

At the same time, many communication professionals continuously monitor and assess what stakeholders think of an organization, whether this is in line with the projected corporate identity of the organization, and whether the organization is generally accepted and valued. This kind of research is not limited to a particular campaign or activity, but is carried out on a continuous basis to gauge stakeholder support towards the organization. As such, it is more general in scope: it is focused on the general profile, or reputation, that the organization enjoys in the minds of stakeholders, rather than being tied to a particular activity such as a programme or communication.

Communication professionals also carry out reputational research to find out which organizational values are respected and whether the values that the organization projects in communication, symbolism and behaviour are indeed salient in the minds of stakeholders. This provides them with an important strategic indication as to whether the company's identity is valued at all and whether the organization's identity has been successfully communicated. In the first scenario, when a company's identity is not valued enough, managers may want to redefine their organization, strategies and operations with values that do matter to stakeholders and make a difference in the marketplace. A good example of this in the petrol sector are corporate giants BP and Shell, when they restyled their identities into responsible businesses. When an organizational identity is not effectively communicated or understood, as in the second scenario, managers need to rethink their stakeholder engagement programmes, and the visibility and effectiveness of the communication campaigns that the organization has previously used (Chapter 6). Getting feedback from reputation research is an important step in the process of developing and refining corporate identity strategies, including stakeholder engagement and communication programmes (Chapter 5).

Such feedback can be gathered through two broad types of reputation research: (1) publicly syndicated rankings; and (2) company-specific reputation research. Table 7.1 provides a summary of three publicly syndicated reputation rankings – the *Fortune*, *RepTrak Pulse* and *Financial Times* reputational surveys. Each of these rankings enjoys popularity with managers but all have obvious limitations in that they fail to account for the views of multiple stakeholder groups, and appear to be primarily tapping a firm's financial performance and assets. The *Fortune* measure, for instance, is known for its financial bias and the high correlation between all of the measure's nine (previously eight) attributes. This means that these nine attributes, when measured, relate to one factor, so that a company tends to rate high, or average, or low, on all nine attributes.[3]

These publicly syndicated rankings converge on a number of areas, including financial performance, product quality, employee treatment, community involvement, environmental performance, and a range of other organizational issues (such as supporting equality of opportunity and diversity, good environmental performance, improved ethical behaviour, and so on).[4] But these rankings do not take into account the fact that stakeholder opinions vary and that stakeholder groups attend to very different cues when forming an opinion of an organization. Some stakeholder groups would not be at all interested in some of these areas, or would in any case not rate them in their evaluation of the company. Furthermore, the distinctive values that a company may project, and that are extracted from its organizational identity or corporate personality, are not necessarily captured by these publicly syndicated measures.

When communication practitioners plan to set up their own company-specific reputation research, they need to be conscious of the fact that a corporate reputation

TABLE 7.1 Overview of the *Fortune, RepTrak Pulse* and *Financial Times* reputation surveys

	Fortune's 'most admired corporations'	*RepTrak Pulse*	*Financial Times*' 'world's most respected companies'
Method and sample	Annual survey of over 10,000 senior executives, outside directors and financial analysts	Annual survey of a large sample of consumers (approx. 60,000) who are asked to evaluate the 600 largest companies in the world	Annual questionnaire to 1,000 CEOs/senior executives in over 20 countries and 22 business sectors, complemented by a selected cross-section of fund managers, non-governmental organizations (NGOs) and media commentators
Measure	Ranking is based upon the compilation of assessments given by respondents of the ten largest companies in their own industry on nine criteria of 'excellence'	Ranking is based upon averaging perceptions of trust, esteem, admiration, and good feeling obtained from a representative sample of 100 local respondents who are familiar with the company	Simple ranking on the basis of nomination by CEOs, and weighted by GDP of the respondent's country
Attributes included	Quality of management, quality of products and services, innovativeness, long-term investment value, financial soundness, ability to attract, develop and keep talented people, responsibility to the community and the environment, wise use of corporate assets, global acumen	Four attributes: trust, esteem, admiration, and good feeling about a company	Most important unprompted reasons given behind nominations are business performance (growth and long-term profitability), clear leadership and people management, effective strategy of market capitalization, high-quality products and services, and policies and procedures to assess business' environmental impact

is not just a general impression but an evaluation of the firm by stakeholders. According to reputation expert Charles Fombrun, a corporate reputation is 'a perceptual representation of a company's past actions and future prospects that describe the firm's overall appeal to all of its key constituents when compared to other leading rivals'.[5] Whereas corporate images concern the immediate impressions of individual stakeholders when they are faced with a message that comes from an organization, reputations are more endurable evaluations that are established over time. Conceptually, a corporate image may be defined as the immediate set of associations of an individual in response to one or more messages from or about a particular organization. In other words, it is the net result of the interaction of a subject's beliefs, ideas, feelings and impressions about an organization at a single point in time. Corporate reputation can be defined as a subject's collective representation of past images of an organization (induced through either communication or past experiences) that is established over time. Images might vary in time due to differing perceptions, but reputations are more likely to be relatively inert or constant, as individuals and stakeholders retain their assessment of an organization built up over time. Gray and Balmer, two academics, illustrate this distinction between the image and reputation constructs:

> Corporate image is the immediate mental picture that audiences have of an organization. Corporate reputations, on the other hand, typically evolve over time as a result of consistent performance, reinforced by effective communication, whereas corporate images can be fashioned more quickly through well-conceived communication programmes.[6]

The properties of the reputation construct provide the basis for developing operational measures and for surveying opinions of important stakeholder groups. First, the time dimension (as reputation is an established perception over time) needs to be factored into the measurement process. This can be achieved by having respondents evaluate a company (*vis-à-vis* its nearest rivals) *generally* instead of having them reflect upon a single instant (e.g., at a time of crisis) or image (e.g., during a specific campaign). Second, reputation is a perceptual construct, so simple proxy measures of the assets, performance or output of a particular organization will not be enough to capture stakeholders' views of an organization. Third, measurement, and also the sampling of respondents, needs to account for the various attributes upon which an organization is rated by different stakeholder groups.

Different types of research techniques may be used to gather reputational data. These techniques exclude the publicly syndicated measures, such as the *Fortune* 'most admired companies' and the *Financial Times'* 'most respected companies', which are a secondary source of research that managers and communications practitioners can tap into to gain information about the standing of their organizations (when these are included in the rankings). Better still is for a company to set up and conduct reputation research of its own with applied research techniques and its own stakeholder groups. In doing so, a company will be able to account for the diversity of opinions of its stakeholder groups and will have a clearer view of the attributes that these different groups actually find important and on which they rate the organization. Table 7.2 displays the two broad classes of research techniques, qualitative and quantitative, that may be used either separately or in combination for reputation research.[7]

Qualitative research, such as in-depth interviews with individual stakeholders or focus group sessions with selected groups of stakeholders, are one option. These qualitative techniques are more open in nature; they allow selected stakeholders to delve into their associations with the organization as they see them. This usually provides very rich and anecdotal data of stakeholder views of the company. Quantitative

TABLE 7.2 Corporate reputation research methods

Methodology	Techniques	Data collection	Number of respondents	Ease of analysis	Costs
Qualitative	Unstructured interview	Oral interview: each respondent is asked to reflect upon his/her views of an organization and explain why (with or without use of visual aids)	10–40	Moderate/ low	Moderate
	Focus group	Group discussion: in a group, respondents discuss their views of the organization and explain why (with or without use of visual aids)	5–10 (each group)	High	Moderate
	Repertory grid	Oral interview: each respondent is asked to pick two out of three statements which match the organization best or worst and explain why	10–40	Moderate	Low
	Laddering	Oral interview: each respondent is asked to reflect upon beliefs about the organization aimed at discovering means–ends relations	10–25	Low	High
Quantitative	Attitude scales/ attribute rating	Questionnaire: respondent ratings of attributes on Likert scales	50 or more	Moderate/ high	Moderate
	Q-sort	Oral interview: each respondent is asked to rate and rank statements about the organization written on cards	30–50	Low	Moderate

research, where stakeholders are asked to rate the organization (and its nearest rivals) on a number of pre-selected attributes, is another option. Quantitative research leads to more discrete data that can be statistically manipulated, but is less rich and may also be less insightful (i.e., it reflects to a lesser extent the particular view of the individual stakeholder). The choice of whether qualitative or quantitative research techniques are used is based on content issues as well as pragmatic and political considerations. Qualitative techniques are chosen when the attributes upon which an organization is rated are simply not yet known, or when there is a need for a comprehensive, detailed and rich account of stakeholders' perceptions of and associations with the organization. Quantitative surveys are preferred when the attributes upon which an organization is rated are to a large extent known, allowing for a structured measurement across large sections of stakeholder groups. Many organizations also opt for quantitative surveys as these are relatively easy to administer and process, and as they provide them with a 'tangible' indication (i.e., a number). Figure 7.3 illustrates the reputations of two organizations through an attribute rating that produces such numerical values. A 'tangible' indication is also one of the motives for organizations to buy into panel studies such as the *RepTrak Pulse*, which provides them with a score that they can work with, and sets a benchmark for future years.

Surveying the opinions of external stakeholders regarding the organization is essential for capturing their views of the organization and its relative standing in the

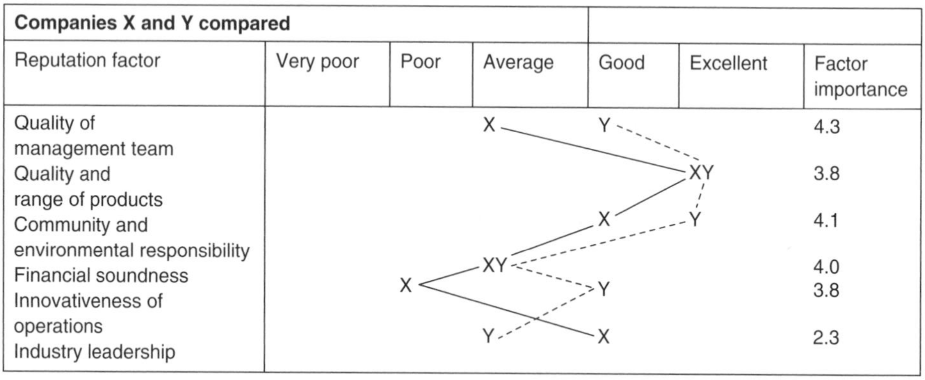

Companies X and Y compared						
Reputation factor	Very poor	Poor	Average	Good	Excellent	Factor importance
Quality of management team			X	Y		4.3
Quality and range of products					XY	3.8
Community and environmental responsibility				X	Y	4.1
Financial soundness			XY			4.0
Innovativeness of operations		X		Y		3.8
Industry leadership			Y	X		2.3

FIGURE 7.3   The corporate reputation of two companies compared

sector in which it is operating; and to offset a strict internally held view upon the company's core values in its vision and culture. Organizations cannot myopically focus internally on their identities alone and trust that on the back of their identity's strength they will achieve glowing reputations. Equally, organizations should not be led only by stakeholder opinions (and opportunistically manufacture and fashion a corporate identity for it), as such opinions may be fickle and can sometimes be short-lived. Therefore, an internal orientation on organizational identity, which may be a source of inspiration and differentiation, needs to be balanced with an external stakeholder orientation, so that a company avoids shortsightedly focusing on solely one.[8]

Polaroid, for example, is a case in point. The company had from its beginnings created a strong and distinctive identity around its business model and core competence of instant photography. Conforming to this identity, the focus was originally on self-developing film technology, garnering healthy profits on the film technology while earning relatively little on the cameras. This worked well until the advent of digital photography, which offered instant photographs but made film unnecessary.

Digital photography altered investors' and consumers' expectations, and as Polaroid was rather slow in following suit (and redefining itself as an imaging company and moving into digital photography), it had to file for Chapter 11 bankruptcy protection in October 2001. Surveying and being attuned to the reputation that an organization has with its stakeholders provides an important strategic indication as to whether the company's identity is at all valued and whether it has been successfully communicated.

MEASURING CORPORATE IDENTITY

7.4 Communication practitioners and other managers within the organization are responsible for opening up a dialogue about the core values of the organization with employees and discussing them systematically and concretely.[9] This often involves a kind of soul-searching exercise in which senior managers and communications practitioners should engage and that is aimed at producing and triggering the attributes and values of the organization (see Table 7.3 below) that are perceived as authentic, that characterize it, are unique to it, and set it apart from other companies in its sector. Wal-Mart offers a good example. Its credo of 'giving working people the opportunity to buy the same things previously available only to wealthier people' is wonderful, but is just a generic aspect of its positioning and pricing strategy; it is not the one specific feature that is differentiating or hard to imitate by rival firms. What is unique to Wal-Mart, however, are its core values of 'community' and 'partnership' that lie at the root of its founding and has led to the company's success. 'Community' and 'partnership' are values that are meticulously carried through in its stores, advertising campaigns, employee ownership schemes, and supply chain management. Wal-Mart has, for instance, changed the role of their suppliers so that they are now partners with them in their stores, thereby cunningly shifting inventory responsibilities back to the suppliers.

Without doubt, the values that an organization, through its members, considers to be true, authentic and differentiating stretch beyond corporate communication and the remit of communication practitioners alone. The CEO and the senior management team are the most obvious patrons of organization-wide identity questions as well as of the way in which these are translated into mission and vision documents and spread throughout the organization. When Carlos Ghosn, for instance, took the helm at Nissan in 1999 he personally led the restoration and strengthening of Nissan's identity, which had become sloppy, weak and insufficiently exploited.[10] Alongside a restructuring and cost-cutting programme to boost productivity and profitability (for which he took a lot of flak), Ghosn revamped Nissan's identity of quality engineering and the uniquely Japanese combination of keen competitiveness and a sense of community. He ensured that through his own performance and commitment as well as through internal communication, these values trickled down through the ranks to embrace all employees.

As the example of Nissan shows, it is important that a sense of organizational identity is internalized by members of the organization, so that they can live and enact the company's values in their day-to-day work. Particularly those members of the organization who represent the organization in the eyes of stakeholders, such as the CEO, front-office personnel and front-line staff (salespeople, retail staff), and of course those who are responsible for marketing and communication, need to have a fine grasp of the organization's core ideology and values. Senior managers, with the help of senior communication practitioners, as experts on stakeholder management, can facilitate this understanding by articulating and actively communicating the company's values to all staff within the organization through policy documents, briefings, identity workshops and internal communication (see Chapter 9).

TABLE 7.3 Organizational identity research methods

Method	Participants	Data collection	Ease of analysis	Expert analysts needed	Costs
Cobweb method	Group of senior managers	Brainstorm session	High	No	Low
Focus group	Groups of senior managers and employees	Brainstorm session	High	No; but group facilitator (consultant)	Low– moderate
Projective techniques	Groups of senior managers and employees	Interviews with use of visual aids	Low	Yes; trained psychologist/ researcher	Low– moderate
Laddering/ critical incident	Groups of senior managers and employees	Open interviews	Low	Yes; trained researcher	Low– moderate
Audit/survey	Groups of senior managers and employees	Questionnaire	High	Yes; trained researcher	Low– moderate

A number of analytical tools, ranging from management exercises to more psychological projective tests, are available to senior managers and senior communication practitioners for drawing out and articulating the organizational identity (Table 7.3). These different tools vary in what and how they measure identities (open versus closed measurement) and in pragmatic considerations, such as the ease of analysis and the costs involved in their use:

1   *Cobweb method*: This method consists of a group of senior managers coming together and sharing their views on the organization's key characteristics. At the beginning of the session, these managers are asked to name those attributes which, in their opinion, best characterize and define the organization. This is a brainstorming exercise, so there are no right or wrong answers. After this brainstorming session, managers have to choose the eight attributes that they consider to be most relevant and to have most value in describing the organization. These eight attributes can be visually displayed in the form of a wheel. Each attribute is then rated on a scale of

1–8, further defining the organization's key characteristics, and allowing further comparisons with stakeholder views of those attributes. The method is very easily carried out, but has obvious limitations in that it only captures the views of managers regarding the key characteristics of the organization.

2 *Focus group*: This method has the advantage over the cobweb method in that a broader group of representatives from the organization can be selected, and their views of the key characteristics of the organization can be captured in a more detailed manner. A focus group starts with a brainstorming session in which all participants are asked to write down (on Post-It notes or cards) the characteristics of their organization and share their views on the identity of the organization. When each participant has articulated his or her views, these Post-Its/cards can be grouped and arranged into a map or plan on a tabletop or stuck/pinned to a noticeboard (or similar display space), providing a synthesis of each participant's views upon the identity of the organization. Further analysis and group discussions then follow to select the key characteristics that, according to the group, best define the organization.

3 *Projective techniques*: These techniques stem from psychotherapy and aim to generate rich ideas and to involve individual members of the organization in a discussion of a subject such as organizational identity that may be difficult to verbalize in discrete terms. Visual aids, such as pictures, cards, diagrams or drawn-out metaphors, may be used to elicit a response. These visual aids are usually designed to be ambiguous so that respondents will 'project' their own meaning and significance on to the visuals. By doing so, they will declare aspects of their deeper values, beliefs and feelings concerning the organization, and this can be used for a further discussion of the key aspects of the organization. A common form of projective technique is the Thematic Apperception Test (TAT). This approach asks individuals to write a story about an image that depicts a work situation. The researcher's task is then to find themes in what people say about their organization.[11]

4 *Laddering or critical incident*: this widely-used management technique can also be applied to organizational identity, where it is used to infer the basic values that guide people's work in an organization. The method involves open interviews where employees are asked to describe what they do on a daily basis and how they look upon their work. Such descriptions of critical work incidents can then be further analysed to decipher the underlying values. The method can, when aggregated, give important insights into the general values that people working within an organization seem to share.[12]

5 *Audit or survey*: A more structured research method involves an audit or survey that asks members of the organization to select from lists of attributes those characteristics that best define the organization. The selected characteristics can then be further screened by asking respondents in the same survey to evaluate the importance and value of each of the selected characteristics in describing the organization. Surveys are easy to administer, but may not be able to capture the richness and detail of organizational identity that more open methods can.

Once the values and attributes that make up an organizational identity are drawn out and made explicit, senior managers and communication practitioners need to consider whether the identified values are inspiring and stand out, whether they offer potential for differentiation in the marketplace, and whether they are likely to be appreciated by stakeholders of the organization. In other words, it needs to be decided whether the elicited core values are to play a role in the corporate identity mix and are to be made public through products and services, through communication and through employee behaviour. Some of the values expressed through the corporate identity mix will in fact derive from the organizational identity; other values may be included because of the sector in which the organization is operating or because of the expectations of its stakeholder groups.

Reputation expert Charles Fombrun proposed that companies should systematically map their identities and their 'messaging profile'; that is, how identities are projected and communicated through print, visual, video and web-based communications.[13] Compiling such a profile involves collecting and analysing all official communication issued by an organization, including press releases, speeches and corporate adverts, and analysing their content. Content analysis may focus on certain keywords and expressions to assess whether the key identity attributes are in fact projected and communicated to stakeholders.

CHAPTER SUMMARY

7.5 The chapter has outlined practical issues and principles around research and measurement, including methods associated with campaign-based research and evaluation as well as standardized methods for measuring corporate reputations and corporate identity. One important distinction that was made is between one-time studies of effects after a campaign and standardized benchmarking studies of the reputation of an organization, which essentially measures stakeholder evaluations that have been built up over time. Research on both campaigns and general corporate reputations is useful for practitioners to guide and inform the formulation of communication strategies (Chapter 5) and messaging within campaigns (Chapter 6) and, more generally, to demonstrate the effectiveness of communication in changing stakeholder opinions and their support towards the organization.

 ## DISCUSSION QUESTIONS

1   Describe the advantages of using quantitative versus qualitative methods of reputation research.

2   What are the main weaknesses of *Fortune*'s well-known ranking of corporate reputations?

3   What is the difference between the concepts of corporate image and corporate reputation?

KEY TERMS

Benchmark studies

Corporate identity

Corporate image

Corporate reputation

Focus group

Formal research techniques

Formative evaluation

Informal research techniques

Laddering

One-time studies

Projective technique

Publicly syndicated rankings

Q-sort

Qualitative methods

Quantitative methods

Repertory grid

FURTHER READING

Cutlip, S.M., Center, A.H. and Broom, G.H. (2008), *Effective Public Relations* (10th edn.) London: Prentice-Hall.

Fombrun, Charles J. and Van Riel, Cees B.M. (2004), *Fame and Fortune: How Successful Companies Build Winning Reputations.* London: FT Prentice-Hall.

Stacks, Don and Michaelson, David (2010), *A Practitioner's Guide to Public Relations Research, Measurement and Evaluation.* Business Expert Press (http://www.businessexpertpress.com/).

NOTES

1   Lauzen, M.M. (1995), 'Public relations manager involvement in strategic issue diagnosis', *Public Relations Review*, 21: 287–304.

2   Cutlip, S.M., Center, A.H. and Broom, G.M. (2000) *Effective Public Relations*, 8th edn, page 437.

3   Dowling, G.R. (2001), *Creating Corporate Reputations*. Oxford: Oxford University Press.

4   Fryxell, G.E. and Wang, J. (1994), 'The Fortune Corporate Reputation Index: reputation for what?', *Journal of Management*, 20: 1–14.

5   Fombrun, C. (1998), 'Indices of corporate reputation: an analysis of media rankings and social monitors ratings', *Corporate Reputation Review*, 1 (4): 327–340.

6   Gray, E.R. and Balmer, J.M.T. (1998), 'Managing image and corporate reputation', *Long Range Planning*, 31 (5): 685–692, quote on p. 687.

7   Dowling, G.R. (1988), 'Measuring corporate images: a review of alternative approaches', *Journal of Business Research*, 17: 27–34, Van Riel, C.B.M., Stroeker, N.E. and Maathuis, O.M. (1998), 'Measuring corporate images', *Corporate Reputation Review*, 1 (4): 313–326.

8   Bouchikhi, H. and Kimberly, J.R. (2003), 'Escaping the identity trap', *Sloan Management Review*, Spring: 20–26; see also Hatch, M.J. and Schultz, M. (2001), 'Are the strategic stars aligned for your corporate brand?', *Harvard Business Review*, February: 128–135; Cheney, G. and Christensen, L.T. (2001), 'Organizational identity: linkages between "internal" and "external" organizational communication', in Jablin, F. and Putnam, L. (eds), *The New Handbook of Organizational Communication*. Thousand Oaks, CA: Sage, pp. 231–269.

9   Edmonson, A.C. and Cha, S.E. (2002), 'When company values backfire', *Harvard Business Review*, November: 2–3.

10 Ghosn, C. (2002), 'Saving the business without losing the company', *Harvard Business Review*, January: 37–45.

11 Thorpe, R. and Cornelissen, J.P. (2002), 'Visual media and the construction of meaning', in Holman, D. and Thorpe, R. (eds), *Management and Language: The Manager as a Practical Author*. London: Sage, pp. 67–81.

12 Van Rekom, J. (1997), 'Deriving an operational measure of corporate identity', *European Journal of Marketing*, 31 (5/6): 410–422.

13 Fombrun, C. (1996), *Reputation: Realizing Value from the Corporate Image*. Cambridge, MA: Harvard University Press, p. 72.

SPECIALIST AREAS IN CORPORATE COMMUNICATION

4

Part 4 explores four of the most important specialist areas in corporate communication: media relations, internal communication, issues management and public affairs, and crisis communication. These four areas involve stakeholder groups whose goodwill is important to an organization and its corporate reputation. Each of these areas also involves specialist knowledge, tools and techniques around communicating to these stakeholder groups, such as journalists and media organizations, investors and shareholders, activist groups and NGOs, and an organization's managers and employees.

After reading Part 4 of the book, the reader should be familiar with effective approaches to media relations, internal communication, issue management and crisis communication.

MEDIA RELATIONS

8

Chapter Overview

Communicating with the media is a central area of activity in corporate communication. Drawing on theories from mass communication and from developments in practice, the chapter outlines how journalists and media organizations work and how news coverage and content may have an impact on corporate reputation. The chapter also explores the use and effectiveness of specific media relations techniques (media monitoring services, press releases and press briefings) as well as strategies around new media, Web 2.0 and digital communication platforms.

INTRODUCTION

8.1 Working with the media is what most people associate with corporate communication. Media relations involves managing communication and relationships with the media; all the writers, editors and producers who contribute and control what appears in the print, broadcast and online news media. From a corporate communication standpoint, these news media are vital as channels for generating publicity and because their coverage of business news may influence many important stakeholders, including investors, customers and employees. Many corporate communication professionals therefore see the news media as a 'conduit' for reaching their stakeholders, rather than as a stakeholder or audience themselves.

This chapter explores how journalists and news organizations operate and how corporate communication professionals can best liaise with them and can develop effective communication strategies to influence their news coverage in broadcast, print and online media. The aims of the chapter are, first, to provide an introduction to the roles and values of news journalists and news media organizations, and to discuss their importance in terms of the impact of news coverage on corporate reputation. Based on this overview, the chapter continues by exploring the relationship between corporate communication professionals and journalists and discusses various traditional tools and techniques, such as media research and press releases, that communication professionals can use to manage this relationship. The final section considers the changing media landscape with the explosion of new Web 2.0 media, such as blogs, social networking sites, and other powerful digital communication platforms. These new media present clear challenges to organizations in terms of presenting the company image and telling the company's story, and require organizations to develop digital corporate communication strategies.

JOURNALISM AND NEWS ORGANIZATIONS

8.2 The news media involve a variety of organizations, with the production and dissemination of news content through various media (newspapers, radio, TV and the internet) as a core operational process. The production of news content typically involves two levels: (1) journalists, who on an individual basis consult sources and write news stories; and (2) other parties within the news organization (e.g., copy-editors), who, based upon their news routines, edit stories before they make it into print.[1] This distinction between journalists and news routines is important for corporate communication professionals because it illustrates the variety of influences on the production of news content and points to the limited degree of control that journalists producing stories about organizations actually have on the whole process, including the final printed words that make up the news story.

Journalists may talk to sources, cover a beat, and write a story, but then not even recognize their own story when it goes to print. This is because, at the level of *news routines*, there are many other people involved in the writing process who affect the story, such as the fact checker, who verifies that the names of people, organizations and places mentioned are all spelled correctly. Copy-editors may check that quotes are appropriately attributed to sources in a way that minimizes conflict and controversy. Layout and design specialists may be involved to check that news stories do not go over a certain word limit and that the story is designed within the format of the outlet and probably with an idea of how to attract readers. Moreover, the newspaper editor may decide that what was once a business news story should be a front page article for a much broader audience. In such a case, the lead paragraphs would need to be rewritten from a business or strict financial perspective into a public interest perspective, attracting a much wider reading audience typical of the front page. When there is a strong set of news routines within a news organization, it means that the journalist is to an extent writing for the needs of the editorial desk to which they are assigned: a national news desk, a local news desk, the financial/business news desk, or perhaps even an international news desk or the arts. On the other hand, when news routines are absent or less strong, there may be more flexibility for a journalist to write the story from a preferred angle and in a way in which he or she would like to write it. For example, an internet blog written by an individual journalist is subject to less rigorous scrutiny and further editing than an article published in a daily newspaper.

For journalists, writing for the needs of the desk is their way of ensuring that their story makes it into print. While no journalist ever writes a story without the intent of it getting picked up, whether the story is published or not is not their call. Moreover, journalists do not have a say on the final printed story, what the headline of the story is, or which photographs will be included (if any) with their story. Those decisions lie with their editors, including the front page editor, national editors, business/financial editors, and arts/community editors, among others. For journalists themselves, the pressure of writing for a news desk is sometimes experienced as a hindrance in their work and produces conflict with their professional ideals of objectivity, fairness and impartiality. Many journalists share a set of values based on seeking information and maintaining a measure of independence from all organizations, including their own.[2]

News routines within a media organization may also reflect a certain ideology (a set of normative principles and values) or political orientation that is shared by journalists and editors of that organization. For example, *The New York Times* has been characterized as 'the editor's paper' and *The Washington Post* as the 'reporter's paper', referring to the levels of bureaucracy that exist in them. Similarly, articles in *The Guardian* newspaper are generally in sympathy with the middle-ground, liberal to left-wing end of the political spectrum. This ideology may have a direct bearing upon the way in which news about organizations is reported. For example, a recent study commissioned by the BBC Trust found that programmes on the BBC (e.g., *The Money Programme*, *Radio Five Live* and the *10 O'Clock News*) failed to represent shareholders' and employees' perspectives on corporate stories in favour of a consumer perspective. The study criticized the BBC business editors' often rather negative and narrow views on business, and made three recommendations:

1 The BBC should address the lack of knowledge of business issues among editorial staff.
2   It should widen 'the range of editorial ideas and programming about business'.
3 It should 'ensure compliance in business coverage with standards of impartiality'.[3]

Hence, ideology matters in terms of how organizations are covered in the news media and whether this will largely consist of 'good' or 'bad' news coverage.

NEWS AND CORPORATE REPUTATION

8.3 In general, media coverage of an organization can have a strong influence on the corporate reputation of that organization. Ranging from reports on annual results to investigations of corporate issues, media coverage often has an 'amplifying' effect on a company's reputation when 'good' or 'bad' news is reported.

While media coverage does not strictly determine a company's reputation or the way in which stakeholders think about an organization, it does have an impact in terms of highlighting an issue or increasing the already held positive or negative view of an organization.[4]

This amplifying effect has often been studied through the lens of agenda-setting theory. This theory was traditionally developed in mass communication and public opinion research but has recently been extended to the domain of corporate reputation. The agenda-setting hypothesis underlying the theory is that the frequency with which the media report on a public or political issue determines that issue's salience in the minds of the general public.[5] In other words, 'The press may not be successful much of the time in telling people what to think, but it is stunningly successful in telling its readers what to think about'.[6]

The basic idea behind agenda-setting theory is that news media communicate a wealth of information when they report on organizations, politics, the economy or issues of social and human concern. In doing so, they also signal to their viewers, readers or audience what issues are salient about these topics. Over time, and through repeated mention of the same issues, these issues may become lodged in the public's mind. The public will use the input from the media to decide which issues are important. The news media 'set' the public agenda.

Agenda-setting theory distinguishes two levels of agenda setting. The first level relates to the salience of an organization, and the second level deals with the attributes or associations related to that organization. Taking Shell as an example, first-level agenda setting occurs when Shell is the first oil company to come to mind for members of the general public because Shell receives more media attention than other petroleum companies. The media report on certain organizations and in doing so enhance the public's awareness of an organization and certain aspects and characteristics about that organization. Second-level agenda setting is apparent when the public associates Shell primarily with a particular issue (e.g., renewable energy) that has received much attention in the news during a particular period. Craig Carroll, a mass communication scholar, tested both levels of agenda setting in relation to US corporations.[7] Carroll analysed the content of coverage of those corporations in *The New York Times*, which he used as a proxy for all reporting on those companies in the USA. He then correlated the findings of news content with data on the public's awareness of those corporations and their associations with those corporations. Positive results were found for both levels of agenda setting. Results revealed that news coverage influences which corporations were salient in the public's mind and the amount of media coverage devoted to certain corporate issues or attributes of the organization (e.g., workplace environment) were roughly in line with the public's associations regarding those corporations.

A further study by May-May Meijer confirmed the same agenda-setting effects of media coverage. She also extended these results by testing the hypothesis that the higher the salience of an issue associated with a company in media coverage, the better the reputation of the company that is seen to 'own' that issue. For example, news coverage on environmental issues in the petroleum sector may have benefited the reputation of BP for a number of years as this organization was seen to take a leadership role in recognizing the ecological impact of business and in reducing carbon emissions.[8] However, the company's recent retreat from investments in alternative energy and the 2010 oil spill in the Gulf of Mexico have generally dampened its environmental image. As a result, BP is now more likely seen as a 'bad guy' in relation to environmental issues in the sector.

The second level of agenda-setting also suggests that news coverage not only reports facts and neutral observations, but also conveys feelings through its stance and tone on the issue. This affective dimension has been talked about in terms of media favourability – 'the overall evaluation of a firm presented in the media … resulting from the stream of stories about the firm'.[9] Reputation expert David Deephouse used this term to suggest that the media not only convey information, they actually make and represent reputational assessments to their audiences. Deephouse referred to 'favourable' news coverage when an organization was praised for its actions or was associated with activities that should raise its reputation, while 'unfavourable' coverage referred to reporting in which an organization was criticized for its actions or associated with actions that should decrease its reputation.[10] Deephouse found evidence suggesting that the higher the level of media favourability, the higher the level of an organization's performance. While the media does not directly impact upon an organization's performance (the media are an intermediary between organizations and stakeholder opinions and actions), this finding has one central implication for corporate communication professionals: they should seek to cultivate positive evaluations by the media through releasing well-placed stories that report on organizational actions (e.g., charitable giving, CSR initiatives) or significant newsworthy events.

Agenda-setting theory may also explain why certain companies are higher in reputation rankings (e.g., the *Fortune* or *Financial Times* rankings) than others. Companies making these rankings are prominent on the media agenda and are more likely to be prominent on the public agenda, while those companies that are outside these rankings are far less likely to be prominent in the public's mind.[11] The news media often also rely upon large and well-known organizations for their information subsidies, and there is evidence to support the claim that only companies with significant corporate reputations – whether good or bad – are used as sources of information.[12] Organizations that are not well known are often ignored because of their low levels of newsworthiness, or simply because the media are not familiar with them. This has significant implications for the media's role as a watchdog, when only certain organizations are monitored and covered in the news and other organizations are simply ignored and stay outside the public eye.

Agenda setting thus points to a powerful paradox for news organizations: on the one hand, their watchdog role means that they have to systematically report on news across the economy and across all types of organization, ranging from small and medium-sized enterprises to multinational corporations and public sector organizations. On the other hand, news organizations cannot wholly perform this role because of a lack of information on smaller companies and the lack of visibility of these organizations – which makes them less interesting to the general public.

FRAMING NEWS STORIES

8.4 The relationship between communication professionals and journalists has often been described as adversarial. Journalists often have a negative opinion about communication professionals, in part because they feel that there is a clear divide between their interests. According to journalists, communication professionals think about the needs of their companies first and less about what journalists need. Past research has also found that journalists felt that professionals withheld information, were not always objective and certainly not focused on issues of public interest.[13] On the other hand, communication professionals are less negative about journalists and are often eager to work with them. However, professionals also realize that journalists have their own agenda and may frame news about the company in line with their news routines and the ideology of the news organization that they work for (see section 8.2). While both professionals and journalists have different agendas and thus different angles on news related to a company, they do realize that they are interdependent: journalists need and often use information provided by professionals and, equally, professionals and the companies that they work for often need the media as a conduit to generate coverage on the company and to reach important stakeholders, such as the financial community, customers, prospective employees, government and the general public. According to some reports, as much as 80 per cent of news reports about companies is prompted and delivered by communication professionals.[14] The realization of this interdependence has led to a further specialization of media or press relations within corporate communication: many large companies have a dedicated press office or media team that deals with the general media and that subsumes or is separate from investor relations professionals, who deal only with financial media, such *as The Wall Street Journal* and *The Financial Times*.

When corporate communication professionals propose a particular story (e.g., in the form of a press release) to a journalist, they engage in two separate but related processes. The first is to solicit interest in the story itself. The second is to make sure that the story is framed in a way that is consistent with the organization's preferred framing (i.e., how the organization would like to have its story told). Exchanges between professionals are essentially *negotiations* about how news is *framed*.[15]

Framing theory is a theoretically rich approach that has been used to understand and investigate communication and related behaviours in a wide range of disciplines, including psychology, speech communication, organizational decision-making, economics, health communication, mass communication and political communication. Framing theory focuses on how messages are created in such a way that they connect with the underlying psychological processes of how people digest information and make judgements. Because people cannot possibly attend to every little detail about the world around them, framing in communication is important because it helps shape the perspectives through which people see the world. The notion of framing is best understood metaphorically as a window or portrait frame drawn around information that delimits the subject matter and thus focuses attention on key elements within it. Hence, framing involves processes of *inclusion* and *exclusion* of information in a message as well as emphasis. The communication scholar Entman summarized the essence of framing as follows:

Framing essentially involves selection and salience. To frame is to select some aspects of perceived reality and make them more salient in the communicating text, in such a way as to promote a particular problem definition, causal interpretation, moral evaluation and/or treatment recommendation for the item described.[16]

In the context of corporate communication, framing theory suggests that communication professionals *frame* a particular corporate decision, issue or event in such a way that it furthers and promotes the interests of the organization. This frame, which features in a press release or in corporate reports on the company's website or in speeches of spokespersons and the CEO, is labelled the *corporate frame* that is provided to the media and to the general public. Journalists and editors, on the other hand, may interpret and represent the same decision, issue or event in a different way. *News framing* refers to the way in which news is selectively portrayed by the media in an effort to explain news or ideas about organizations in familiar terms for a broader audience. How a news item is framed also largely depends on the political views and ideology of journalists and their news organizations. Much research in mass communication has documented how journalists use dominant frames on politics, society and corporations to construct an understanding for their audience. Journalists often use such frames unconsciously as they relate to deeply ingrained assumptions about the social world.[17]

Because of their different interests, communication professionals and journalists may frame the same decision, issue or event in completely different ways. For example, when the industrial gases corporation BOC (now part of Linde) released its first quarter earnings in February 2006, the company framed the news in terms of 'record first quarter earnings', which the company said indicated that BOC was 'well positioned for growth' as an independent company. The news media, including *The Financial Times* and *The Guardian*, however, framed the earnings as increasing the likelihood that the company would be taken over by one of its competitors. In other words, journalists from these newspapers selected some elements of the press release (the actual recorded earnings) but reinterpreted them in the light of BOC as a takeover target, which was the frame that was made salient in their news coverage.

Skilful communication professionals play on journalists' knowledge and views to propose stories that follow dominant news frames, fit certain categories of content and resonate with a journalist's notion of the expectations of their audience. Publicists such as Max Clifford are often very skilful in aligning a story proposal (corporate frame) with a story expectation (news frame) which leads to a greater probability of the story being placed and reported. The skill in media relations, in other words, is often in spotting the stories or the angles that can turn corporate news into media news or bring a corporate story into a global news story. This process is referred to as the *alignment* of frames between professionals and journalists.

Because not all journalists are necessarily going to frame a story in the same way, communication professionals often find themselves engaged in *frame contests* with journalists. Market models of journalism suggest that journalists will deliberately strive to frame stories in ways that resonate with what journalists perceive to be the largest segment of their audience. For example, in July 2006, a trader with Citigroup committed suicide by jumping from the 16th floor of the bank's Canary Wharf offices. Despite evidence that the trader had committed suicide because of mental depression, many newspapers (including *The Daily Telegraph*) framed the suicide in inverted commas (i.e., as 'suicide') and openly suggested a link to work pressures in the investment banking industry. Journalists from these newspapers chose to frame the news in what turned out to be a biased and inaccurate way because of a link with reader expectations and despite any evidence of trading irregularities or substantial losses.

How, then, can professionals avoid such frame conflicts? Alignment of frames is more likely when the substance of the corporate frame relates to common norms and expectations about business and society. For example, the Body Shop's long-standing focus on social equality and fair trade aligns with some journalists' expectations of the role of business in society (see Case Study 8.1 at the end of this chapter). Frame alignment is also more likely when professionals and journalists openly discuss an issue, decision or event so that a journalist is more likely to understand the other side. The opportunity for such an open discussion presupposes of course that communication professionals have developed a relationship with journalists in which both parties respect each other.

Media relations techniques

Communication professionals use a wide range of tools and techniques to obtain news coverage and to monitor reporting on their organization over time. These include press releases, press conferences, interviews, and media monitoring and media research. We'll briefly discuss each in turn.

1 *Press release*: The aim of press releases is to transfer news to journalists so that it can be made public. Press releases are more likely to be used and placed in a news medium when they refer to newsworthy events or items that are current and have a human interest or appeal, when the release is written in a factual (as opposed to judgemental) manner and with a clear heading and lead (first paragraph) into the topic.

When writing a press release, communication professionals should keep the expectations, preferred frames and deadlines of the different media in mind. Different media organizations and media forms (TV, print, internet) involve different reporting styles, timetables and deadlines. The print journalist, for example, will employ a pyramid scheme where the most important information is shared first in the article, and as the article increases in length, the information appearing further down in the news article will be deemed less important. In contrast, the radio journalist will try to share all of the information early on. Moreover, a reporter who is assigned to a business or financial desk will be concerned about angles from the perspective of business audiences and the implications for financial performance and financial markets. The public affairs reporter will be more concerned about the public angle. A feature writer will be more concerned about the human interest angle.

As mentioned, it is important that professionals are sensitive to the dominant frames and interests of journalists and their news organizations so that there is a greater likelihood of frame alignment. Another point is the time-frame of different news media. Television and the internet are 'fast' media in the sense that a topic or article is published directly, whereas newspapers are slower in that they wait until the next deadline to publish.

Magazines even have longer deadlines. This time-frame, which can be short for internet and television, is of importance to corporate communication professionals because the chance of incorrect reporting is greater for these fast media.

2 *Press conference*: Another tool of disseminating information to the news media involves inviting journalists to a press conference. Press conferences are normally organized around fixed periods in the calendar, when organizations release financial results or share corporate information at the annual general meeting with shareholders. There may also be *ad hoc* press conferences around a particular issue or crisis (e.g., product defects, accidents) (see Chapters 10 and 11) that are called to provide journalists with up-to-date information. A key element of the press conference is that it allows journalists to ask questions of the company executives gathered at the event. This 'interactive' aspect distinguishes a press conference from a press release. A press conference is therefore more applicable when information cannot be conveyed in a standardized, written form or when the information involves a controversial or sensitive issue (Chapter 10). In preparation for a press conference, professionals need to draw up a list of journalists and editors whom they would like to invite to the conference and brief them about the conference in time.

3 *Interviews*: Journalists often request an interview with official spokespersons or with the CEO or other senior executives of the organization. For this purpose, communication professionals need to offer executives advice and training on news angles in relation to corporate themes and on specific guidelines regarding the interview format. Such guidelines may consist of advising staff to keep 'control' of the interview by asking the journalist to call or come at a pre-arranged time, to brief them about the interview topics in advance, and to ensure that the journalist supplies them with a copy of the interview transcript and final article so that facts, opinions and attributions can be checked.

In addition, CEOs and other executives who are likely to be interviewed by journalists over the telephone, face-to-face or in front of a camera need to be trained to be skilled communicators. Many organizations therefore instruct their CEO and senior executives in media training so that they stay 'on message', synchronize their body language with their verbal messages, and can anticipate questions from journalists. When a CEO becomes an effective communicator, that can translate into admiration, respect and trust and a stronger overall corporate reputation.[18]

4 *Media monitoring and research*: The most common type of media research consists of monitoring media relations efforts. Two of the most commonly used monitoring techniques are gate-keeping research and output analysis. In addition, many corporations also use syndicated media monitoring services such as Carma International and Media Tenor:

(a) *Gate-keeping research*: A gate-keeping study analyses the characteristics of a press release or video news release, allowing them to 'pass through the gate' and appear in a news medium. Both content and style variables are typically examined. For example, previous research has found that press releases dealing with financial matters (e.g., annual results) are more likely to be used than those dealing with other topics. Press releases that are aimed at the specific interests of the newspaper to which they are sent are also more likely to be published than general releases. Furthermore, editors typically shorten news releases and rewrite them to make them easier to read before publication.[19]

(b) *Output analysis*: The objective of output analysis is to measure the amount of exposure or attention that the organization receives as a result of media relations. Several techniques can be used in output analysis. One way is simply to measure the total amount of news coverage (i.e., total number of stories or articles) that appears in selected mass media. It is also possible to examine the tone (positive or negative) of stories or articles. Many communication professionals systematically collect press clippings (copies of stories or articles in the press) and record the degree of exposure in terms of column inches in print media, the number of minutes of air time in radio and TV media or the number of sites or 'hits' on the Web in electronic media.

An often-used measure for exposure is the 'advertising value equivalent' (AVE), which consists of counting the column inches of press publicity and seconds of air time gained and then multiplying the total by the advertising rate of the media in which the coverage appeared. It is not uncommon, using this measure, for communication campaigns and well-placed press releases to generate many hundreds of thousands of pounds (euros or dollars) worth of advertising. However, AVE does not incorporate an evaluation of the tone of the stories or articles or the exposure of the organization compared to competitors. Another form of output analysis is to calculate the reach and frequency of media reporting on an organization. 'Reach' is usually based on the total audited circulation of a newspaper or the estimated viewing or listening audience of TV or radio, while frequency refers to the number of times a story or article about an organization is carried in the same medium.

(c) *Syndicated media monitoring services*: Countering the shortcomings of output analysis, a number of media research agencies (e.g., Carma, Media Tenor) have developed media monitoring packages. These packages focus on measuring the total circulation or audience reached; the tone of the news stories or articles on the organization; the extent to which key messages (e.g., in a press release) were picked up and communicated; and the share-of-voice compared to competitors or other comparable organizations. Philips, for example, uses the Carma media monitoring tool to monitor news coverage on the firm compared to competing consumer electronics firms (e.g., Samsung, Sony) and other relevant firms (e.g., Shell, which is similarly a Dutch corporation). The advantages of these tools are that they focus on outcome (share of voice and tone) as opposed to mere exposure or output, the automated analysis of mass media around the world and easy-to-use web portals, which allow a communication professional to view real-time developments in media coverage.

THE NEW MEDIA LANDSCAPE

8.5 Recent years has seen an explosion in the opportunities and use of 'new' media in society, including social media sites such as *Facebook* and *YouTube* and Web 2.0 applications. These advances in media and web technology provide new challenges and opportunities for organizations to communicate and engage with their stakeholders, including the news media. The basic trend associated with the development of these new media is that it highlights the democratization of the production and dissemination of news on organizations. Rather than the classic model of communication professionals liaising with official news channels, blogs and social networking sites now also offer content on organizations, and indeed may influence stakeholders or the general public in their perceptions and subsequent behaviours. Equally, employees can nowadays distribute their own information about an organization electronically to outside stakeholders, sometimes without any gate-keeping or control from corporate communication professionals. Indeed, with access to email, blogs, and social networking sites for sharing corporate information, many employees become somewhat like corporate communication professionals themselves, as demonstrated by the case example from General Electric (Case Example 8.1 below).

Case Example 8.1

General Electric: Campaigning through new media

In 2008, General Electric (GE) redeveloped its digital communication platforms, including the intranet and social networking tools for employees as well as its external-facing website. The intranet came to include *GE Connect*, a *Facebook*-like internal network, that allows staff to maintain personal sites and profiles, to write blogs and develop knowledge-sharing and discussion sites. GE also has an interactive external website, where employees post videos about their work and thus act as brand ambassadors. A particularly popular feature is a correspondence site on the intranet (called *InsideGE*), where employees can debate stories and issues in an unfettered manner. In 2009, GE Aviation faced a threat to funding for the F–35 fighter-jet engine it was developing for the US military, an issue that sparked huge interest with employees inside the firm. Debating the issue on *InsideGE*, employees decided that they should collectively lobby politicians on the issue. Rather than a more traditional corporate communication approach of telling GE's story via the media or via a targeted public affairs strategy, employees initiated their own grass-roots approach. About 12,000 employees from all parts of GE sent letters to the senators of their own state, asking the US government to keep funding the engine. Employees wrote a personal letter and framed the appeal

(Continued)

(Continued)

around their own interests, as individual citizens, and also argued for preserving jobs and local technology expertise. The initiative not only helped in getting the resolution passed, it also marked a new dawn for internal and external communication within GE. It has led to the realization that employees can collectively voice issues and communicate with external stakeholders. As in this instance, there may be ways in which the traditional news media can also be circumvented to get a message across to stakeholders, such as government. According to Sangita Malhotra, corporate communication manager at GE, companies like GE need to grow with these developments rather than attempt to turn back the clock. New media are not only here to stay, but also offer new opportunities internally, in terms of harnessing employees' creativity and identification, and externally, in terms of crafting conversations about the company and its activities.

Source: This case study was informed by Palmer, M. (2010) 'Time to connect', *Financial Times*, 22 March 2010.

From a corporate communication perspective, the developments in new media and web-based technologies may be seen as both a challenge and an opportunity. It is seen as a challenge when professionals take the view that the new media landscape blurs the picture between content providers and makes news-gathering and dissemination increasingly fragmented, for themselves as well as for stakeholders. As a consequence, they may feel that these developments challenge them in managing or even controlling the corporate messages and news coverage that an organization receives. The development of new media can also be seen as an opportunity. Involving the organization somehow in these developments may create new ways of reaching and engaging with stakeholders, including news media organizations. It provides an organization with the opportunity to engage in conversations, and to tell and elaborate its story or key messages to stakeholders or the general public in an interactive manner, a real advance compared to the standard and arms-length messaging model associated with traditional media relations. The simultaneous challenge and opportunity provided by new media is tied into the democratizing nature of these media. It is therefore less about control and more about proactive engagement within digital and web-based conversations and communities. The information scientist Komito describes this development as follows:

> Where discussion previously focused on the consumption of digital information, as individuals accessed information provided by organizations, these popular new Internet applications enable sharing of information amongst users who are now individual information providers. ... There is good empirical evidence that the Internet is, decreasingly, a means by which corporate information is provided to users than a means by which user-generated information is shared amongst other Internet users. This collection of applications enables individuals to share information (including videos, photos, news items, and audio footage) and create virtual communities on the web. The previous growth in the amount of information in digital form has been replaced by growth in the communication of that digital information.[20]

While it is too early to tell how these emerging media developments will change corporate communication in the long run, their explosive use in recent years suggests that these technologies are driving a shift in how people engage with one another and with organizations. It is quickly changing how dialogues occur, how news about organizations is generated and disseminated, and how stakeholder perceptions are shaped and relationships forged. Consider, for example, the increasing internet access of individuals around the world. Every one of those individuals with access, as well as every connected organization, can in principle become a global publisher of new content. Additionally, the widespread use of technologies such as camera phones and digital cameras means that individual citizens can instantly become a potential photojournalist or, with the spread of video capabilities, a documentary filmmaker. For example, at the G20 protests in London in 2009, a fund manager from New York, who was in London on business, used his digital camera to film the protests and captured the moment when Ian Tomlinson, a newspaper vendor, was assaulted by the police and, as a result, later collapsed and died. The footage, while shot by an amateur, created a huge news story.

Besides this shift in news production towards 'citizen journalists', a further notable development is the decline in the usage of traditional news media. Newspapers have suffered a significant decline in interest and use, as readers and users flock to the internet and to alternative news sources. Whatever the long-term developments may be, approaches to corporate communication will require at least some reinvention as these new media continue to evolve. Two recent examples of these changes involve the use of blogs and online newsrooms as part of media relations:

1 *Blogs*: Blogs are a controlled web-based medium that enable an individual or group of individuals (bloggers) to publish information in a diary or journal style. Bloggers control the information that they publish, and moderate comments that viewers (non-authors) add to the blog. Increasingly, 'citizen journalists' as well as traditional journalists host blogs themselves, and also many major news outlets support blogs that cover topics around business and the economy. The statistics in blog usage point to an increasingly proactive and prolific population: approximately more than 175,000 new blogs are created every day. These developments suggest that corporate communication professionals have to monitor and engage with influential bloggers, regardless of whether they are citizen or traditional journalists.

   The other response, although arguably more time-consuming, is for an organization to maintain or sponsor a corporate blog that opens the organization up to conversations with all stakeholders, including the media. One of the first companies to start a corporate blog was Microsoft. Robert Scoble, when he was still employed at Microsoft, wrote a daily blog on technology which often promoted Microsoft products, such as Tablet PCs and Windows Vista, but he also frequently criticized his own employer and praised its competitors. His blog was read by many independent software developers and technology journalists around the world and made Microsoft's image more humane with this particular community. In February 2005, he became the first person to earn the newly coined term of 'spokesblogger', defined as an official spokesperson for an organization in that he or she develops, writes and edits an organization's blog.[21] Spokesbloggers, while seemingly publishing an independent blog, often do not speak only for themselves, but also on behalf of their employer or the organization that they represent. Generally speaking, the advantage of corporate blogging is that it allows stakeholders, including journalists, to engage in a direct and unfiltered conversation with the organization. Increasingly, journalists are also actively searching the blogosphere for information on organizations. According to a 2008 *PR Week* survey, nearly 73 per cent of responding journalists admitted using blogs when researching stories.[22] This provides a powerful argument for organizations to have a presence with its own sponsored blog.

2 *Online newsrooms*: In order to connect different platforms and media content, corporate communication professionals have also increasingly developed online newsrooms, as a dedicated part of the company's website. These newsrooms are a one-stop shop for media relations. They typically include standard reports, speeches and press releases, but also tend to host dynamic content, including videos, news feeds, widgets, podcasts, and searchable archives of content. The general advantage of these newsrooms is that it provides journalists with information when they need it and it also helps drive traffic to the company's website. In addition, it allows the company to get its message out in a way that responds to the methods used by journalists searching for company information on the internet. To stimulate usage by journalists, the design of these newsroom sites needs to be user-friendly and easy to navigate. Dynamic content, including image libraries and videos, also significantly enhance the experience of using the site. A good example of a company that quite early on developed an online newsroom with dynamic content is the Body Shop. Case Study 8.1 documents how the video releases hosted on the newsroom site helped the company announce and rationalize its take-over by L'Oréal.

CASE STUDY 8.1

L'ORÉAL'S TAKE-OVER OF THE BODY SHOP

On 17 March 2006, the Body Shop International PLC (the Body Shop), a retailer of natural-based and ethically-sourced beauty products, announced that it had agreed to be acquired by the beauty giant L'Oréal in a cash deal worth £652 million. The Body Shop had been put up for sale two years prior to the take-over by L'Oréal. Although there were a few interested parties at the time, no formal offer was made.

The Body Shop

The Body Shop, a cosmetics retailer which promotes itself based on ethics, fair trade and environmental campaigning, was founded in 1976 by Dame Anita Roddick.

(Continued)

(Continued)

Roddick had copied the business model for the Body Shop from a Californian outfit with the same name that she had visited in 1970. Roddick modelled the look of her shops, the colour scheme, the products, her brochures and catalogues upon the Californian chain. In 1987, when Roddick's the Body Shop entered the US market, the company offered the Californian owners $3.5 million as compensation for use of the name. They also agreed to change the name of their six shops in California to Body Time.

Roddick started her first Body Shop in 1976 in Brighton in the UK. The store sold around 15 lines of homemade cosmetics made with natural ingredients such as jojoba oil and rhassoul mud. From its early days, the Body Shop was associated with the social activism of Roddick. The windows of the early Body Shop outlets, for example, featured posters of local charity and community events. Roddick was, from the start, also very critical of the environmental insensitivity of big business and called for a change in corporate values.

Profits-with-a-principle

The Body Shop's core brand identity is its 'profits-with-a-principle' philosophy and the brand was closely marketed in combination with a social justice agenda. This was a revolutionary idea at the time, and the Body Shop developed a loyal customer base. By the late 1970s, the company had grown into a number of franchise stores around the UK. Growing at a rate of 50 per cent annually, the Body Shop was getting a lot of media attention in the 1980s and Roddick hired a PR firm to handle the media attention.

The Body Shop became fully listed on the London Stock Exchange in 1986. At the same time, the company formed an alliance with Greenpeace for the 'Save the whales' campaign. Following some disagreements with Greenpeace, Roddick discontinued the relationship and formed instead an alliance with Friends of the Earth in 1990. The Body Shop also teamed up with Amnesty International, and from the 1990s onwards became very vocal in its support for international human rights.

The company had its fair share of critics during the 1980s and 1990s. They accused the company of hypocrisy as they felt that it was making profits under the guise of endorsing social equality. Some shareholders also complained that instead of maximizing profits, the company was diverting money into 'social work' projects. For example, Jon Entine, an award-winning journalist, published a damning critique of the Body Shop in an article in 1994. Entine reported that the Charity Commission records in the UK did not show any charitable contributions from the company in its first 11 years of operation and only a less than average contribution (1.5 per cent of pre-tax profits) in subsequent years. He also said that the company made false claims that its products were natural, as chemicals were still used in the production of many of the Body Shop's products at the time. In 1998, McSpotlight and Greenpeace put forward similar criticisms that the Body Shop exploited the public by championing a social agenda. They said that the Body Shop's products were not completely free from chemicals, and although the company claimed that it was against animal testing, its products contained ingredients that had been tested on animals by other companies.

Throughout the 1990s, the company continued to grow in size, although its market value declined. The Board of the Body Shop had also got tired of Roddick's radicalism,

(Continued)

(Continued)

her combative stance on globalization and her vocal criticism of anti-wrinkle cream. In 1998, Roddick was forced to step down as the CEO. In 2000, Roddick announced that she would quit the Board in two years but that she would continue to carry out media functions for the Body Shop and would keep travelling around the world in search of new product ideas. Anita Roddick became a Dame in 2003 in recognition of her social campaigning and passed away on 10 September 2007.

The take-over by L'Oréal

L'Oréal is one of the largest and most successful cosmetics companies in the world with 17 global brands in its portfolio. By 2004, L'Oréal had achieved 19 years of consecutive double-digit growth. The company had successfully strengthened its market dominance by promoting its major brands, such as L'Oréal Paris and Lancôme, and by acquiring and internationalizing popular local brands such as Ralph Lauren, Redken, Maybelline and Garnier. Advertising was focused on the superior quality of the company's products and endorsements by successful career women and celebrities. L'Oréal became interested in the acquisition of the Body Shop as the take-over would provide the company with a new perspective on retailing (speciality stores, direct-sales business), a brand capable of generating publicity in developing markets (China, Russia, India), an entry into the 'masstige' market (premium mass cosmetics), a foothold in the Fair Trade movement, as well as additional revenues. At the same time, L'Oréal realized that it had not been previously associated with ethics or Fair Trade and had been criticized in the past for its use of animal testing in the production of cosmetics. Therefore, a take-over of the Body Shop would present L'Oréal with some communication challenges.

When the deal was finalized between the two companies, both L'Oréal and the Body Shop published press releases and video clips to announce and rationalize the deal and to communicate the advantages to both parties. These press releases and video clips were made available on an online newsroom. L'Oréal's chairman and CEO, Lindsay Owen-Jones, issued a written statement. Adrian Bellamy (Chairman of the Body Shop), Peter Saunders (CEO of the Body Shop) and Anita Roddick (Non-executive Director) all issued pre-recorded video clips with answers to questions about the take-over. The transcripts of these video releases were also made available as press releases. Adrian Bellamy said: 'I'm extremely positive about the deal. We'll be stronger as part of the L'Oréal group than by sailing our own boat. We'll be able to share its global platform and experience.' Similarly, L'Oréal's Chairman and CEO Owen-Jones said: 'We have always had great respect for the Body Shop's success and for the strong identity and values created by its outstanding founder, Anita Roddick'. He also added:

> A partnership between our two companies makes perfect sense. Combining L'Oréal's expertise and knowledge of international markets with the Body Shop's distinct culture and values will benefit both companies. We are delighted that the Body Shop has agreed to unanimously recommend our offer to the company's shareholders. We look forward to working together with the Body Shop management, employees and franchisees to fulfil the Body Shop's independent potential as part of the L'Oréal family.

(Continued)

(Continued)

L'Oréal also said that the management team at the Body Shop would be retained and that the company would continue to operate as a separate company to preserve its own identity.

In her own press release, Roddick justified the deal by saying that L'Oréal wanted to learn from the Body Shop's value-based management. She denied that she had sold out and maintained that the Body Shop's values and focus on social development would not change. As she stated in the press release:

> I do not believe that L'Oréal will compromise the ethics of the Body Shop. That is after all what they are paying for and they are too intelligent to mess with our DNA. … I want to make things happen, to spread human values wide in business if I possibly can. And this sale gives us the chance to do so. The campaigning, the being maverick, changing the rules of business – it's all there, protected. And it's not going to change. That's part of our DNA. But having L'Oréal come in and say we like you, we like your ethics, we want to be a part of you, we want you to teach us things, it's a gift. I'm ecstatic about it. I don't see it as selling out.

Roddick also mentioned that she hoped that the Body Shop values would rub off on the way in which L'Oréal does business.

> But with L'Oréal now, the biggest cosmetics company in the world, for them to partner with us on our projects in 35 countries in the world, I think it's amazing, amazing. They could work with our Nicaraguan farmers who sell us 70 tons of sesame oil. How many tons could they use? A thousand? I mean it's mind-blowing in terms of poverty eradication.

Media reporting

The media reported the take-over on the same day (17 March 2006) that the deal was finalized and announced. Initially, news coverage consisted of reports on the details of the take-over with quotes from the press releases of L'Oréal's Owen-Jones and Anita Roddick. The BBC, for example, quoted from Roddick's press release in which she said that 'This [the take-over] is the best 30th anniversary gift the Body Shop could have received'. *The Guardian* published the same quote from Roddick along with another demonstrating the complementary link that Roddick mentioned in her press release: 'L'Oréal has displayed visionary leadership in wanting to be an authentic advocate and supporter of our values.' However, later that afternoon, *The Guardian* online edition published an article on a call by animal welfare activists to boycott the Body Shop. A coalition of activist groups, including Naturewatch, opposed L'Oréal's policy on the testing of cosmetics ingredients on animals. None of the other newspapers reported the same or a similar story on the same day.

Editorial pieces in subsequent weeks occasionally picked up on the nature of the relationship between the two companies. For example, an article in *The Economist* on 25 March 2006 questioned the complementary but independent link between the two companies. The article suggested that it would be difficult for L'Oréal not to adopt any cross-selling practices across Body Shop outlets. Rhetorically, the article asked: 'Will L'Oréal really be able to resist slipping its ethically challenged wrinkle cream onto the shelves next to the bracing and naturally inspired body scrubs offered by the Body Shop?'

(Continued)

(Continued)

However, by and large, the news media and the general public accepted the claim from Roddick and Owen-Jones that the Body Shop would remain an independent entity with the upshot that its value-based practices and social change campaigns could have a wider impact with the support from L'Oréal. Part of this news framing may be attributed to the strong media presence of Roddick, who with her frank style of communicating convinced many journalists of the rationale of the deal. While early indications showed that the brand of the Body Shop had dropped somewhat in brand indices, such as YouGov BrandIndex, the Body Shop's image is making a comeback and on its own terms.

QUESTIONS FOR REFLECTION

1   Discuss the framing of the take-over of the Body Shop by L'Oréal in terms of the concepts of frame alignment and frame contests. Why do you think that some media reported frames and quotes from corporate press releases while others published alternative frames about the take-over?

2   When the take-over was announced, the Body Shop issued pre-recorded interviews to journalists. In your view, should the Body Shop have done anything else (e.g., face-to-face interviews, a press conference) to influence the news coverage and framing of the take-over?

Source: This case study is based upon www.thebodyshopinternational.com; 'The Body Beautiful', *The Economist* (www.economist.com), 25 March 2006; and articles downloaded from www.jonentine.com.

CHAPTER SUMMARY

8.6 This chapter started with an overview of journalists and news organizations and of the production of news content. Given the importance of the news media for a company's reputation, the chapter continued by discussing ways in which professionals can frame news items in such a way that they are picked up by the press. The chapter also outlined various practical tools and techniques that communication professionals use to obtain media coverage, build relationships with journalists and monitor reporting on their organization over time. Finally, the chapter concluded with a discussion of the new media landscape and of how organizations can develop digital communication platforms to support media relations.

 ## DISCUSSION QUESTIONS

1   Describe the main tenets of the agenda-setting role of the news media.

2   What can communication professionals do to increase the chances of a story being covered in the news media?

3   The new media landscape is drastically changing the production and dissemination of news, including news on corporate organizations. What are the main challenges in this respect for organizations and what can communication professionals do in response?

KEY TERMS

Agenda setting

Blogging

Corporate frame

Frame alignment

Frame conflict

Frame contest

Frame negotiation

Gatekeeping research

Ideology

Interviews

Journalist

Media favourability

Media monitoring

News desk

News frame

News routines

Online newsroom

Output analysis

Press conference

Press release

FURTHER READING

Argenti, Paul A. and Barnes, Courtney M. (2009), *Digital Strategies for Powerful Corporate Communications*. New York: McGraw-Hill.

Arthur W. Page Society (2007), *The Authentic Enterprise: Relationships, Values and the Evolution of Corporate Communications*. New York: Arthur W. Page Society.

Henderson, David (2006), *Making News: A Straight-Shooting Guide to Media Relations*. New York: Harlem Writers Guild Press.

NOTES

1   Deephouse, D.L. and Carroll, C.E. (2007) 'What makes news fit to print: a five-level framework predicting media visibility and favourability of organizations', Working paper, Alberta School of Business.

2   See, for example, Lorimer, R. (1994), *Mass Communications*. Manchester: Manchester University Press.

3   Conlan, T. (2007), 'BBC business news failing impartiality test, says report', *The Guardian*, 26 May, p. 18.

4   Fombrun, C.J. and Shanley, M. (1990), 'What's in a name? Reputation building and corporate strategy', *Academy of Management Journal*, 33: 233–258.

5   McCombs, M. and Shaw, D. (1972), 'The agenda-setting function of mass media', *Public Opinion Quarterly*, 36: 176–187.

6   Cohen, B.C. (1963), *The Press and Foreign Policy*. Princeton, NJ: Princeton University Press, p. 120.

7   Carroll, C. (2004), 'How the mass media influence perceptions of corporate reputation: agenda-setting effects within business news coverage', unpublished doctoral dissertation, University of Texas at Austin, TX, USA.

8   Meijer, M. and Kleinnijenhuis, J. (2006), 'Issue news and corporate reputation: applying the theories of agenda setting and issue ownership in the field of business communication', *Journal of Communication*, 56: 543–559.

9   Deephouse, D.L. (2000), 'Media reputation as a strategic resource: an integration of mass communication and resource-based theories', *Journal of Management*, 26: 1091–1112, quote on p. 1097.

10   Deephouse (2000), p. 1101.

11   Carroll, C.E. and McCombs, M. (2003), 'Agenda-setting effects of business news on the public's images and opinions about major corporations', *Corporate Reputation Review*, 6: 36–46.

12   Carroll (2004), p. 2.

13   See, for example, Belz, A., Talbott' A.D. and Starck, K. (1989), 'Using role theory to study cross perceptions of journalists and public relations practitioners', *Public Relations Research Annual*, 1: 125–139; Neijens, P.C. and Smit, E.G. (2006), 'Dutch public relations practitioners and journalists: antagonists no more', *Public Relations Review*, 32 (3): 232–240.

14   Merten, K. (2004), 'A constructivist approach to public relations', in van Ruler, B. and Vercic, D. (eds), *Public Relations and Communication Management in Europe*. Berlin: Mouton de Gruyter, pp. 45–54; Elving, W.J.L. and Van Ruler, A.A. (2006), *Trendonderzoek communicatiemanagement* [*Trend Research Communication Management*]. Amsterdam: University of Amsterdam.

15   See, for example, Hallahan, K. (1999), 'Seven models of framing: implications for public relations', *Journal of Public Relations Research*, 11: 205–242.

16   Entman, R.M. (1993), 'Framing: toward clarification of a fractured paradigm', *Journal of Communication*, 43 (4): 51–58, quote on p. 55.

17   See, for example, Hallahan (1999) and Entman (1993).

18   See, for example, Gaines-Ross, L. (2003), *CEO Capital: A Guide to Building CEO Reputation and Company Success*. Hoboken, NJ: Wiley; Hayward, M.L., Rindova, V.P. and Pollock, T.G. (2004), 'Believing one's own press: the antecedents and consequences of CEO celebrity', *Strategic Management Journal*, 25: 637–653.

19   Morton, L. and Ramsey, S. (1994), 'A benchmark study of the PR news wire', *Public Relations Review*, 20: 155–170; Morton, L. and Warren, J. (1992), 'Proximity: localization versus distance in PR news releases', *Journalism Quarterly*, 69: 1023–1028; Walters, T., Walters, L. and Starr, D. (1994), 'After the highwayman: syntax and successful placement of press releases in newspapers', *Public Relations Review*, 20: 345–356.

20   Komito, L. (2008), 'Information society policy', in Hearn, G. and Rooney, D. (eds), *Knowledge Policy: Challenges for the 21st Century*. Cheltenham: Edward Elgar, pp. 87–101.

21   *The Economist* (2005), 'Robert Scoble, Microsoft's celebrity blogger', 10 February.

22   Washkuch, F. (2008), 'State of transition: media survey 2008', *PR Week*, 30 March.

INTERNAL COMMUNICATION

9

| Chapter Overview |

Employees are a crucial stakeholder group for any organization. Organizations need to communicate with their employees to strengthen employee morale and their identification with the organization and to ensure that employees know how to accomplish their own, specialized tasks. The chapter discusses general strategies for communicating to employees within the organization. These strategies range from communication that makes employees feel comfortable speaking up and providing feedback to managers, to using communication to stimulate innovation and creativity within communities of practice.

INTRODUCTION

9.1 Organizations require employees to cooperate with one another to achieve the company's goals. Most organizations have divided complex activities up into more specialized tasks for individual employees. While efficient, the pay-off of such specialization depends almost wholly on coordinating tasks and activities across employees. If an organization controls its members through top-down command and delegation, the individual needs of employees for autonomy, creativity and sociability may be frustrated. But, at the same time, if the organization fails to control its employees, it loses the ability to coordinate its employees' activities, and will ultimately fail. Hence, organizations must find ways to meet their employees' individual needs and stimulate their creativity while persuading them to act in ways that meet the organization's overall objectives. Organizations do so by adopting various strategies for communicating with employees. In the next section, we define the general scope of internal communication. The chapter then goes on to discuss how internal communication may strengthen employees' identification with their organization. The degree to which managers communicate to employees and involve them in decision-making has a direct impact on employee morale and their commitment to the organization. The final section of the chapter outlines how social media can be used internally within organizations to encourage employees to form communities of practice that stimulate knowledge-sharing, learning and innovation.

DEFINING INTERNAL COMMUNICATION

9.2 Contemporary organizations realize that their employees need to be communicated with. The terms that have often been used to label this area of corporate communication are 'employee communication', 'staff communication' and 'internal communication'. Traditionally, internal communication, which is the term used in this chapter, was defined as communication with employees internally within the organization. Internal communication was distinguished from forms of external communication with stakeholders such as customers and investors. However, the advent of new technologies (e.g., internet blogs and emails) has meant that messages to employees do not always remain 'inside' the organization. These new technologies have blurred the boundaries between 'internal' and 'external' communication. Employees can nowadays distribute their own information about an organization electronically to outside stakeholders, sometimes without any gate-keeping or control from corporate communication professionals. On an internet blog, for example, employees can share their views and publish their grievances as well as organize and demand action from the organization. Indeed, with access to email, blogs and social networking sites for sharing corporate information, many employees become somewhat like corporate communication professionals themselves.

Clearly, communication technologies have led to many changes in the workplace. Computer technologies have made it easier to produce, multiply, distribute and store written documents, to exchange messages over long distances and to work together and to execute meetings relatively independently of time and space. Employees are now often connected to each other by electronic means rather than through close physical proximity. Emails, the intranet, video-conferencing and podcasting are used by managers to communicate with employees and by employees themselves to stay informed of company news. IBM, for example, offers more than 5,000 audio and video podcast 'episodes' to employees, who can download these files and watch or listen to them at a convenient time. IBM feels that these podcasts are a useful way to disseminate corporate information in an efficient and engaging way.

If we look at the use of communication technologies within organizations, we can distinguish two central areas of internal communication: (1) management communication; and (2) corporate information and communication systems. Management communication refers to communication between a manager and his or her subordinate employees. Communication in this setting is often directly related to specific tasks and activities of individual employees as well as to their morale and well-being.

Research on what managers do has demonstrated that managers spend most of their time communicating, and much of that time is spent in verbal, face-to-face communication.[1] Besides face-to-face communication, managers also increasingly use email, video-conferencing and enterprise software to communicate to their employees. While the responsibility for management communication lies with managers themselves and not with the corporate communication department, communication professionals often advise and support managers in their communication to staff. Communication professionals in AstraZeneca, for example, have developed training materials for senior and middle managers to help them become better communicators.

Corporate information and communication systems (CICS) have a broader focus than the manager–employee dyad. CICS refers to the broadcasting of corporate decisions and developments to all employees across the organization. The emphasis is on disseminating information about the organization to employees in all ranks and functions within the organization in order to keep them informed about corporate matters. CICS is often the preserve of the communication department, which is charged with releasing information to employees through the intranet, emails and so-called 'town hall' meetings (i.e., large employee meetings where senior managers announce and explain key corporate decisions or developments). Corporate TV, such as the digital FedEx Television Network or Nokia's digital broadcasting systems, are also used as communication channels for reaching employees around the world.

Whereas management communication is often restricted to the specific interpersonal work setting of a manager and employee, CICS may not differentiate content between employees and typically relates to more general organizational developments rather than specific areas of work. Although different, both areas of internal communication complement each other in ensuring that information flows vertically, horizontally and laterally across the organization. Without both forms of internal communication, a company's overall communication effort will be ineffective and its employees demotivated.

The complementary nature of both can best be understood through the concepts of downward and upward communication. Downward communication consists of electronic and verbal methods of informing employees about their organization, its performance, and their own contribution and performance in terms they can comprehend. In other words, downward communication involves 'information flowing from the top of the organizational management hierarchy and telling people in the organization what is important (mission) and what is valued (policies)'.[2] Both management communication and CICS are central to downward communication. Together, they provide employees with general information from the top of the organization (CICS) as well as with more specific information from their managers (management communication).

A good example of this kind of downward communication is the corporate calendar system within Siemens. The corporate calendar (Figure 9.1) lists events throughout the year at which the corporate strategy and corporate objectives are communicated to employees from different parts of the company. The calendar was developed by corporate communication professionals who realized that employees were not always informed about the company's strategy in a timely and consistent manner. Communication professionals raised the issue with the CEO and senior executives, who agreed that the calendar system could be usefully incorporated into the corporate strategy as a way of implementing the better communication structures. The CEO and senior executives felt that the calendar would make an important contribution to the achievement of the corporate objectives as it provides a medium to report on the past year's targets and for setting binding priorities and objectives for the new fiscal year.

As displayed in Figure 9.1, the Siemens Business Conference (SBS) marks the start of each fiscal year. This central communication event provides a platform for senior managers to report on the past year's targets and to set priorities and objectives for the new fiscal year. The SBS event is followed by management conferences in the business divisions, regions and corporate units. By streamlining management events, the corporate calendar ensures that all managers and employees hear about the past year's results and are given objectives for the coming period.

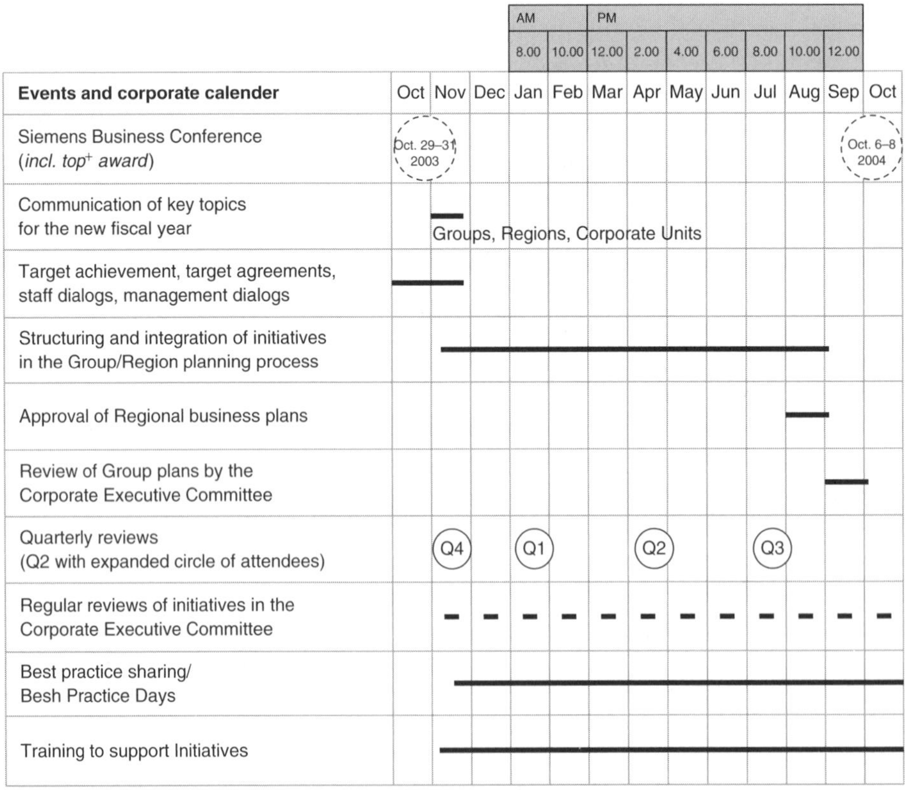

Events and corporate calender	Oct	Nov	Dec	Jan	Feb	Mar	Apr	May	Jun	Jul	Aug	Sep	Oct
Siemens Business Conference (incl. top+ award)	Oct. 29–31 2003											Oct. 6–8 2004	
Communication of key topics for the new fiscal year		Groups, Regions, Corporate Units											
Target achievement, target agreements, staff dialogs, management dialogs	—												
Structuring and integration of initiatives in the Group/Region planning process		—	—	—	—	—	—	—	—	—			
Approval of Regional business plans										—			
Review of Group plans by the Corporate Executive Committee												—	
Quarterly reviews (Q2 with expanded circle of attendees)		Q4		Q1			Q2			Q3			
Regular reviews of initiatives in the Corporate Executive Committee		- -	- -	- -	- -	- -	- -	- -	- -	- -	- -	- -	-
Best practice sharing/ Besh Practice Days		—	—	—	—	—	—	—	—	—	—	—	—
Training to support Initiatives		—	—	—	—	—	—	—	—	—	—	—	—

Time scale: AM — 8.00, 10.00, 12.00; PM — 2.00, 4.00, 6.00, 8.00, 10.00, 12.00

FIGURE 9.1 The corporate calendar system in Siemens (calendar dating from 2003). Reprinted with permission

Upward communication involves information from employees that is sent upwards towards managers within the organization. It often involves information about the employee him or herself, information about co-workers, information about organizational practices and policies, and information about what needs to be done and how it can be done. Allowing employees to communicate upwards is important because employees' ideas, responses to their working environment, or critiques of the plans and ideas announced by managers may be used to find ways to improve an organization's overall performance and profitability. Upward communication is typically facilitated within the interpersonal setting of management communication. Managers can stimulate employees to voice concerns and to provide them with feedback on practices, procedures and new organizational changes. At the same time, CICS may include communication systems such as message boards on an intranet and 'town hall' meetings, allowing employees to ask questions of senior managers and to ask for further information on corporate decisions or organizational developments.

INTERNAL COMMUNICATION AND ORGANIZATIONAL IDENTIFICATION

9.3 Generally speaking, when employees strongly identify with the organization they work for, they are more satisfied in their work, they will be more cooperative and they will also demonstrate behaviour that is helpful to the organization.[3] Organizational identification, in other words, plays a significant role in many organizations. Organizational identification can be defined as: 'the perception of oneness with or belongingness to an organization, where the individual defines him or herself in terms of the organization(s) of which he or she is a member'.[4] Academic research has shown that organizational identification increases as a result of the perceived external prestige of the organization[5] and as a result of the degree of overlap between the personal identity of the employees and the identity of the organization. When employees perceive their organization to be associated with a strong reputation and prestige in the eyes of outsiders, they often feel proud to belong to that organization and may feel inclined to bask in its reflected glory. Employees identify with an organization partly to enhance their own self-esteem: the more prestigious an individual employee perceives his or her organization to be, the greater the potential boost to self-esteem through identification. Employees also identify more strongly with their organization to the degree that the corporate values and attributes of the organization (organizational identity) correspond with one's own personal values. In other words, the higher the perceived fit between the values of an individual employee and the corresponding organization, the stronger the degree to which that employee identifies with his or her organization (see Case Example 9.1 below).

Internal communication, in particular, has a significant impact on organizational identification. Recent studies demonstrate that downward communication enhances organizational identification when the information transmitted is perceived as adequate and reliable.[6] Adequate information involves receiving useful and sufficient information about what is expected of employees in their work and regarding their contributions. The more adequate or specific the information to the employee involved, the higher the level of identification with that organization. Reliable information involves the perception that managers release information that is trustworthy and instrumental to the accomplishments of tasks. When information coming from management is perceived as reliable, employees are more likely to identify with their organization.[7] A further factor that has a significant impact on organizational identification involves the degree to which employees feel that they are listened to and are involved by managers when decisions are made. When employees feel that they participate in decision-making and are able to exert some control over their working life, they identify more strongly with their organization and are also generally more committed. Good internal communication, therefore, combines upward and downward communication in such a way that employees are well informed about the future directions of the organization (in particular the organization's strategies and policies), are allowed to interact with management about their policies, and where this interaction has an impact on managerial decisions. In other words, internal communication is most productive in the sense of eliciting employee commitment and organizational identification if it is a two-way process of communication, rather than a one-way flow of feedback and instructions. The role of corporate communication professionals and managers is therefore to use management communication and ICIS in such a way that internal communication provides each employee with adequate information and the opportunities to speak out, be listened to, and get actively involved in the organization.

Case Example 9.1

From ABN-AMRO to Fortis and back again

ABN-AMRO is a global retailing and investment bank that was taken over in 2007 by a consortium comprising the Royal Bank of Scotland, Fortis and Banco Santander. The operations of the bank were to be split between the banks in the consortium. The most visible part of the bank, its retail operations, was going to be subsumed within Fortis.

Prior to the take-over, ABN-AMRO had been known as an aggressive market player. Its past successes had led to a culture of confidence and a feeling of superiority over other banks within its local Dutch market and Western Europe. Employees within ANB-AMRO shared international ambitions and an interest in deal-making. This particular culture presented communication professionals within Fortis with significant challenges surrounding the take-over. Generally speaking, it was going to be a hard task to shift employees from identifying with an aggressive Dutch bank to what was seen as a largely Belgian banking and insurance corporation that had grown because of clever acquisitions as opposed to real market acumen.

The newly merged corporation was rebranded as Fortis overnight, phasing out the old ABN-AMRO branding and design. Fortis management also attempted to frame the cultural integration as one that would be easily accomplished and would fit a global corporation like Fortis. Jean-Paul Votron, the CEO, emphasized that 'at Fortis we have more than 100 different nationalities. Instead of national cultures, we are growing

(Continued)

(Continued)

towards one company culture.' However, the cultural integration proved much more difficult. A number of former ABN-AMRO bankers left the company, and cultural conflicts surfaced on top of the usual uncertainty surrounding mergers and acquisitions.

An interesting twist, however, came a year later when, due to the worldwide financial crisis, the Dutch government was forced to nationalize the banking operations owned by Fortis in the Netherlands. The government decided to change the name of the new bank back to ABN-AMRO, in order to capitalize on its strong brand in the Dutch market. A transition team under the leadership of Gerrit Zalm, a former finance minister, began the work of integrating the former ABN-AMRO and Fortis operations. The team consisted of managers from both organizations, signalling the importance of merging the two cultures under the new ABN-AMRO umbrella.

Source: This Case Example was informed by Reuters (2007) *Fortis CEO seeks new culture with ABN buy*: report, 30 October 2007.

VOICE, SILENCE AND STIMULATING EMPLOYEE PARTICIPATION

9.4 Voice, silence and employee participation are terms used to refer to the degree to which employees speak up, are listened to and participate in organizational decision-making. Employee participation involves organizational structures and processes that are designed to empower and enable employees to identify with organizational goals and to exert power over decision-making. Unionization of the workforce, for example, is one way in which the interests of workers are represented and communicated to senior managers. In some organizations, participation is anchored in the very identity and corporate governance of the organization. Cooperative organizations, for example, are jointly owned and democratically controlled by all those who work for the organization. John Lewis, a successful cooperative chain of department stores in the UK, attributes much of its success to employee co-ownership, which the company feels has led to 'sky-high' levels of employee engagement.[8]

While most organizations are not based on a form of employee co-ownership like John Lewis, employee participation has been an issue of concern as long as organizations have existed. Employees want a say in shaping their work lives, and organizations equally often feel that participation is desirable for a number of reasons, including genuine concern for the welfare of employees to a desire for the productivity benefits that can follow from employees engaging with the organization. However, even though participation is desirable, enabling employee participation is by no means straightforward.

The management scholars Morrison and Milliken have argued that there are often powerful forces in many organizations that prevent employees from participating and that force them to withhold information about potential problems or issues.[9] They refer to such withholding of information as 'organizational silence'. When employees share a perception that speaking up is unwise or without any consequence, they remain silent. Such silence in turn may mean that vital upward information is not passed on to managers.

Morrison and Milliken pointed to two factors that often systematically cause employees to feel that their opinions are not valued and that thereby discourage them from speaking up. The first factor relates to managers' fear of receiving negative feedback from employees. There is evidence to suggest that senior and middle managers often feel threatened by negative feedback, whether this information is about them personally or about a decision or a course of action with which they identify. Managers often feel a strong need to avoid embarrassment, threat, and feelings of vulnerability or incompetence. Therefore, they are likely to avoid any negative information and negative feedback coming from subordinates. The second factor that may influence organizational silence involves a set of managerial beliefs which suggest that managers know best about organizational matters. The basic assumption underlying such beliefs is that, because of information asymmetries, employees will not have a broad enough understanding of the organization. The information that employees therefore provide about organizational matters is seen as not relevant or up to date compared to the knowledge that managers already have. This particular belief is quite strong in managers who view their role as one of directing and controlling, with employees assuming the role of unquestioning followers.

If the dominant belief of managers in an organization is that employees are not sufficiently knowledgeable about what is best for the organization, then it is reasonable for managers not to involve them in decision-making processes. In turn, participative forms of decision-making that involve employees will be seen by managers as not worth the time and effort they require. Excluding employees from decision-making is also a way to avoid dissent and negative feedback and, thus, will also stem from fear of negative feedback. In many organizations, although there may be the appearance of some forms of participative decision-making (e.g., task forces, committees, etc.), managers still often attempt to hold on to their decision-making authority. And when managers fear negative feedback from employees, they are unlikely to engage in seeking much informal feedback from subordinates. Instead, managers may be more inclined to seek feedback from those who are likely to share their perspective and who are, thus, unlikely to provide negative feedback.

The fear of negative feedback and the belief that upward information is often of little value will also be associated with a lack of mechanisms for soliciting employee feedback after decisions are made. Using procedures such as employee surveys or 360-degree feedback will be unlikely because there will be a tendency to believe that little of value will be learned from them and because negative upward feedback will be seen as a challenge to management's control. It is important to realize that these various managerial beliefs and practices, which contribute to silence, may operate at multiple levels of an organization. For example, middle managers and work supervisors may hold these beliefs and exhibit the day-to-day practices that impede upward communication, while corporate communication professionals and senior executives feel that employee feedback and involvement is a key performance indicator.

Organizational silence can damage the organization in that it blocks negative feedback, and hence an organization's ability to detect and correct errors. Without negative feedback, errors within an organization may persist and may even intensify because corrective actions are not taken when needed. The quality of decision-making may also be affected by organizational silence. Potentially useful viewpoints and alternatives from the perspective of employees are not considered. The effectiveness of organizational decision-making will be compromised because of the restricted information available to managers. The tendency of managers to discourage employee opinions and feedback is also likely to elicit negative reactions from employees. Employees may come to feel that they are not valued and that they lack any control in their work. When employees feel that they are not valued, they will also be less likely to identify with the organization.

The concept of organizational silence is closely related to the concept of communication climate. 'Communication climate' is defined as the internal environment of information exchange between managers and employees through an organization's formal and informal networks.[10] A communication climate is characterized as 'open' when information flows freely between individuals, groups and departments, and it is characterized as 'closed' when information is blocked. Organizational silence corresponds to a 'closed' communication climate because it involves a shared and widespread feeling among employees that speaking up is of little use, leading them to withhold potentially valuable information. In an 'open' communication climate, in contrast, employees feel free to express opinions, voice complaints, and offer suggestions to their superiors. In such a climate, information also passes without distortion upward, downward and horizontally throughout the organization. Employees feel that they have enough support from their managers that they can give information to them without hesitation, confident that superiors will readily accept it, whether good or bad, favourable or unfavourable. In an 'open' communication climate, employees also know that their information will be seen as valuable, and hence sending communication upward may have an effect.

SOCIAL MEDIA AND COMMUNITIES OF PRACTICE

9.5 Downward and upward communication largely reflect the hierarchy of the organization, with managers communicating to employees on an individual basis or in work teams, and with employees speaking up and potentially participating in decision-making at higher levels in the organization. Hierarchy often stems from the vertical structure, as depicted in the organizational chart of an organization (see Figure 2.5). The vertical structure refers to the way in which tasks and activities are allocated to employees and located in the hierarchy of authority within an organization. The solid vertical lines that connect the boxes on an organization chart depict this vertical structure and the authority relationships involved, with senior and middle managers being located higher up in the hierarchy than employees. Communication that strictly follows such hierarchical lines, either downwards or upwards, is often, by its very nature, about control and command, and about supporting the coordination of specialized tasks across employees and departments.

Besides such vertical communication, many organizations have started to cultivate 'communities of practice' that draw together employees from various parts of the organization. Communities of practice are based on the idea of self-organization through coordinated activity. Lave and Wenger, who popularized the idea, defined a community of practice as a group of people informally bound together by common interests.[11] Such communities are not only self-managing, similar to self-managing work teams, but also self-designing in pursuit of social connections and a common social identity as well as mutual learning and knowledge development. An organization can consist of many different communities of practice that, once formed, can cross departmental and divisional boundaries, or any other dimension of formal hierarchical structure. Structure exists in emerging networks of social connections between individuals and groups.

The community model suggests that although the group itself may not literally be in one and the same place, they are connected as a group and bound together through their common interests. Wenger suggests in this respect that 'members of a community are informally *bound* by what they do together – from engaging in lunchtime discussions to solving difficult problems – and by what they have learned through their mutual engagement in these activities'. He also argued that 'communities of practice are not a new kind of organizational unit' but that they are 'a different cut on the organization's structure – one that emphasizes the learning that people have done together rather than the unit they report to, the project they are working on, or the people they know'.[12] In other words, communities of practice 'set their own boundaries' around themselves and largely through collaborating together. Examples of communities of practice are found in many organizations and have been called by different names, including 'learning communities' at Hewlett Packard, 'family groups' at the Xerox Corporation, 'thematic groups' at the World Bank, 'peer groups' at BP, and 'knowledge networks' at IBM Global Services (see Case Study 9.1 below). According to Wenger, it is important that 'boundaries' of communities of practice remain fairly 'flexible' so that the expertise within them is not sheltered from other communities and so that a community avoids becoming insular.

With flexible boundaries, communities of practice learn through the knowledge that they develop within them as well as through any further knowledge from other communities that they may bring in and assimilate. In recent years, a growing list of interactive digital platforms, often labelled as Web 2.0, give employees the ability to communicate freely with one another and to build communities around shared interests. Much like *Facebook* and *LinkedIn*, internal social networks allow users to create personal profiles, post messages and correspond with other community users. These networks can be password-protected and can be grown organically, based on the interests shared between employees. The IBM case study provides a good example of how digital platforms can be used to support the development of communities of practice.

CASE STUDY 9.1

TRANSFORMING IBM

International Business Machines (IBM) is one of the largest information technology and services companies in the world with almost 400,000 employees and operations in more than 170 countries. Through the development of the personal computer in the 1980s, the company became an industry leader. In the 1990s, however, IBM moved from being the most profitable company in the world and an industry leader to one with negative earnings and sliding revenues. This had a major impact on the workforce of more than 400,000 employees at the time, who had grown accustomed to a tradition of life-long employment at the best place to work in the world. However, the total workforce had to be cut over the course of several years.

After these crisis years, culminating with an $8.1 billion net loss in 1993, IBM began a steady climb towards profitability with a net income of $7.7 billion in 2001. In 2002, IBM found itself in a solid position again, given its wide range of products and its unparalleled research excellence (IBM had received more patents than any other company for each year in the previous decade). However, Sam Palmisano, who became CEO in 2002, recognized that these capabilities would not be enough. He felt that he also needed to unite IBM's vast resources to create customized solutions on behalf of its customers, and to do that, he needed to develop a deep level of social integration within IBM.

In 2002, this was a huge challenge given the changes and turmoil that the company had gone through in the previous decade. As he assumed control in 2002, Palmisano recognized that the task would be one of uniting IBM's global workforce behind a common set of values and through stimulating collaborative work. When employees shared strong connections with one another, and were united in purpose, horizontal interaction and innovation at the behest of customers would be a lot easier.

Changing the internal culture

However, as a result of the turmoil of the 1990s, whatever values the employees had previously shared between them had been lost. By 2002, many of IBM's more than 325,000 employees had no idea that there were any common IBM values other than driving up profits. Longer-term employees had also become disenfranchised from the company, their trust in the company shaken by lost job security and reduced benefits. Palmisano and his top executives recognized that something had to be done.

From the start, they reasoned that a top-down approach would not work with a highly educated and cynical workforce. IBM employees generally have strong feelings about their work and would probably not appreciate a prescriptive approach that circumscribes the company's values for them. Palmisano's team therefore decided to set up an online discussion forum, using a technology that was pioneered by IBM in 2001. The forum was open to all IBM employees and facilitated the free and open expression of ideas. The team felt that this forum would be the right venue for

(Continued)

(Continued)

focusing IBM's global workforce on a recommitment to corporate values. It fitted with the mobility of IBM's workforce and their flexible work arrangements.

The team initially produced a set of three proposed value phrases (commitment to the customer; excellence through innovation; integrity that earns trust) that were put online in 2003 to start the online discussion. On 21 July 2003, Palmisano announced the exercise on the IBM intranet, inviting IBMers across geographies, divisions, levels and functions to participate in the discussion. Over the next three days, an estimated 50,000 IBMers monitored the discussion and 10,000 comments were posted. Many of these comments revolved around how to realize and live particular values, not around the wording or the substance of the values themselves. Besides many cynical comments, employees also posted comments for the formulation of common values that could bring the company together. As Palmisano recalls:

> IBMers by the tens of thousands weighed in. They were thoughtful and passionate about the company they want to be a part of. They were also brutally honest. Some of what they wrote was painful to read, because they pointed out all the bureaucratic and dysfunctional things that get in the way of serving clients, working as a team or implementing new ideas. But we were resolute in keeping the dialog free-flowing and candid. And I don't think what resulted – broad, enthusiastic, grass-roots consensus – could have been obtained in any other way.

At the end of the online session, the executives collated and analysed the comments, which led to an announcement in November 2003 of the new company values. These were 'dedication to every client's success', 'innovation that matters – for our company and the world', and 'trust and personal responsibility in all our relationships'. When these values were posted on the intranet as 'our values at work', more than 200,000 IBMers viewed it within a few weeks and employee responses indicated that there was strong support for the three chosen values.

In October 2004, IBM held a second values-related online discussion, this time on the practical issues involved in the implementation of the values. Many ideas for how this could be done were posted by employees. After this session, Palmisano announced with his trademark clarity a range of initiatives, both internal and external, that would help in realizing the hard work of living these values. These initiatives included efforts to overhaul corporate programmes, align performance management and compensation with the values, invigorate training, and support individuals in forming innovation-driven communities of practice.

Once the key values had been identified, Palmisano and his communication executives also recrafted the IBM story in the image of these values. The IBM story details how IBM and its predecessor companies have always been infused by human values, focused on developing innovations that matter to the world and that support progress, and defined by the best customer service. While these values may not have been more or less prominent at various stages in the company's history, the IBM story suggests that they have always been there at a deeper level. As such, they can also act as a guide to the future direction of the company.

(Continued)

(Continued)

Communities of practice

Besides this value-driven initiative, Palmisano also recognized the importance of communities of practice within IBM. These communities consist of informally connected groups of employees who discuss, often in an online setting, different areas of expertise. Although they are formed informally, the company supports them through software tools that facilitate the interaction of employees across the globe. Communities of practice within the organization were initially started in 1995, with informal networks of professionals managing domains of knowledge around IBM's technological competencies (such as enterprise systems management, application development, testing methods and practices), marketing competencies (such as e-business, package integration, mergers and acquisitions) and industry sector competencies (such as automotive, chemicals and petroleum, distribution, finance and insurance, and health care). In 2000, there were over 60 unique communities of practice and about 76,000 professionals who participated through a web-based software (ICM asset web), connecting individuals into different communities. These professionals were also supported through an information portal that allowed them direct access to different IBM data sources.

Within these communities, professionals handle knowledge in the above domains as well as intellectual capital. They gather, evaluate, structure and disseminate knowledge that is shared among community peers and across customer projects and they also manage related intellectual capital, consisting of methods, processes, tools, assets, reported experiences, and any other documentation associated with delivering services and considered of value by the business or community. All of these communities evolve with some assistance from the corporate organization. While they are self-managing, they tend to seek support from the organization, usually to obtain some level of organizational recognition, support, and access to the common technology infrastructure.

Many of these communities, particularly ones that are fully formed, are characterized by a lot of development and learning within its boundaries with professionals working together to build and sustain the community as well as to solve business problems and exploit business opportunities. Indeed, professionals in such fully-formed communities often see it as their joint responsibility to pool knowledge and work together to address the business issues presented to it and create new products (new solutions, new offerings, new methods) in the process.

Recognizing the importance of these communities of practice, the company introduced the *On Demand Workplace* in 2003, an online technology which centralized the support for communities of practice and allowed employees across the globe to share and transfer knowledge. This online workplace helps employees to search for the profile of other IBMers, and also provides products and technologies that connect people and business processes.

These communities of practice, together with the value-based initiative, help bring IBMers together, creating stronger social connections between them and providing

(Continued)

(Continued)

a platform for collaboration and innovation. They are thus a central part of the company's market-driven strategy. Palmisano explains: 'If three fifths of your business is manufacturing, management is basically supervisory ... but that no longer works when your business is primarily based on knowledge'. Instead, he argues: 'If you are going to build a business based on continual innovation and new intellectual capital, you are signing up for total dependence on the creativity and adaptive skills of your workforce.'

Hence, common values and communities of practice that cut across divisions, departments and levels are key to developing innovative solutions for clients. Again, in the words of Palmisano: 'How else can we get our people in far-flung business units with different financial targets and incentives working together in teams that can offer at a single price a comprehensive and customized solution – one that doesn't show the organizational seams?'

QUESTIONS FOR REFLECTION

1   Reflect upon internal communication within IBM from the perspective of employees. How can communication with staff be characterized in terms of upward and downward communication and in terms of employee participation and voice?
2   IBM has supported the development of communities of practice within their organization. Would you expect such communities to be equally useful in other organizations and industry sectors that are to a lesser extent focused on constant innovation?

Source: This case study is based on Weeks, J. and Barsoux, J. (2010) IBM: *The value of values*. IMD case study; and on Kanter, R. and Bird, M. (2009) *IBM in the 21st century: The coming of the globally integrated enterprise*. Harvard Business School Case Study.

CHAPTER SUMMARY

9.6 The chapter started by defining the importance of internal communication in terms of its impact on employee commitment, morale and organizational identification. One important message in the chapter has been the importance of combining downward and upward communication between management and employees in such a way that employees feel valued, feel that they are listened to and feel that they can speak up about organizational decisions, practices and relationships with their colleagues. Besides upward and downward communication, organizations may also support employees with digital communication platforms for setting up communities of practice to support learning and innovation.

DISCUSSION QUESTIONS

1 Describe in your own words how, in an ideal scenario, communication flows between managers and employees in an organization.

2 Social media and new work-based technologies are changing internal communication. How in your view can these media and technologies be used to improve learning and innovation as well as cohesion among employees?

KEY TERMS

Communication climate

Communities of practice

Corporate information and communication systems

Downward communication

Employee participation

Employee voice

Management communication

Organizational identification

Organizational silence

Prestige

Social media

Upward communication

FURTHER READING

Birkinshaw, Julian (2010), *Reinventing Management: Smarter Choices for Getting Work Done*. New York: John Wiley and Sons.

Cheney, George, Christensen, Lars Thøger, Zorn, Ted and Ganesh, Shiv (2004), *Organizational Communication in an Age of Globalization: Issues, Reflections, Practices*. Prospect Heights, IL: Waveland Press.

NOTES

1 See, for example, Hales, C.P. (1986), 'What do managers do? A critical examination of the evidence', *Journal of Management Studies*, 23: 88–115; Tengblad, S. (2006), 'Is there a "new managerial work"? A comparison with Henry Mintzberg's classic study 30 years later', *Journal of Management Studies*, 43: 1437–1461.

2 Andrews, P.H. and Herschel, R.T. (1996), *Organizational Communication: Empowerment in a Technological Society*. Boston, MA: Houghton Mifflin Company.

3 See, for example, Dutton, J.E., Dukerich, J.M. and Harquail, C.V. (1994), 'Organizational images and member identification', *Administrative Science Quarterly*, 39: 239–263.

4 Mael, F.A. and Ashforth, B.E. (1992), 'Alumni and their *alma mater*: a partial test of the reformulated model of organizational identification', *Journal of Organizational Behavior*, 13: 103–123, quote on p. 104.

5 Dutton, et al. (1994); Smidts, A., Pruyn, A.T.H. and Van Riel, C.B.M. (2001), 'The impact of employee communication and perceived external prestige on organizational identification', *Academy of Management Journal*, 44: 1051–1062.

6 Smidts et al. (2001); Bartels, J. (2006), 'Organizational identification and communication: employees' evaluations of internal communication and its effect on identification at different organizational levels', PhD dissertation, University of Twente, Enschede, The Netherlands.

7 Christensen, L.T., Cornelissen, J.P. and Morsing, M. (2007), 'Corporate communications and its reception: a comment on Llewellyn and Harrison', *Human Relations*, 60: 653–661.

8 De Vita, E. (2007), 'John Lewis: partners on board', *Management Team*, August: 44–47.

9 Morrison, E.W. and Milliken, F.J. (2000), 'Organizational silence: a barrier to change and development a pluralistic world', *Academy of Management Review*, 25: 706–725.

10 See, for example, Conrad, C. and Scott Poole, M. (2002), *Strategic Organizational Communication in a Global Economy*. Fort Worth, TX: Harcourt.

11 Lave, J. and Wenger, E. (1991), *Situated Learning: Legitimate Peripheral Participation*. Cambridge: Cambridge University Press.

12 Wenger, E. (1998), 'Communities of practice: learning as a social system', *Systems Thinker* (http://www.co-i-l.com/coil/knowledge-gardern/cop/css.shtml).

ISSUES MANAGEMENT AND PUBLIC AFFAIRS

10

Chapter Overview

Public issues of concern and government regulation directly affect corporate activities. Issues management is an increasingly important function within corporate communication. For communication practitioners, it is important that they understand how issues evolve and may affect their organizations and know how best to respond through different communication strategies. The chapter discusses principles of issues management, ranging from reactive communication strategies to proactive advocacy to influence public policy and government regulation.

INTRODUCTION

10.1 Issues management is a rapidly growing subfunction within corporate communication. It has grown partly as a result of many high-profile public issues that have emerged in recent years. While such issues have always existed within the public domain, the past decade has been particularly taxing on business leaders. The turn towards a so-called 'risk society' has led to an emphasis on health and safety, environmental concerns, security and terrorism, and financial risk and regulation.[1] All of these issues are to a greater or lesser extent alive in the public mind. Indeed, the general public often expects a corporate response on these issues. Corporate organizations therefore increasingly realize that instead of fighting public opinion, a more effective approach is to advocate its own positions to the public and to key political decision-makers. Organizations have begun investing in issues management programmes, including corporate advertising campaigns, well-crafted lobbying and negotiation tactics. By being knowledgeable about issues and government regulation and by getting involved in the development of public policy, corporate

organizations are better able to protect themselves from potentially damaging regulations while taking advantage of any positive opportunities that government regulation
creates. In this chapter, we describe the scope and principles of issues management.
Before outlining these principles in greater detail, we begin with a brief introduction
to the topic.

DEFINING ISSUES

10.2 An issue can negatively affect the reputation of the organization. A fraud
allegation, for example, may damage a company's reputation as a financially solid and reliable investment target. Similarly, a product recall may lead to
public concern about the safety and reliability of a company's products. Strictly
speaking, an issue can be defined as: (1) a public concern about the organization's
decision and operations, which may or may not also involve (2) a point of conflict in
opinions and judgements regarding those decisions and operations. For example,
when Mattel recalled millions of toys in 2007 because of dangerously high levels of
chemicals and toxins, the recall became an issue of public concern about the safety of
the company's supply chain and manufacturing in China. Mattel, however, acknowledged the problem. As a result there was no difference of opinion between customers
and members of the general public about the severity of the issue and about the
necessity of a product recall.

In many instances, before issues become connected to an organization and before
activists, the public or stakeholders campaign for a specific organization to change,
such issues already exist within society and are often a matter of concern in public
debates. For example, in many contemporary societies, healthy eating and obesity
were already issues of public concern before they became connected to organizations such as Coca-Cola and McDonald's. Similarly, there has been an ongoing concern about executive pay and remuneration in many Western societies which has
often led to direct action against large corporations. When in 2009 shareholders of
Shell voted against a payment plan that would include financial bonuses for the
company's top executives, they acted upon a 'mood' against 'fat cat pay' and 'per-
formance-related pay' that was already present in investment circles and the wider
public domain.

Howard Chase, a well-known expert on issues management, defines an issue as 'an
unsettled matter which is ready for a decision'.[2] Chase emphasizes that an issue often
involves a point or matter in contention between an organization and another party,
and often requires decisive action on the part of the organization in order to protect
its reputation. He also suggests that issues and crises are closely related as an issue
may develop into a crisis.

A *crisis* is defined as an issue that requires not just decisive action but also immediate action from the organization. The necessity of immediate action may be triggered
by, for example, mounting public pressures, intense media attention or because of the
direct danger (in case of an accident, product tampering or faulty products) to employees, customers or members of the general public. The organization theorist Karl Weick
defines a crisis as a critical and intense issue that threatens the very existence of an

organization in terms of its basic assumptions, values and ways of operating.[3] For example, when Shell attempted to dispose of the Brent Spar oil rig in the North Sea, its actions led to a public boycott and to legislation that not only damaged its reputation, but also challenged the company to change its basic assumptions and values regarding the environmental impact of its business (see Case Study 10.2).

A useful way of thinking about the distinction between issues and crises is to consider the process of how issues develop over time. Figure 10.1 displays how issues emerge and how they may become more salient and potent as a result of media attention and greater public concern. As indicated on the left in the figure, there are many 'latent' issues that may become 'active' because of media attention or because of a coalition of stakeholders mobilizing themselves in relation to the issue. At this stage, it is important for organizations to monitor and scan the environment for shifts in public opinion on latent issues that stakeholders may connect with the organization and its industry. AstraZeneca, for example, continuously monitors opinions around the world towards animal testing for medical purposes. This issue of animal testing is seen as 'latent' or dormant because of the generally positive attitude towards responsible animal testing in the developed world. In addition, many governments often side with pharmaceutical companies against extreme acts of aggression by some animal rights activist groups. However, there is always the potential for the 'latent' issue to evolve into an 'active' issue when opinions towards animal testing change. When that happens, the issue becomes salient in the public domain. The media often play a crucial role in this process of making issues 'active'. The media may magnify interest in the issue through news coverage or may be the party that brought the issue up in the first place.

After an issue has become 'active', it may develop into an 'intense' issue that increases the pressure on an organization to do something about it. An 'intense' issue

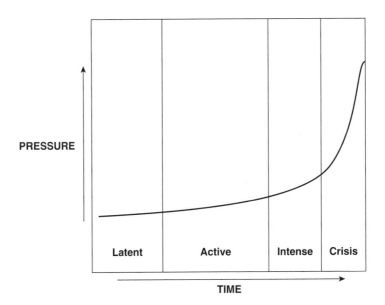

FIGURE 10.1 The development of an issue into a crisis

is very closely related to a 'crisis' that dominates the organization's agenda and requires immediate action. An example may illustrate the distinction between 'intense' issues and 'crises' (see Case Example 10.1).

Case Example 10.1

How an issue may evolve into a crisis

In March 2005, a leak of nuclear material was detected in one of the plants of British Nuclear Fuels (BNFL). The leak involved highly radioactive nuclear fuel dissolved in concentrated nitric acid and about 20 tons of uranium and plutonium fuel. As the leak was contained within the plant, it was not of any direct danger to the public. The company therefore decided that the leak had very little newsworthiness to the general public. BNFL had started an investigation into the cause(s) of the leak and only informed local residents and local media of the leak. As far as the company was concerned, it was a 'latent' issue of little concern to the general public. However, the issue became 'active' when *The Guardian* newspaper published a front-page article in May 2005 on the leak and questioned the company's ability to process nuclear fuel in a safe and secure way. The issue subsequently intensified when it transpired that BNFL had already been warned by the European Commission (EC) that it was in breach of EU rules and was urged to tighten controls to ensure that nuclear materials 'are not diverted from the peaceful uses for which they have been declared'. The warning had followed EC inspections of the plant, which had led inspectors to conclude that 'accounting and reporting procedures presently in place do not fully meet Euratom (EU) standards'.[4] The already 'intense' issue became a 'crisis' of legitimacy for BNFL when the media broke the news on the 'culture' in the plant, which had led to staff ignoring more than 100 warnings over six months that the plant had sprung a catastrophic leak. The crisis thus consisted of a direct challenge from the media and the government to the company's very existence as a safe and reliable operator of nuclear energy. BNFL came under direct and intense pressure to respond to the challenge by putting new safety procedures in place, by recovering the leaked material and by retraining staff in the nuclear plant.

Source: Brown, P. (2005) Huge radioactive leak closes Thorp nuclear plant, 9 May 2005, *The Guardian*.

MANAGING ISSUES

10.3
The aim of this section is to present guidelines for the management of issues so that 'latent' and 'active' issues do not morph into 'intense' issues or a crisis. Although it may not be always possible to completely 'manage' issues, as communication practitioners cannot always foresee or control how an issue evolves,

it is important that professionals are prepared and have communication strategies in place. The starting point of issues management involves scanning and monitoring the environment and detecting potential and actual issues. Environmental scanning and an analysis of the issue form the basis for deciding on an appropriate issue response strategy. The entire process of managing issues consists of the following stages: (1) environmental scanning; (2) issue identification and analysis; (3) issue-specific response strategies; and (4) evaluation.

Environmental scanning

All organizations exist in the context of a complex commercial, economic, political, technological, social and cultural world. This environment changes and is more complex for some organizations than for others. How this affects the organization can include an understanding of historical and environmental effects as well as expected or potential changes in environmental variables. This is a major task for communication practitioners because the range of variables is so great. Many of those variables will give rise to *opportunities* and others will exert *threats* on the organization. Whether environmental forces have such an impact on the organization depends furthermore on how the organization itself, in terms of the *strengths* and *weaknesses* in its values, resources and competencies, can respond to them. A problem that has to be faced is that the range of variables is likely to be so great that it may not be possible or realistic to identify and analyse each one. Thus, there is a need to distil a view of the main or overarching environmental impacts on the organization. Two analytical tools can be used for this: DESTEP analysis and SWOT analysis.

A DESTEP analysis is a broad analysis of the various *d*emographic, *e*conomic, *s*ocial, *t*echnological, *e*cological and *p*olitical developments and factors that are expected to have an impact upon the organization and its operations. This includes a summation of factors such as government regulations (political) that affect the industry in which the organization operates, changing societal attitudes towards certain industries and increasing demand for 'corporate citizenship' (social), and the effects of an economic slump and recession for the organization's supply and pricing strategies (economic). The DESTEP analysis provides a framework for summarizing and prioritizing all these factors. Through such a guided analysis of the environment, practitioners are able to describe the most important current environmental changes and to predict future ones.

A SWOT analysis stands for an investigation of the *s*trengths, *w*eaknesses, *o*pportunities and *t*hreats. The first half of this analysis – strengths and weaknesses – examines the company's position, its capabilities, operations and products *vis-à-vis* stakeholders, competitor activities, environmental trends and company resources. The second half of the SWOT takes this review further to examine the opportunities and threats identified within the environment, including, for instance, market opportunities, political regulation and shareholder activism. The result of the SWOT analysis should be a thorough understanding of the organization's status, of its standing with important groups in its environment and of the factors in the environment that may impinge upon it. A SWOT analysis should be carried out in an objective and detailed manner, with evidence provided to support the points cited.

Together, these two analytical tools can help practitioners identify trends and detect potential issues in relation to the organization's operations and in relation to important stakeholder groups.

Issue identification and analysis

Through environmental scanning, communication practitioners will identify potential and emerging issues that they need to keep an eye on. A number of these emerging issues may become active. Once they become active, they will have to be further analysed. The aim of issue analysis is to determine the present intensity of the issue in the public domain: how likely is it to trigger government action or impact on public opinion?; what is the likelihood of the issue continuing?; can the organization influence its resolution?; and which key stakeholder groups and publics are involved with the issue? 'Active' issues may concern stakeholders of the organization but also publics (e.g., activist groups) that the organization would not count as legitimate stakeholders but who nonetheless have mobilized themselves in relation to the issue and against the organization.

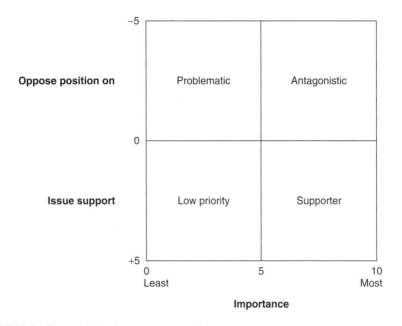

FIGURE 10.2 The position–importance matrix

A useful device for analysing stakeholder and public opinions on a particular issue is the position–importance matrix (Figure 10.2). The position–importance matrix is very similar to the power–interest matrix (Figure 3.4) but is less concerned with the general salience or interests of stakeholders and is specifically concerned with the position of a stakeholder or public in relation to a particular issue. Stakeholders and publics are categorized in the matrix according to their position on a particular issue and according to their importance to the organization. Relevant stakeholders and publics are identified on the vertical axis and assessed in terms of whether they oppose the organization on the issue or support it. A numerical value of 0 to −5 is assigned to those stakeholders and publics opposing the issue and a value of 0 to +5 to those supporting it. The importance of stakeholders and publics to the organization and towards an effective resolution of the issue is measured on a horizontal axis and varies from a value of 0 (least important) to a value of 10 (most important). After stakeholders and publics are positioned on the two values, the location of the stakeholders and publics in the matrix is plotted. As displayed in Figure 10.2, four categories of stakeholders and publics result from this analysis:[5]

1 *Problematic stakeholders/publics*: Those stakeholders or publics who are likely to oppose or be hostile to the organization's course of action, but are relatively unimportant to the organization because they are not normally recognized as important stakeholders or publics and have little power to exert strong pressure on the organization.

2 *Antagonistic stakeholders/publics*: Those stakeholders or publics who are likely to oppose or be hostile to the organization's course of action and hold power or influence over the organization.

3 *Low priority stakeholders/publics*: Those stakeholders or publics who are likely to support the organization's course of action but are relatively unimportant in terms of their power or influence on the organization.

4 *Supporter stakeholders/publics*: Those stakeholders or publics who are likely to support the organization's course of action and are important to the organization in terms of their power or influence.

After the analysis and categorization are completed, the idea is that communication practitioners can work out communication strategies to most appropriately deal with each stakeholder or public. For example, practitioners may use educational programmes with 'problematic' stakeholders and publics to change their opinions on an issue and may prepare defensive statements or crisis plans in case problematic stakeholders and publics form a coalition and together voice their discontent about the organization. Strategies for 'antagonistic' stakeholders or publics typically involve anticipating the nature of their objections and developing and communicating counter-arguments as well as bargaining with selected stakeholders or publics to win their support. Strategies for 'low priority' stakeholders or publics often consist of educational programmes and promoting the company's involvement with these supporting stakeholders while strategies for 'supporter' stakeholders or publics often involve providing information to reinforce their position and possibly asking them to influence indifferent stakeholders.[7]

Besides analysing the opinions of stakeholders and publics on a particular issue, it is also important for communication practitioners to identify the current 'stage' of an issue. For example, it will be useful to know whether an issue can be classified as 'active' or 'intense', based on the amount of public debate about the issue and the pressure upon an organization to do something about it. The issues expert M.C. Healey provides a useful framework of the 'life cycle' of an issue (Figure 10.3) which consists of four stages: (1) emergence; (2) debate; (3) codification; and (4) enforcement.[7]

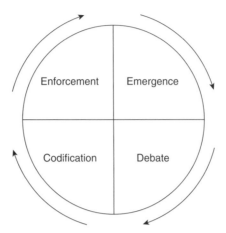

FIGURE 10.3   The life cycle of an issue

The basic idea behind the framework is that it is important for organizations to detect issues when they first 'emerge' and to engage publicly in the 'debate' on the issue. In doing so, organizations may be able to influence opinions in a favourable direction before the issue becomes 'codified' or defined within the public domain and 'enforced' through government legislation, industrial action or consumer boycotts. For example, when Greenpeace first tabled the issue of Shell's disposal of the Brent Spar oil rig in the North Sea, Shell ignored the *emerging* issue and defended the disposal decision as 'business as usual' and as the 'best option with the least environmental damage'. The scientific evidence behind the decision convinced Shell that the company did not need to engage in any *debate* about the issue and explain its decision to the general public. The result was that Greenpeace's framing of the issue as an 'ecological disaster' and 'toxic dump' came to define how the general public viewed the issue (*codification*), a view that was subsequently enforced through consumer boycotts and political action by many European governments (*enforcement*) (see Case Study 10.2). The general principle that arises from the framework is that organizations need to detect issues early on because only in the early stages of 'emergence' and 'debate' can stakeholder or public opinions on an issue be influenced.

Issue-specific response strategies

The analysis of an issue provides the basis for identifying an appropriate response. The repertoire of issue–response strategies involves the following three options: (1) a buffering strategy; (2) a bridging strategy; and (3) an advocacy strategy. The choice of any one of these three options is based upon the 'intensity' of the issue, the importance of the issue to the organization's stakeholder groups, values and beliefs of managers in an organization, and costs.

   1   Buffering strategy: This is essentially an attempt to 'stonewall the issue' and delay its development. Organizations attempt to continue with their existing behaviour by postponing decisions or by remaining silent. Buffering involves trying to keep claims from stakeholders or publics in the environment from interfering with internal operations. A good example of buffering involves Exxon Mobil's initial attempt to remain silent on the issue of climate change and avoid organizational ownership of the issue.

2 Bridging strategy: This involves organizations being open to change and recognizing the issue and its inevitability. Bridging occurs when organizations seek to adapt organizational activities so that they conform to external expectations of important stakeholders and publics. In response to those expectations, organizations attempt to find a way to accommodate them within the organization's plans and operations. For example, both BP and Shell have emphasized their investments in alternative energy to respond to stakeholder expectations. Both organizations are also trying to be more transparent in reporting progress on their environmental performance and actively engage in a dialogue with their stakeholders about environmental issues and expectations.

3 Advocacy strategy: This is an attempt to try to change stakeholder expectations and public opinions on an issue through issue campaigns and lobbying. Organizations do not directly 'stonewall' an issue (buffering) or adapt to external expectations (bridging), but use campaigning and lobbying to alter stakeholder opinions and expectations on an issue, and often in such a way that these conform to the organization's present practices, output and values.[8] The aim is to persuade external stakeholders and publics that the organization's position on an otherwise controversial issue is both rationally acceptable and morally legitimate. For example, Exxon Mobil has lobbied governments on climate change and has sponsored think-thank and campaigning organizations that have directly or indirectly taken money from the company. These organizations take a consistent line on climate change: that the science is contradictory, that scientists are split and that if governments took action to prevent global warming they would be endangering the global economy for no good reason. In other words, Exxon Mobil has lobbied and campaigned to sow doubt about whether serious action needs to be taken on climate change.[9] In doing so, the company attempts to change public opinion on climate change and on the necessity of the company having to take direct action to curb carbon emissions.

Broadly speaking, organizations can choose between these three strategy options. BP and Shell both 'bridged' on the issue of climate change and their own environmental impact because of mounting public pressure and because their own stakeholders were calling for change. Exxon Mobil, on the other hand, has not bridged on this particular issue, because the company's dominant coalition of senior managers and shareholders dispute the evidence on climate change and feel that an environmental stance would be in conflict with the company's economic principles. To choose any of these strategies determines how the organization communicates about the issue. For example, with a buffering strategy, organizations often communicate very little publicly on the issue but may issue defensive statements to the media that defend the company's policy or stance on a particular issue. A bridging strategy often involves extensive communication in the form of a corporate advertising campaign on the issue, dialogue forums with stakeholders and the publication of progress on the issue. An advocacy strategy will typically consist of lobbying and campaigning on the issue. This may involve sponsorship of campaigning organizations or NGOs, a mass-media corporate issue campaign and face-to-face presentations to key opinion leaders on the issue.

The way in which organizations communicate about issues, from either a buffering, bridging or advocacy angle, involves specific acts of framing. Issue framing refers to the purposeful efforts that communication practitioners take, while communicating, to shape the frames of interpretation of stakeholders or publics. The underlying process by which frames are evoked in a text (speech, campaign, report) involves choices of selection and salience whereby some aspects of a perceived reality are selected and made more salient in a communicating text, in such a way as to promote a particular problem definition, causal interpretation, moral evaluation, and/or treatment recommendation. Shell framed the Brent Spar issue as a sensible and legitimate 'business decision', supported by the UK government and scientific studies. Communication professionals defended the decision to the media and the general public and were told by senior executives to treat the situation as 'business as usual'. Greenpeace, on the other hand, framed the same event as a 'toxic time bomb' and as an 'environmental disaster' (see Case Study 10.2). Typically, by selecting particular salient points, frames organize or hold together certain ideas that the organization wants to communicate, diagnosing a situation and prescribing a course of action. This organizing function is often based on an "underlying logic" that manifests itself in stock phrases, keywords or metaphors that signify the larger frame and "that [together] provide thematically reinforcing clusters of facts or judgments".[10]

Frames also presuppose culturally familiar categories of understanding. Indeed, prototypical cultural phenomena may function as the central organizing theme or underlying logic of a frame, including cultural archetypes (e.g., heroes or victims), myths or mythical figures (e.g., David versus Goliath in Brent Spar), and ideologies or values (e.g., freedom of speech, environmental care). The invoked cultural frame may also to a greater or less extent be understood by stakeholders and considered as salient or 'taken for granted' in relation to a specific issue. Case Study 10.1 illustrates the framing debates that are often involved in publicly important corporate issues.

CASE STUDY 10.1

THE FRAMING OF BONUS PAYMENTS AFTER THE CREDIT CRISIS

An interesting example of the framing debate is the issue of bonus payments in banks after the global financial crisis from 2007–2010. Billions of taxpayers' money was used to bail out many banks, supplying them with credit in the wake of the collapse of a global housing bubble, which brought about a shortage of credit and a decline in trade. Governments around the world have since been developing

(Continued)

(Continued)

schemes and legislation to create better oversight and more stringent regulation of the banking sector. In an open letter in the *Wall Street Journal* on 9 December 2009, Gordon Brown, the Prime Minister of the UK, and the French President Nicolas Sarkozy argued that:

> a huge and opaque global trading network involving complex products, short-termism and too-often excessive rewards created risks that few people understood. We have also learned that when crises happen, taxpayers have to cover the costs. It is simply not acceptable for them to foot the bill for losses in a deep downturn, while institutions' shareholders and employees enjoy all the gains as the economy recovers.

Both men argued for stricter regulation that would ensure that compensation systems, and bonus payments in particular, limit the kind of excessive risk-taking that was partly to blame for the financial crisis. In line with this view, the UK government announced a plan in December 2009 to tax bankers' bonus payments. The rationale for this was framed as being in the public interest. Besides recouping some of the investments made by taxpayers, it would also demotivate or curb excessive risk-taking associated with the bonus culture.

However, executives of banks in the UK, including ones that benefited from the government bail-out, condemned the plans. On behalf of the British Bankers' Association (BBA), Angela Knight pointed out that the banking industry generated significant jobs and taxes for the UK. She was concerned that London's reputation as a financial capital could be damaged and that it might lead to an exodus of companies: 'We need to think about the message this will send outside the UK about Britain being a place to do business in'. Her main point was that banking is a viable industry that already does its fair share for the UK economy. She also questioned the practical consequences of such a measure, something that was echoed by other bank executives.

The Board of the Royal Bank of Scotland, which is almost wholly owned by the British taxpayer, for example, threatened to resign *en masse* if the Treasury of the UK government blocked bonus payments. Other executives have suggested that governments, even when they are a shareholder, should not interfere in remuneration decisions that are market-driven. Lloyd Blankfein, the CEO of Goldman Sachs, feels strongly that his people must be rewarded for their efforts and skills. John Varley, CEO of Barclays, has drawn the analogy with premiership football – he has to pay superstar salaries to his best staff because otherwise they may go and work for the competition.

The debate about bonus payments, as commercially crucial and legitimate rewards or as incentives to excessive risk taking, still rages on. While no one would deny that exceptional effort, creativity or hard work deserves an exceptional payment, the difficulty with bank bonuses may be that they are not necessarily associated with exceptional effort or ingenuity, nor do such payments always translate into long-term social and economic benefits. A recent paper by two economists, Thomas Philippon and Ariell Reshef (NBER working paper 14644) demonstrates that since the 1980s bankers' pay has risen by 80 per cent compared with the average wage. Only half of

(Continued)

(Continued)

that rise, they argue, can remotely be justified by the increasing complexity and skills needed for modern-day banking, which in turn makes the average job in banking 40 per cent overpaid. A key issue in this respect is that the very system or market for talent and effort which bankers claim to be a part of is at least in part one of their own making: bankers transact with themselves for huge fees and commissions and, on the back of that, attribute bonus payments to themselves.

QUESTIONS FOR REFLECTION

1   How would you yourself frame the issue of bankers' pay? What kind of conceptualization or ideology does this presuppose?
2   Generally speaking, is it possible to combine frames around market competition and fairness and equality?

Source: This case study is informed by Brown, G. and Sarkozy, N. (2009) 'For Global Finance, Global Regulation', *Wall Street Journal*, 9 December 2009; Judge, E. (2009) 'Bankers hit back at "populist" bonus supertax', *The Times*, 7 December 2009 (quote from Angela Knight); and Philippon, T. and Reshef, A. (2009) 'Wages and Human Capital in the US Financial Industry: 1909–2006'. *NBER Working Paper* No. 14644. January 2009.

Evaluation

The final stage of the issues management process involves an evaluation of how the issue has developed and how stakeholder expectations and public opinions have changed. First, it is important for organizations to know what the 'stage' of the issue is and whether there is still an opportunity to influence public debate on the issue in question. In addition, depending on the strategy chosen by an organization, communication practitioners need to evaluate the success of their buffering, bridging or advocacy strategy. They need to find out whether and how stakeholder expectations and public opinions have changed, whether their activities contributed to a change in public opinion on the issue and whether the organization's response strategy has been appreciated by stakeholders and the general public.

INFLUENCING PUBLIC POLICY

10.4 One important part of issues management involves influencing public policy formation. Such influence may be indirect, through advocating a certain framing of an issue that may in turn influence government, or direct, through lobbying, political action committees and industry coalitions. In 2003, for example,

Fannie Mae, a mortgage provider in the USA, spent $87 million on an advertising campaign to help curtail the US Congress's efforts to create a more stringent regulator to oversee its operations and to have the authority to alter its capital standards. Together with direct lobbying, its efforts paid off and the legislation was never passed. While the company had successfully campaigned and lobbied, the lack of stringent oversight led to accounting problems that had a big role in the 2007 crisis. Eventually, Fannie Mae was bailed out by the US government, in order to secure loans to home-owners.

Investments in commercial lobbying and representation through political action committees and coalitions have grown significantly in recent years. Shaping or influencing government and public policy in this way is commonplace. The relevance of such activities stems from the fact that there is hardly an item of legislation which does not in some way encroach upon business interests or impinges on organizational goals. A former Secretary to the Treasury in the UK government, Michael Portillo, observed that political lobbyists are 'as necessary to the political process as a thoroughly efficient sewage system is to any city'.[11] Despite its connotation, the analogy suggests that lobbying is not necessarily about 'spin doctoring', or indeed unethical or against the public interest. Instead, lobbying is a crucial part of the public policy process. Generally speaking, there are two competing views on the legitimacy of the corporate lobbying of government. There is the view that lobbyists, and the corporate organizations they work for, abuse the democratic system for their own selfish interests and that the growth in the industry, particularly in the use of political consultants, requires the imposition of greater controls over lobbying activities. The alternative position is that lobbying is genuinely an intrinsic part of the democratic process because it can create a counterbalance to potentially ill-informed or badly thought out policy decisions. Furthermore, it can be argued that government, including civil servants, actually depend on lobbyists for information and advice.

Besides direct lobbying, organizations also use political action committees and industry coalitions, and grass-roots campaigning to influence government legislation. Together, these four tools are considered as the main techniques for influencing government and public policy. *Lobbying* involves an individual (a lobbyist), designated by an organization or interest group, to facilitate influencing public policy in that organization's or interest group's favour. Lobbying is typically done through directly contacting government officials. *Political action committees* (PACs) represent a fund for political donations made up of money from an organization's members or employees. The donations go to candidates and legislators who demonstrate favourable perspectives or behaviours towards an organization's public policy goals. In principle, PACs are a means for organizations to support public policy in a way that agrees with their own political and legislative beliefs. In practice, many organizations use PACs to obtain access to government officials and to pursue their own direct interests.

Industry coalitions are an alliance of organizations in the same industry who, through direct lobbying or donations, attempt to have a voice in the policy formation process. Many coalitions are permanent, with representatives located in political centres such as Washington, Beijing and Brussels. While coalitions often adopt names and frame their mission in terms of the public interest, they may often be led and financed by narrow interests. For example, The National Wetlands Coalition in the

USA, contrary to what its name may suggest, comprises oil drillers, land developers and major gas corporations. Other coalitions may be more straightforward representations of an industry, such as the British Bankers' Association (BBA), mentioned in Case Study 10.1.

Finally, *grass-roots campaigning* involves organizations engaging with members of its own group and/or others with a stake in an issue to persuade legislators to support its public policy goals. Because legislators depend on voters in elections, constituent grass-roots input is a powerful tool to influence legislators. There are several varieties of grass-roots campaigning. Organizations, particularly public sector or not-for-profit organizations, may mobilize their own employees and/or association members. 'Third-party' grass-roots campaigning is a term used for engaging public groups that may be impacted by an issue. Organizations may, for example, mobilize community groups affected by pending legislation.

CASE STUDY 10.2

ISSUES MANAGEMENT IN SHELL

Shell is one of the first truly international corporations and has been one of the ten largest companies in the world for nearly a century. Historically, its regional operating units were the dominant elements in a decentralized management structure. The company is now more centrally controlled through a committee of managing directors and is organized globally into five lines of business: exploration and production, chemicals, gas and coal, renewable energy, and oil products.

Shell historically had a strong technical and engineering orientation in all its strategies and operations, and placed a strong emphasis on long-range planning based on the construction of competing 'scenarios' of major long-term market trends that would affect its economic status and market operations. By the late 1980s, top executives within Shell were particularly concerned about environmental issues and wished the corporation to be seen by the general public as more progressive and as making headway on these issues, rather than adopting a business-as-usual approach. They decided to use the scenarios approach as a way of communicating this aspiration to the rest of the organization. This became known as the 'sustainable world' scenario.

Initially, they were successful in influencing the organization's culture forcing every middle and top manager to think through how their investment proposals and projects would survive in an environmentally conscious world. However, the overall culture of the corporation was not significantly affected, as became clear in 1995 in the way in which Shell handled two environmental issues (the Brent Spar and Niger Delta). That year, Shell found itself in heated debates with a whole range of critics, including The Movement for the Survival of the Ogoni People, Greenpeace, the Sierra Club, Amnesty International, the German government and the media, over the environment and associated human rights. These debates were played out in a variety of public forums. These two issues resulted from public dismay around Shell UK's proposed action to dispose of Brent Spar, an enormous oil storage and

(Continued)

(Continued)

loading platform, in the waters of the North Sea, and Shell's failure to take a high-profile public stance against the Nigerian government, Shell's local business partner in Nigeria, when it executed nine environmentalists, including Ken Saro-Wiwa, an internationally acclaimed journalist and writer who had spearheaded protest against Shell's environmentally destructive operations in the Niger Delta.

Brent Spar and Greenpeace

The first environmental issue arose in May 1995 when Greenpeace occupied the Brent Spar. Greenpeace's aim was to mobilize resistance to Shell UK's plan to sink the installation in the North Sea. The Brent Spar had been decommissioned in 1991 as there was no longer any use for the installation platform. Shell had investigated the various options for disposing of the platform and had negotiated a deal with the British government to legally approve disposal of the Brent Spar in the North Sea. Shell spent over £1 million on environmental studies, which had concluded that deep-sea disposal was the 'best practical environmental option', with less harm to the environment than any other options, such as dismantling the platform on land. In October 1994, the British government approved the plan for deep-sea disposal. Greenpeace, however, opposed Shell's plans for a number of reasons. They disputed the environmental studies and argued that deep-sea sinking would release heavy metal, oils and radioactive material into the sea and would also set a precedent for other petroleum companies to do the same. To voice its concerns, Greenpeace then decided to occupy the Brent Spar before the platform was dismantled and sunk.

Shell's strategic planners and communication staff had contemplated a number of worst-case scenarios, including challenges from environmental groups, but no response plans had been formulated. Shell was focused on ensuring that the process of disposal would go ahead and decided to respond first with a series of civil court cases for trespassing. Shell got a court order to forcibly remove the people occupying the Brent Spar. But while Shell won the battle to evict Greenpeace off the platform, it was losing ground in public opinion on the issue. Shell had decided to lie low and did not want to appear too defensive in the media. The company also felt that it had sound legal, economic and environmental support for its actions. The company had done all the necessary planning and research before the decision was taken.

Greenpeace, however, argued that harmful chemical residues and radioactive wastes remained in the Brent Spar's storage tanks. Greenpeace called it a 'toxic time bomb' and a platform 'laden with toxic cocktails'. It accused Shell of 'contempt for public concern about its operations, fishermen's livelihoods and for the health of the North Sea', and said that the company was hiding behind a 'veil of secrecy'.

In response, John Wybrew, Director of Public Affairs and Planning at Shell UK, defended the company's plan and actions, arguing that the 'case' for deepwater disposal had been 'sound'. From the company's perspective, deep-sea disposal represented the 'best practicable environmental option'. On the basis of cost–benefit analysis, Shell had concluded that sinking the Brent Spar would have 'negligible impacts on the marine environment, but the safety and occupational health risks

(Continued)

(Continued)

of injury during onshore disposal would be six times higher'. Wybrew said that 'painstaking analysis and over 30 studies' supported this assessment, and it had been 'endorsed by independent experts and oceanographers, and supported by environmentalists, conservationists, and fishermen during extensive consultations'. He criticized Greenpeace for relying on 'single-issue' campaigning, which freely exploited dramatic visual stunts, and accused them of being 'adept at packaging misinformation in ready-to-use word snips'.

Nonetheless, Greenpeace succeeded in turning the Brent Spar into a symbol of man's misuse of the oceans, irrespective of the reality. It aroused powerful emotions connected with 'litter-louting' on a grand scale, and astutely played the 'David versus Goliath' card. Such powerful emotions brought in its wake escalating violence (e.g., there were three violent attacks on Shell service stations in Germany and physical damage to others) and a widespread consumer boycott of Shell across Europe. Major media coverage and public protest, especially in continental Europe, eventually led several European heads of government to criticize Shell and the British government for backing the Shell proposal. Although at first rejecting criticism, by the end of June 1995 Shell agreed to change its plan. The Brent Spar was towed to Norway, where it was dismantled while stationed in a deep-sea fjord.

Nigeria and the Ogoni

The second major environmental issue for Shell emerged in relation to its operations in Nigeria. Shell has been operating in the Niger Delta since the 1930s and is by far the largest operator in the area, with an output of more than one million barrels a day. But the company's 90 oil and gas fields have suffered spills and sabotage, damaging the livelihood of farmers and fishermen and threatening half a million Ogoni people, who live in the Niger Delta. The Ogoni people have seen almost no return of Shell's revenues. Moreover, because of weak environmental regulation, these indigenous peoples, who live traditionally by fishing and farming, have suffered severe ecological and health impacts from oil spills. In Nigeria, much of the gas by-products from oil drilling were flared (i.e., burned off in the open air), which caused some of the worst local environmental pollution. Flaring is held responsible for acid rain in the Niger Delta, which is said to corrode roofs, pollute lakes and damage vegetation. Together oil spills and gas flaring have threatened the Niger Delta, which is one of the largest and most ecologically sensitive wetlands in the world.

In 1993, a non-violent protest organized by the Movement for the Survival of the Ogoni People (MOSOP) against Shell and other oil companies led Shell to withdraw its staff and close operations in that part of the Niger Delta where the Ogoni lived. The Nigerian government, as Shell's business partner, blamed the MOSOP leadership for local resistance. The government tried Ken Saro-Wiwa and others in a military tribunal. Nine Ogonis, including Saro-Wiwa, were executed on 10 November 1995.

From the early 1990s, Ogoni environmental activists and Delta tribal chiefs had documented the environmental degradation stemming from oil company activity. Their accounts were taken up in the African media and in the media around the world. Saro-Wiwa's high public profile within the worldwide environmental

(Continued)

(Continued)

movement forced a response from Shell. Shell expressed 'shock' and 'sadness' over Saro-Wiwa's death. However, in the first instance, Shell also tried to minimize and displace blame for both the political and ecological problems in Nigeria. Shell Nigeria released a briefing statement that was mainly argumentative and defensive in nature. Overall, Shell characterized itself as a victim, arguing that the company had been 'unfairly used to raise the international profile' of the MOSOP campaign against the Nigerian government. While the company acknowledged that there had been environmental problems, it downplayed the issue. Shell admitted that its facilities needed upgrading, but blamed sabotage rather than the corrosion of ageing pipes for the oil spills. It said that Ogoni claims of environmental 'devastation' were grossly exaggerated, citing conclusions of journalists who said that Shell's limited presence in the Delta area meant that the damage was only a tiny 'fraction' of that 'routinely claimed by campaigners'. Shell also cited a 1995 World Bank study that characterized the problem of oil pollution as 'only of moderate priority' in comparison to other poverty-related factors that contributed to environmental deterioration (i.e., population growth, deforestation, erosion and over-farming). It further relied on the World Bank study and a report by the World Health Organization to dispute the connection between gas-flaring and health. Thus, it claimed a lack of 'evidence' that such problems as asthma and skin rashes were due to its activities. Shell Nigeria also claimed that it had 'some influence' with the government but that applying 'force' was impossible: 'What force could we apply – leaving aside the question of whether it would be right for us to do so?' This mirrored the position of Shell Group Chairman at the time, Cor Herkströter, who defined Shell's role as strictly economic and commercial and said that the company lacked 'licence' to interfere in politics or the sovereign mandate of government.

Since the initial issue emerged in 1995, Shell has continued to remain under fire over its environmental record in Nigeria. In January 2007, advertisements calling on Shell to 'clean up its mess' appeared in *The Guardian* and the Dutch newspaper *De Volkskrant*. The adverts were signed and financially supported by more than 7,000 people worldwide in an effort to encourage Shell to live up to the aims of its corporate social responsibility (CSR) policies. Nnimmo Bassey, from Environmental Rights Action in Nigeria, said: 'Despite Shell's public commitment to CSR and specific promise it has made to communities, life on the fence line can too often be likened to hell. From Nigeria to Ireland, the Philippines to South Africa, Shell still too often fails to respect the environment or the needs of local communities.'

Shell's poor environmental record in Nigeria is given prominence in the adverts, which demand that the company pay US$10 billion to clean up oil spills and compensate communities in the Niger Delta. Environmental Rights Action, Friends of the Earth and others estimate that as much as 13 million barrels of oil have been spilled into the Niger Delta ecosystem over the past fifty years by Shell and its partners, an amount they say is 50 times more than that associated with the infamous *Exxon Valdez* tanker grounding off Alaska. 'The spills pollute the land and water of the communities. Drinking water is affected, people get sick, fish populations die and farmers lose their income because the soil of the land is destroyed.' Shell has since responded to the adverts and has stated that they 'neither reflect the realities

(Continued)

(Continued)

of the situation and the very real progress made, nor represent the views of the wider communities around these locations. Shell is committed to being a good neighbour and maintains productive relationships with many local communities and their representatives.'

Both the Brent Spar and Ogoni issues forced Shell to reflect upon its identity and effectively challenged the company's modernist, technical and rational way of approaching its operations. In one sense, these issues have moved the company from a taken-for-granted discourse of economic development towards a cautious adoption of the language of sustainable development, with attempts to balance the interests of economic development with environmental well-being. Shell has since adopted a stakeholder orientation in its business principles and has set up platforms for stakeholder engagement and dialogue. The company also publishes an annual report documenting its environmental and social progress and has made much of its focus on sustainable development and renewable forms of energy in recent advertising campaigns. Shell claims to 'listen' to all its stakeholders, who have explicitly told the company that 'a commitment to sustainable development is key to a company's reputation'.

QUESTIONS FOR REFLECTION

1 Describe the way in which these two environmental issues evolved into crises for Shell.
2 Discuss the way in which Shell identified and managed both issues. Should the company have opted for a different response?

Source: This case study is based upon Terry Macalister (2007) 'Campaigners urge Shell to put profits into clean-up', *The Guardian*, 31 January 2007; and Livesey, S.M. (2001) 'Eco-identity as discursive struggle: Royal Dutch/Shell, Brent Spar and Nigeria', *Journal of Business Communication*, 38: 58–91.

CHAPTER SUMMARY

10.5 Issues management is an increasingly important specialist discipline within corporate communication. Effectively, issues management starts with scanning the environment and with identifying latent and emerging issues even before they become salient in public debates and may potentially result in government legislation. However, when issues have become active and salient, it requires that communication practitioners decide on a response (buffering, bridging or advocacy) in line with the 'intensity' of the issue and its importance to the organization's stakeholder groups.

DISCUSSION QUESTIONS

1 Describe the life cycle of issues and how they may develop into active and intense issues for organizations.

2 Reflect upon the strategies of buffering, bridging and advocacy around issues. Using examples of organizations that you know, when is the one or the other strategy more appropriate? What generally determines the feasibility of each of these options?

 # KEY TERMS

Active issue

Advocacy

Bridging

Buffering

Crisis

DESTEP

Environmental scanning

Grass-roots campaigning

Industry coalitions

Intense issue

Issue

Latent issue

Lobbying

Political action committee

Public affairs

SWOT

 # FURTHER READING

Harris, Phil and Fleisher, Craig S. (2005), *The Handbook of Public Affairs*. London: Sage.
Heath, Robert L. and Palenchar, James Michael (2008), *Strategic Issues Management: Organizations and Public Policy Challenges* (2nd edn). London: Sage.

NOTES

1 Giddens, A. (1990), *Consequences of Modernity*. Cambridge: Polity Press; Beck, U. (1992), *Risk Society: Towards a New Modernity*. London: Sage.
2 Chase, W.H. (1984), *Issue Management: Origins of the Future*. Stamford, CT: Issue Action Publishers.

3   Weick, K.E. (1988), 'Enacted sensemaking in crisis situations', *Journal of Management Studies*, 25: 305–317.

4   European Commission, 'European Commission issues nuclear safeguard obligations warning to British Nuclear Group Sellafield', Brussels, 15 February 2006. (www.europa. eu/rapid/pressReleasesAction.do?reference=IP/06/171&format=HTML&aged=0&language=EN&guiLanguage=en).

5   Nutt, P.C. and Backoff, R.W. (1992), *Strategic Management of Public and Third Sector Organizations: A Handbook for Leaders*. San Francisco: Jossey-Bass, p. 191; Bryson, J.M. (1995), *Strategic Planning for Public and Nonprofit Organizations: A Guide to Strengthening and Sustaining Organizational Achievement* (rev. edn). San Francisco: Jossey-Bass, p. 284.

6   Nutt and Backoff (1992), pp. 196–198; Bryson (1995), pp. 285–286.

7   Healey, M.C. (1978), 'The dynamics of exploited lake trout populations and implications for management', *Journal of Wildlife Management*, 42: 307–328.

8   Dowling, J. and Pfeffer, J. (1975), 'Organizational legitimacy: social values and organizational behavior', *Pacific Sociological Review*, 18: 122–136; Heugens, P.M.A.R., Van Riel, C.B.M. and Van den Bosch, F.A.J. (2004), 'Reputation management capabilities as decision rules', *Journal of Management Studies*, 41: 1349–1377.

9   Monbiot, G. (2006), 'The denial industry', *The Guardian*, 19 September.

10   Entman, R.M. (1993), 'Framing: toward clarification of a fractured paradigm', *Journal of Communication*, 43 (4): 51–58, quote on p. 52.

11   *Marketing*, 16 February 1995, p. 16.

CRISIS COMMUNICATION

11

Chapter Overview

Crises have the potential to damage an organization's reputation and the relationships with its stakeholders. It is therefore important that organizations anticipate and plan for probable crisis scenarios and prepare crisis communication plans. Drawing on frameworks and principles from theory and practice, the chapter discusses how organizations can prepare and plan for crises and can identify appropriate communication strategies that match stakeholder expectations in relation to different crises.

INTRODUCTION

11.1 The current information age has created a challenging environment for many organizations. Because of modern communication and information technologies, people are increasingly aware of the issues and risks associated with organizations and their industries. These technologies also afford a way of voicing concerns and of dialoguing on these issues, providing a direct challenge to organizations and their attempts to manage health, safety and environmental risks. These risks and issues may form the bedrock for crises. The public concern around the safety of airlines and flying in the aftermath of the 9/11 attacks on the World Trade Center in New York, for example, led to a crisis for the airline industry and contributed to the bankruptcy of airlines such as Sabena and Swissair.

The objective of crisis management and crisis communication is to exert control, in so far as possible, over events and organizational activities in ways that reassure stakeholders that their interests are cared for and ensure that the organization complies with social, safety and environmental standards. Such control requires that organizations develop contingency plans to prepare for possible crises as well as communication plans to effectively respond to crisis scenarios when they emerge. While some crises can be prepared for in advance, organizations may be confronted by natural accidents or terrorist attacks that cannot be prevented or avoided. But being prepared is half the battle. The other half is about the skills in communicating effectively and responsibly, and about taking actions to contain the crisis and limit any negative consequences for stakeholders and for the company and its reputation.

This chapter defines crisis management, discusses crisis scenarios, and presents principles for effective crisis communication. Before we outline these communication principles in greater detail, the chapter starts with a brief introduction to crises and crisis management.

PREPARATION FOR CRISES

11.2
Broadly speaking, a *crisis* is defined as an event or issue that requires decisive and immediate action from the organization. The necessity of immediate action may be triggered by, for example, mounting public pressures, intense media attention or because of the direct danger (in case of an accident, product tampering or faulty products) to employees, customers or members of the general public. While organizations may not foresee every possible crisis that may affect them, they can develop crisis contingency plans in advance.

Communication practitioners have a role to play in working with others in the organization to identify probable crises and to develop contingency plans. Such identification may involve some kind of scenario planning and an organization-wide consultation of risks and issues surrounding company operations. Based on such planning and consultation, professionals and other executives can identify the most probable crisis scenarios (rather than wasting time working through solutions to problems that have a low probability of occurring) for which they can develop contingency plans.

Crisis experts Mitroff and Pearson highlight five different levels of contingency plans.[1] Stage 1 involves minimal planning around a few contingency plans drawn up for an emergency response. This may comprise a limited set of plans, such as evacuating a building during a fire or giving first aid to employees who suffer injury or sudden illness. Stage 2 involves more extensive planning but is limited to natural disasters and potential human errors. Planning at this stage entails measures for damage containment and business recovery. Stage 3 involves extensive contingency plans with crisis procedures for probable natural disasters and human errors and with training of personnel so that employees can implement these crisis procedures. Stage 4 is similar to Stage 3 but involves an organization-wide consultation of potential crises and their impact on stakeholders. The scope of Stage 4 is wider than typical natural disasters and human errors and includes products defects, tampering and social issues regarding the company's supply chain, operations and contributions towards society. Finally, Stage 5 involves all of the previous stages but also incorporates environmental scanning and early warning systems to identify crises as early as possible.

The case example of Maclaren (11.1) demonstrates the vulnerabilities to organizations when they have no crisis contingency plans in place. Company executives had not anticipated concerns about the safety of its products, nor had they prepared themselves in advance. As a result, executives did not communicate quickly enough and demonstrated a general lack of care and responsibility in the eyes of consumers.

Case Example 11.1

Being prepared: the crisis surrounding Maclaren pushchairs

Maclaren is a well-known global brand of children's pushchairs. The safety standard of its 'umbrella-fold' pushchairs has been one of its strengths, together with the durability of the product. Its folding frames and hinges are generally stronger than the pushchairs produced by its competitors. Nonetheless, the company was caught by surprise in November 2009 when it was widely reported that children's finger tops were being 'amputated' in the pushchair hinges. The company had known of the problems – there had been 15 incidents of fingertip laceration or amputation in the USA over a period of ten years – and Maclaren executives had become particularly concerned when there were eight cases between 2007 and 2009. Maclaren engineers had been working tirelessly since the summer of 2009 on remedying the problem with the hinges. However, when the news was leaked, the company was caught unawares. It did not have any contingency plan in place.

In a reactive way, Maclaren issued warnings to owners emphasizing that they should not let children stick their fingers in the folding mechanism as the pushchairs were opened. Maclaren also issued repair kits to cover the hinges but only to owners of the pushchairs in the USA. Where the company went wrong was to discriminate between US consumers and consumers in other parts of the world. This decision had been made internally and had resulted from differences between safety regulators around the world. Most countries had been happy with a simple warning, whereas the US Consumer Product Safety Commission insisted on a temporary fix.

Eventually, and in response to a consumer backlash, Maclaren also offered the repair kits to consumers elsewhere. But by that point the damage to its image had already been done. Maclaren had also underestimated the power of the internet and social media for the news to spread. Executives had not anticipated the spread of the news nor were they communicating through various channels about the problem and about the steps that the company was taking to address it.

Source: Rastegar, F. (2010) How I Did it: Maclaren's CEO on Learning from a Recall, *Harvard Business Review*, January–February 2011; Kirby, J. (2009) Maclaren's Stroller Recall: What would you do?, HBR online blog, November 10, 2009 (see http://blogs.hbr.org/hbr/hbrcditors/2009).

As we have seen in Chapter 10, when organizations do not deal with issues in a timely or responsible manner a crisis situation may emerge. But not all crises are self-inflicted by organizations or emerge from widely debated public issues. Crisis expert Timothy Coombs defines four types of crises based on two dimensions: internal–external and intentional–unintentional.[2] The internal–external dimension refers to whether the crisis resulted from something done by the organization itself (e.g., the actions of managers) or instead was caused by some person or group outside the organization. The intentional–unintentional dimension relates to the controllability of the crisis. Intentional means that the crisis event was committed deliberately by some actor. Unintentional means that the crisis event was not committed deliberately by some actor. The two dimensions together give four mutually exclusive crisis types, as illustrated in Figure 11.1.

	Unintentional	Intentional
External	*Faux pas*	Terrorism
Internal	Accidents	Transgressions

FIGURE 11.1   Crisis type matrix

A *faux pas* is an unintentional action that an external agent (e.g., a non-governmental organization) unintentionally transforms into a crisis. A *faux pas* often begins as an issue between an organization and a particular external agent who challenges the appropriateness of the organization's actions. When an organization does not engage in debate with this external agent or when public opinion and stakeholder expectations move against the organization, the issue may turn into a crisis. Social responsibility tends to be the focal point of most *faux pas*. The term *faux pas* comes from French and literally means 'false step'. It generally refers to a violation of accepted, although unwritten, social rules and expectations.

Accidents are unintentional and happen during the course of normal organizational operations. Product defects, employee injuries and natural disasters are all examples of accidents. The unintentional and generally random nature of accidents often leads to attributions of minimal organizational responsibility, unless of course the organization was directly responsible for the accident. Accidents can be further divided into acts of nature (e.g., hurricanes, earthquakes, epidemics, etc.) and human-induced errors (e.g., industrial accidents). The rationale for this division is that stakeholders and publics are less likely to attribute blame and react negatively to acts of nature than to human-induced error.[3]

Transgressions are intentional acts taken by an organization that knowingly place stakeholders or publics at risk or harm. Knowingly selling defective or dangerous products, withholding safety information from authorities, violating laws, or 'creative' bookkeeping are all examples of transgressions.

Terrorism refers to intentional acts taken by external agents. These intentional actions are designed to harm the organization directly (e.g., hurt customers through product tampering) or indirectly (e.g., reduce sales or disrupt production). Product tampering, hostage taking, sabotage and workplace violence are all examples of terrorism.

COMMUNICATING ABOUT A CRISIS

11.3 Classifying crises into these four types (*faux pas*, accidents, transgressions and terrorism) is useful because it provides a basis for identifying the most appropriate crisis communication strategy.[4] The principle for choosing an appropriate communication strategy (Table 11.1) is the degree to which the organization is perceived by stakeholders and the general public to be responsible or culpable for the crisis. When the perception is that the organization is not directly responsible or culpable, the organization may attempt to distance itself from the crisis or deny that the crisis exists or is as serious as external actors make it out to be. On the other hand, when the organization is seen as directly responsible or culpable for the crisis, the organization will have to defend its position or may simply have to apologize for the crisis and change its behaviour.

The unintentional nature and external challenge of a *faux pas* may lead to an attribution of minimal organizational responsibility. However, an organization can often change in response to the challenge, which means that the possibility of a perception of organizational responsibility for the crisis does exist. When the perception of organizational responsibility is low or weak, the organization may use a distance strategy to further weaken the linkage between the crisis and the organization (Table 11.1). For example, an organization may excuse itself by scapegoating a third party as responsible for the crisis or may downplay the actual seriousness and scale of the crisis. Exxon Mobil's denial of climate change is a good example of a strategy of downplaying the crisis. Alternatively, an organization may follow an association strategy to remind stakeholders and the general public of past good behaviour that may offset the negatives that the crisis brings to the organization. For example, an organization may associate an unfair dismissal with its past track record of fair worker treatment to put the incident in a wider context. However, when the perception of organizational responsibility for a *faux pas* is high or strong, an organization will have to follow an acceptance or accommodative strategy (Table 11.1). Besides apologizing for the crisis and openly accepting the blame, this may consist of remediation (compensating victims) or rectification (taking corrective action to prevent the crisis from happening again).

TABLE 11.1　Crisis communication strategies

Perception of low level of responsibility	
Non-existence strategies	**Claim of denying the crisis**
1 Denial	A simple statement denying that a crisis exists
2 Clarification	An extension of the denial tactic with attempts to explain why there is no crisis
3 Attack and intimidation	A tactic of confronting the person or group who claims that a crisis exists; may include a threat to use 'force' (e.g., a lawsuit) against the accuser
Distance strategies	**Claim of distancing the organization from direct responsibility for the crisis**
1 Excuse	A tactic of denying intention or volition by scapegoating others for the crisis
2 Downplay	A tactic of convincing stakeholders or the general public that the situation is not that bad in itself or compared to other crises
Association strategies	**Claim of connecting the organization to things positively valued by stakeholders and publics**
1 Bolstering	A tactic of reminding stakeholders and the general public of existing positive aspects of the organization (e.g., reminders of past charitable donations or a history of fair worker treatment) in order to offset the negatives the crisis brings to the organization
2 Transcendence	A tactic of associating the negatives and loss arising from a crisis with a desirable, higher order goal (e.g., animal testing to develop life-saving drugs)
Suffering strategy	**Claim that the organization suffers from the crisis**
1 Victimization	A tactic of portraying the organization as a victim of the crisis in order to win public sympathy
Perception of high level of responsibility	
Acceptance strategy	**Claim accepting responsibility or culpability for the crisis**
1 Full apology	A tactic of simply apologizing for the crisis and accepting the blame
2 Remediation	A tactic of announcing some form of compensation or help to victims (money, goods, aid, etc.)
3 Repentance	A tactic of asking for forgiveness. The organization apologizes for the crisis and asks stakeholders and the general public to forgive its misdeeds
Accommodative strategy	**Claim promising to prevent the crisis from recurring again**
1 Rectification	A tactic of taking corrective action to prevent a recurrence of the crisis in the future

Natural accidents are unintentional and outwit the control of organizations. Such accidents can therefore be easily responded to with a distancing strategy, which serves to reinforce the organization's lack of direct responsibility for the crisis. For example, an organization may legitimately claim that it was not directly responsible for the crisis. *Human-error accidents* are more difficult to justify and will require an apology from the organization and an admission that it will take action to prevent a recurrence of the crisis in the future. BNFL's admission of a nuclear leak in one of its plants in 2005 and the steps that it took in relation to new safety procedures is an example of a full apology and rectification tactic (Table 11.1).

Transgressions are intentional actions taken by organizations which make organizations directly responsible for their impact. A strategy of distancing the organization from the crisis or a non-existence strategy that denies the existence of the crisis is thus futile. Organizations instead need to follow an acceptance strategy where they admit their responsibility but work to atone for the crisis in some fashion. For example, an organization may remediate by willingly offering some form of compensation or help to victims, may repent by publicly asking for forgiveness, or may follow a rectification tactic of ensuring that the crisis will not recur in the future. Ahold, the Dutch retailer found guilty of fraudulent bookkeeping, apologized for the fraud crisis and has since made extensive changes to its corporate governance and accounting. When Anders Moberg took over as CEO, he explained the rectification strategy: 'We learned that as a company you can lose your reputation overnight, but it takes some time to rebuild it and restore trust.' He felt that in order to meet stakeholder expectations, 'we knew we needed to be at the forefront of implementing corporate-governance reforms'.[5]

Terrorist attacks are directed at the organization by external agents and often there is very little direct organizational responsibility or culpability. An organization may therefore adopt a suffering strategy, which portrays the organization as an unfair victim of some malicious, outside actor. Johnson & Johnson's famous portrayal of itself as wounded by product tampering during the 1982 Tylenol crisis is a good example of the suffering strategy.

In short, depending on the degree to which organizations are seen as responsible or culpable for a crisis in the eyes of stakeholders, organizations can employ different communication strategies. It is important to stress at this point that the *perception* of whether an organization is responsible or culpable matters as much as whether the organization is *factually* responsible or culpable. For example, in August 2005, British Airways (BA) had to cancel flights affecting 17,000 passengers as a result of a wildcat strike of BA baggage handlers, who walked out in sympathy with workers sacked by Gate Gourmet, the firm which provides BA's in-flight meals. The crisis cancellation of flights, which left many passengers stranded at Heathrow airport, was effectively outside BA's control; the strike of the baggage handlers was illegal and unannounced, and was the result of the unfair dismissal of workers in another firm (Gate Gourmet). Nonetheless, BA was held responsible for the knock-on effect of having to cancel flights and was pressured to apologize for the crisis situation. BA's CEO at the time, Rod Eddington, said: 'I apologize unreservedly to our customers for the disruption to their travel plans and cancellation of our flights.' BA, however, did not choose to remediate the crisis by giving compensation to the 70,000 stranded passengers, but chose to offer the option that passengers' tickets would be rebooked or refunded. This decision was rationalized by a BA spokesperson as 'We are so, so sorry about all this. We are doing all we can. We have become embroiled in a dispute not of our making'.[6]

Stakeholder and public perceptions of a crisis are thus of central concern. As perceptions of crisis responsibility strengthen, the threat of damage to the organization's image becomes greater. This means that communication professionals need to utilize acceptance and accommodative strategies. Acceptance and accommodative strategies emphasize a damage-limitation approach. Defensive strategies, such as denial or downplaying, logically become less effective as organizations are viewed as more responsible for the crisis.[7] The actual importance of using the right communication strategy depending on the perception of crisis responsibility is furthermore illustrated in the case example of Mattel below (Case Example 11.2).

Case Example 11.2

Crisis Communication: Mattel's effective handling of a product recall

A good example of having a crisis communication plan in place is the way in which the toymaker Mattel handled communication following a product recall.

Mattel faced a number of challenges between August and October 2007 following a recall of products that were found to contain dangerous levels of lead paint. The products were sourced from China, where the manufacturing of these products had not been properly supervised. But Mattel was prepared for this eventuality. Nine years prior to the actual crisis, the Vice President for Corporate Communication and his team had developed a communication plan for this kind of scenario. This ensured that the company was able to hit the ground running when the crisis struck. The company's communication through multiple channels ensured that stakeholders were informed and kept abreast of developments, customers knew how to return their recalled products, and Mattel was able to subtly shift the crisis into an example of the care and responsibility that it feels for its end consumers.

Following the plan, the team systematically targeted consumers, stakeholders and the media. Mattel also provided a constant stream of information on what the company was doing to improve the safety of its products (a rectification strategy). The company had also widely spread the message of the toy recalls through full-page newspaper advertisements, a website, consumer hotlines, online ads and a recall website. Mattel's CEO, Robert Eckert, used the media to his advantage by voicing his personal dedication to product safety and appealing to parents worried about their children. Eckert's most effective communication was the video message he posted online to 'emphasize his concern as a parent and his personal responsibility'. He apologized, publicly admitting responsibility, and described the steps taken to tighten quality assurance requirements on Mattel's suppliers. Mattel's response only fell short in its compensation to consumers. The company offered equivalent value coupons for other Mattel products in exchange for any recalled products. Given the inconvenience caused to consumers and the need to motivate them to return the affected products, this remediation tactic was perhaps somewhat insufficient.

(Continued)

(Continued)

Source: Story, L. (2007) Mattel shifts into crisis mode after quality problems. *New York Times website.* [online]. Available from: http://www.nytimes.com/2007/08/28/business/worldbusin ess/28ihtmattel.4.7289869.html?_r=1; Casey, N. Pasztor, A. (2007) Safety Agency, Mattel Clash Over Disclosures. *The Wall Street Journal: Business website* [online]. Available from: http:// online.wsj.com/article/B118886996338816516.html?mod=hpp_us_whats_news; Fierman, 5. (2007) *Mattel and Crisis Management. Associated Content website* [online]. Available from: http://www.associated.com/article/395446/mattel_and_crisis_management.html; Levick, R. (2009) Lesson From the Mattel Crisis. *Corporate Social Responsibility website* [online]. Available from: http://www.thecro.com/node/544

Once a strategy has been identified, the key to effective crisis management is to maintain effective control of the release of information and to ensure that no unauthorized information or potentially damaging rumours are allowed to circulate. Failure to respond effectively to the media's enquiries about a crisis will invariably lead to journalists seeking information from whatever sources they can (perhaps with only limited regard for the accuracy of information obtained).

It is therefore important to develop communication plans for probable crisis scenarios and establish key responsibilities for communication professionals before a crisis actually happens. This includes:

- the identification of the organization's key spokespersons;
- media training of the CEO, executive directors and key spokespersons;
- establishing a crisis communication team and in major crises a press office to field media enquiries and to handle the release of information;
- establishing safe crisis locations where the media can meet and be briefed in the event of hazardous situations; and the
- identification of contacts at relevant external agencies (e.g., police, fire services) who may need to be contacted in case of a crisis.

The general principles of crisis communication discussed in the chapter including planning and the choice of the right communication strategy are illustrated with the case study of the Metropolitan Police and their handling of an unfortunate incident (Case Study 11.1).

CASE STUDY 11.1

SHOOTING AN INNOCENT CIVILIAN: CRISIS COMMUNICATION WITHIN THE METROPOLITAN POLICE

In the summer of 2005, the City of London was the target of a number of terrorist attacks. On the 7th July that year, London had woken up to an unprecedented series of coordinated suicide bomb attacks in three underground stations and on a bus, killing a total of 52 commuters as well as four suicide bombers, and injuring many

(Continued)

(Continued)

hundreds of civilians. In the aftermath of these explosions, the city's police force, the Metropolitan Police, experienced an intense period in terms of policing activity, investigations, as well as responding to inquiries from the public who were gripped by fear of further attacks. Two weeks later, on 21 July, another terrorist cell attempted to explode bombs at around midday on three underground trains and on a bus in what was seen as a serious copycat attempt to repeat the earlier bombings. The explosives were largely similar to those used two weeks earlier but for reasons as yet unknown did not explode.

On 22 July, the failed bombers were still at large and the Metropolitan Police set up an operation involving specialist firearms teams to assist in the manhunt for these suspects. A designated senior officer (DSO) was appointed to lead the manhunt, which was assumed to involve special anti-terrorist tactics that allow police officers to fire a critical head shot to incapacitate or kill a suspected terrorist (rather than the standard practice of firing at the torso) when authorized by a DSO and without making a verbal challenge. Such a verbal challenge would also alert the suspect to the presence of the police.

One of the failed bombers was identified as Hussein Osman, who lived on Scotia Road in South London. The Metropolitan Police's strategy was to try to control the premises at that address through covert surveillance, and to follow any person leaving those premises until it was felt safe to challenge them and then stop them. The surveillance would be carried out by two surveillance teams and the stop by specialist firearms officers. The movements of these teams were centrally controlled and instructed by the control centre at Scotland Yard, the headquarters of the Metropolitan Police, where the DSO and her team were located. The first of the surveillance teams took up position just after 6am.

At around 9:33, Jean Charles de Menezes, a Brazilian electrician, left the communal entrance at Scotia Road on his way to fix a broken fire alarm in North London. He lived in the flat below Osman. Mr De Menezes was followed by several surveillance officers who had difficulties identifying him to determine whether he was or was not Osman. The officers followed De Menezes getting on a bus to Brixton Road where he got off. He then walked towards the entrance of the Brixton underground station, but saw a notice saying that it was closed for security reasons. He returned to the bus stop and one of the surveillance officers reported to the control room that these movements looked suspicious.

The firearms team were still not in contention, which created a sense of panic when the DSO and other senior officers in the control room realized that there could be a chance that this individual was one of the bombers. Mr De Menezes was again on the bus and on his way to Stockwell tube station, the same station which three of the failed bombers had entered the day before. As these events unfolded, the DSO asked the senior surveillance officer to 'tell them a percentage of identification' – in other words, put a percentage on how sure they were that the man they were following was Osman. The officer replied that it was a ridiculous question. He felt that identification was either fully positive or negative, but he nonetheless asked around his team over the radio. As no one replied, he took it that none could assist in a positive identification. His surveillance team effectively had not been able to make a positive

(Continued)

(Continued)

identification, and the majority of the surveillance officers actually had come to doubt whether Mr De Menezes was the suspect they were chasing. Pressed for an answer, the senior surveillance officer replied 'For what it's worth, I think it's him'. Besides communicating his own intuition, he expresses his ambivalence towards the question and emphasizes again that no one in his team came forward. Nonetheless, on hearing this response, the DSO mobilizes the firearms team to intervene. Effectively, she gives the order to the firearms officers to move in and stop and incapacitate the suspect before he could potentially explode a bomb in Stockwell underground station.

Five cars with specialist firearms officers then set off in line with the overall strategy. Their deployment also confirmed that Mr De Menezes was the suspect and the man they were chasing, despite the fact that in all of the entries in the logs kept in the control room and by the surveillance team he was always described as 'U/I', unidentified. De Menezes had never been directly and positively identified as Hussein Osman.

When the firearms officers arrived at Stockwell tube station, Mr De Menezes had already entered the train. They ran down, believing that they were in pursuit of the suspect who was about to detonate a bomb once he was in a train and underground. When they arrived at the platform, De Menezes was pointed out to them by surveillance officers surrounding him. Two of the firearms officers and one of the surveillance officers stormed into the train carriage and because of the commotion De Menezes stood up at that point. The three officers interpreted this as an act of resistance. In response, the surveillance officer grabbed him and pushed him back in his seat. The firearms officers then leaned over him and fired eleven shots in total. Mr De Menezes was shot seven times in the head and once in the shoulder at close range, and died at the scene. The environment in which these officers had been put had led them to see an individual, who was completely innocent, as a suicide bomber who was about to detonate an explosive device in a crowded underground train. Only a few hours later did they realize that they had shot an innocent civilian.

Crisis communication

Mr De Menezes was shot at around 10:06. Forensic teams on the scene were soon investigating the death, and shortly after the shooting an explosives officer searched the body. No explosives were found. A few minutes later Mr De Menezes' wallet with identification was recovered from the scene. Assistant Commissioner Andy Hayman was in charge of the investigation and around 10:30 advised the Police Commissioner, Sir Ian Blair, that someone had been shot dead at the station and that it was believed that he was one of the bombers. At 10:46 a press line from the Metropolitan Police was agreed and simply stated 'We can confirm that just after 10.00 today (22.07.05) armed officers shot a male at Stockwell LT Station. We are not in a position to release further info at the moment'. Despite the fact that Mr De Menezes had been identified, rumours kept circulating about the deceased man within the Metropolitan Police. In a first meeting with the press, Commissioner Blair reiterated that the 'shooting is directly linked to the ongoing and expanding anti-terrorist operation. ... I understand the man was challenged and refused to obey'. At around 16:30 in the afternoon, Andy Hayman briefed a gathering of journalists.

(Continued)

(Continued)

He was aware of evidence that the deceased was not involved in the previous day's attempted bomb attacks. At 17:07, shortly after the briefing, BBC Television *News 24* reported the following: 'A line just in about the shooting in Stockwell earlier. The man shot dead at the tube station is not thought to be one of the four men shown in CCTV pictures released this afternoon.' This was followed at 17:18 by footage of a BBC reporter outside the Metropolitan Police's headquarters confirming that there had been a special police briefing and stating: 'We don't know any more than the police have said for sure that he was challenged, he refused to obey instructions, he was subsequently shot and he was not one of the four people whose images were released by police a little earlier.' Soon after the briefing, Hayman attended a meeting with Sir Ian Blair. He was directly asked whether he knew anything about the identity of the man who had been shot but chose not to share this information. At a management meeting attended by both men, there was a general discussion about what could be communicated and released into the public domain. A set of notes from that meeting record that those present were advised by Mr Hayman that the press were reporting that the shot man was not one of the four suspected bombers, but he added that it was important to 'present that he was'. Hayman later disputed this but, whether or not this is true, it is clear that he did not tell those present that the reason the media were running the story was because he had briefed a group of journalists to that effect earlier that afternoon. He also again did not choose to share information on the identity of the deceased.

A press statement was issued following the meeting stating the following:

> The man shot at Stockwell station is still subject to formal identification and it is not yet clear whether he is one of the four people we are seeking to identify and whose pictures have been released today. It therefore remains extremely important that members of the public continue to assist police in relation to all four pictures. This death, like all deaths related to police operations, is obviously a matter of deep regret. Nevertheless the man who was shot was under police observation because he had emerged from a house that was itself under observation because it was linked to the investigation of yesterday's incidents. He was then followed by surveillance officers to the station. His clothing and his behaviour at the station added to their suspicions. While the counter terrorist investigation will obviously take pre-eminence, the investigation into the circumstances that led to his death is being pursued and will be subject to scrutiny through the IPCC in due course.

Besides the fact that the identity of the deceased was known, the statement also tries to distance the Metropolitan Police from direct responsibility for the shooting. It even scapegoats Mr De Menezes for acting suspiciously. Another curious feature of the statement is the fact that it acknowledged that an investigation will be started with the involvement of the IPCC (the Independent Police Complaints Commission), which would only happen if an innocent civilian died at the hands of the police. The statement thus apparently seems to contradict itself. It subsequently took another full day for the Metropolitan Police to finally confirm in a press release at 9pm on 23 July that 'the deceased man had been formally identified as Jean Charles de Menezes'

(Continued)

(Continued)

who was 'not connected to incidents in Central London on 21st July 2005 in which four explosive devices were partly detonated'.

In November 2009, after years of legal proceedings in the form of a health and safety trail and a public inquest, the family of Jean Charles de Menezes and the Metropolitan Police finally settled all litigation between them. The family was paid compensation. In the statement that was released with the settlement, it said: 'The commissioner would like to take this opportunity of making a further unreserved apology to the family for the tragic death of Jean Charles de Menezes and to reiterate that he was a totally innocent victim and in no way to blame for his untimely death.'

QUESTIONS FOR REFLECTION

1   Discuss the way in which the Metropolitan Police handled communication in the direct aftermath of the shooting. What, in your opinion, went wrong, and relate this to the available crisis communication strategies discussed in the chapter.
2   Should the Metropolitan Police have followed a different communication strategy?

Source: This case study is based on evidence gathered and presented as part of the Stockwell Inquest into the shooting (see http://www.stockwellinquest.org.uk) and as part of the IPCC's investigation of public statements following the shooting (report known as Stockwell Two; see http://www.mpa.gov.uk/downloads/scrutinites/stockwell/ipcc-two.pdf).

CHAPTER SUMMARY

11.4 Crisis communication is an increasingly important specialist discipline within corporate communication. Managing crises typically starts with developing crisis contingency plans for the most critical crisis scenarios that an organization may encounter. Communication practitioners are involved in the development of these plans and are also responsible for working out the details of crisis communication. One important principle for crisis communication is the degree to which stakeholders and publics hold the organization responsible or culpable for a particular crisis. Based on the perception of organizational responsibility, practitioners can choose between different communication strategies ranging from accommodative strategies to advocacy and defensive strategies.

 ## DISCUSSION QUESTIONS

1   What are the main differences between an issue and a crisis?
2   Select a number of recent crises, such as the BP oil spill in the Mexican Gulf or Tata's handling of the Mumbai terrorist attacks, and reflect upon how each of these

companies communicated about the crisis with the media and its stakeholders. Which of the crisis communication strategies did they follow? Was this successful in the end?

KEY TERMS

Acceptance strategy

Accidents

Accommodative strategy

Advocacy

Association strategy

Crisis

Crisis communication plan

Distance strategy

Faux pas

Non-existence strategy

Suffering strategy

Terrorist attacks

Transgression

FURTHER READING

Anthonissen, Peter (2008), *Crisis Communication: Practical PR Strategies for Reputation Management and Company Survival*. London: Kogan Page.

Coombs, W. Timothy (2007), *Ongoing Crisis Communication: Planning, Managing, and Responding*. London: Sage.

Mitroff, Ian (2006), *Crisis Leadership: Planning for the Unthinkable*. New York: John Wiley.

NOTES

1   Mitroff, I.I. and Pearson, C.M. (1993), *Crisis Management*. San Francisco: Jossey-Bass.

2   See, for example, Coombs, W. Timothy (2007), *Ongoing Crisis Communication: Planning, Managing, and Responding*. London: Sage.

3   Coombs (2007).

4   Coombs, W.T. (1995), 'Choosing the right words: the development of guidelines for the selection of the "appropriate" crisis-response strategies', *Management Communication Quarterly*, 8: 447–476.

5   *Business Week* (2004), 'Royal Ahold: from Europe's Enron to model citizen?', 17 May.

6   *The Guardian* (2005), 'Compensation "unlikely" for stranded BA passengers', 12 August.

7   Benoit, W.L. (1995), *Accounts, Excuses and Apologies: A Theory of Image Restoration Discourse*. Albany, NY: State University of New York Press.

NEW DEVELOPMENTS IN CORPORATE COMMUNICATION

5

Part 5 explores emerging areas of practice within corporate communication, including change and leadership communication and corporate social responsibility (CSR) programmes and community relations. These areas have in recent years evolved into significant areas of activity, in part as a result of the importance of effective communication that is increasingly expected around topics such as change and corporate social responsibility.

After reading Part 5, the reader will be familiar with these significant emerging areas of practice and developing trends as well as with practical principles and frameworks for communicating around these topics in practice.

LEADERSHIP AND CHANGE COMMUNICATION

12

Chapter Overview

Managers need to demonstrate leadership skills and communicate effectively with stakeholders during major organizational changes. The chapter defines leadership communication and discusses various ways in which communication can be used effectively to initiate and realize organizational changes. These strategies range from narratives and stories promoting a change to informational and interactive strategies that allow employees to understand and help realize the change.

INTRODUCTION

12.1 Change is a constant within many organizations. At any one point, organizations initiate changes, ranging from a reformulation of their vision, brand or identity to the implementation of new customer management or software programs, to a restructuring of the organization. Change often implies a disruption of the *status quo* and previously established ways of working and doing things. As such, it may therefore trigger controversy and confusion with employees and thus almost always presents a justification problem. It may also lead to resistance, particularly when managers do not sufficiently communicate about the change. Change *per se* may not necessarily be what worries employees, but the expectation of employees that they will continue to work for the same organization. Denise Rousseau, an organizational psychologist, defined this expectation as a 'sense of continuity', and she argued that it is essential for leaders to frame and emphasize a sense of continuity if employees are to maintain their identification with the organization in the wake of major organizational changes.[1]

Organizational changes require the leadership of managers, who articulate a rationale for why a change is needed and who, also largely through their communication, drum up support from others ('followers') within the organization in order to implement and realize the change. The following section defines the nature of leadership in the context of organizational changes. The subsequent sections then outline various communication strategies during and after major organizational changes (e.g., organizational restructuring) within organizations to reduce employee resistance and to facilitate the implementation and routinization of such changes. The chapter concludes with general observations on characteristics and skills associated with effective leadership communication.

DEFINING LEADERSHIP AND CHANGE

12.2 Leadership is one of those hard-to-define subjects. At one level, our understanding of leadership builds on images of great leaders, including great historical and political leaders. However, most managers working in the more natural surroundings of an organization have relatively little in common with these historical figures.

Nonetheless, these images of great leaders, ranging from Roman emperors to figures such as Churchill and Martin Luther King, have shaped how many people think about leadership. The classic image of leaders is therefore often one of 'born-to-lead'; leaders have natural attributes and skills, such as courage and charisma, which are often 'given'. This means that only some individuals are able to effectively lead from the very top and motivate others in organizations. In fact, you often hear people say things such as 'he is such a natural leader'. Such remarks are often driven by classic and often heroic images of what it means to be a leader.

An alternative, and increasingly popular, perspective on leadership is one which suggests that leadership skills can be acquired and developed, including many of the communication skills associated with leadership roles in organizations. It also recognizes that leadership may be situational, and that within organizations managers or employees may demonstrate leadership in articulating changes or opportunities, and in getting others to follow them. The self-development perspective, in other words, focuses on the ability of individuals to communicate and influence others, as well as on simultaneously being influenced by others in the implementation of a change or a specific task or project. Organizations require groups or teams of people to work together, and effective leaders are those who can focus the efforts of a group or team towards a common goal and can enable individuals to work together. When leading, individual managers influence and shape the interpretations of others in the organization, but ideally are also sensible in not unduly burdening the process with an overlarge ego.

The CEO and most senior executives in an organization naturally need to take on leadership roles in articulating a vision for the organization and any overarching corporate goals. They will also use various platforms, including management and town-hall meetings, to communicate this directly to employees lower down the organization. But middle managers and supervisors or managers of work teams also need to demonstrate leadership skills in their interactions with employees around them. Traditional images of organization and control suggested that managers and supervisors should control and manage employees in strict ways, and from the top down, on the basis of authority relationships. However, models of effective human resource management have highlighted that employees are not merely cogs in a machine or quantities of manpower, but are in fact social beings who look for inspiration and want to be socially involved. Leaders, in turn, are those individuals who, in daily interactions with others, can articulate inspiring visions that marshal support.

One important area where leadership is required involves the management of change. Change is a facet of many organizations. Organizational changes have often been classified in terms of degrees of change. For example, change can be major or radical (e.g., a complete restructuring of an organization) or more minor and convergent (e.g., an adjustment of customer service guidelines as a result of customer feedback). Radical change involves a complete reorientation of an organization, whereas convergent change consists of fine-tuning the existing orientation and ways of working. Change can also be defined in terms of its time-frame: evolutionary changes occur slowly and gradually whereas revolutionary changes happen swiftly and affect virtually all of the organization.[2] Organizational changes can of course also be classified in terms of the primary focus of the change. Changes may involve the adoption of novel or updated *technology* to accomplish work; a *restructuring* and change in *policies* and routine *ways of working*; a change in the *products* and *services* of an organization; or a change in the *organizational identity* and *culture* of the organization.

One particularly helpful way to think about changes is in terms of 'additive' versus 'substitutive' changes. Changes can be seen as either a departure from the old organization (a substitution) or as an addition to, or update of, the old organization (an addition).[3] Substitutive change is a major strategic change that often involves a redefinition of the organization's mission and purpose or a substantial restructuring of the organization. Additive changes are less drastic and may involve, for example, improvements to ways of working. Substitutive changes are obviously more difficult to sell to employees and also more difficult to get support for. Such changes break down the current *status quo*, and therefore require effective leadership communication (see Case Study 12.1 below). Managers, in their role as transformational leaders during such changes, often craft a story or narrative for this purpose, which provides an inspiring image of the new organization (after the change has been enacted), with which employees can engage. For example, when Samuel Palmisano took over as CEO of IBM he set out to change IBM from a profitable multinational corporation into a global integrated enterprise. He managed to achieve the change with the support of his employees. A large part of his success was down to his skills as an effective communicator, his rearticulation of the IBM story and the way in which he involved employees in the transition.

CASE STUDY 12.1

STRATEGIC CHANGE AT BANK MANDIRI

In the aftermath of the Asian financial crisis, the government of Indonesia decided to restructure all seven state-owned banks, with the aim of eventually selling and privatizing each of these banks. In 1998, the government announced that four state banks (Bank Bumi Daya (BBD), Bank Dagang Negara (BDN), Bank Exim and Bapindo) would be merged together into a single banking entity that would be named Bank Mandiri. This was initially criticized because of the costs associated with the merger, but also because it would effectively involve 'bailing out' inefficient banks. However, the Indonesian government argued that closing the four banks or allowing them to fail would have been far more costly.

A few months after the official announcement, Robby Djohan was appointed Chief Executive Officer. Dhojan had a reputation for successfully turning businesses around, including Garuda, the Indonesian state-owned airline, and Bank Niagara. His job was to restructure the new organization, to improve the quality of its assets and to increase efficiency by making improvements to the organization, systems and human resources of the four constituent banks. Dhojan and his team embarked on a comprehensive process of consolidation. They closed 194 overlapping branches and reduced the combined workforce from 26,600 to 17,620. They also rolled out the single corporate brand throughout the network and started to advertise the benefits and values of the new Bank Mandiri brand. The team also tried to establish professional standards for management across the organization, to ensure that the bank would operate under internationally recognized principles of corporate governance, control and compliance.

One of the key challenges facing the new bank was the legacy of a bureaucratic culture which stemmed from its former state-owned status. Dhojan envisaged a clear break from this culture to improve the bank and to meet customer expectations in the private sector. His first move was to strategically place a number of managers as change agents in each of the constituent banks. These managers would bring new thinking and enthusiasm to the bank. Dhojan himself was also open and direct in his management style, and critical of bureaucracy and unclear communication. Despite Dhojan's best efforts, for some time after the merger, Bank Mandiri still consisted of four distinct cultures associated with each of the constituent banks. In response, Dhojan and his team started several communication initiatives to strengthen the ties across the four constituent banks and to forge a new, overarching culture. However, other banking issues around liquidity intervened, which resulted in increasingly less time being spent on communicating to employees about the required transformation.

In May 2000, Robby Djohan was sacked overnight by the Indonesian government and replaced by E.C.W. Neloe, who was an astute manager but less challenging in his management style. Neloe set out to change the culture from the inside, spending his first six months in office evaluating the structures and culture at the bank before taking steps to restructure and change the organizational design. He then set out to create a much flatter organization with fewer layers of hierarchy between the head office and banking operations. Neloe also tried to change the culture within the bank,

(Continued)

(Continued)

although during his tenure he admitted that 'we have not really been able to develop a culture as good as I would like to have [done]. I still hear employees referring to colleagues that are from this or that legacy bank'.

One additional step that the senior management took was to introduce new behavioural guidelines for employees within the bank. Dr Supomo, Executive Vice-President, explains:

> When we introduced the new organization structure, besides restating our vision, mission and shared values, we also introduced new daily behavioural guidelines for our employees. We call it [the] 'Three No's Behaviour': no delays, no errors, and no special payments. This aims to change the old perception of the state-owned banks as bureaucratic and poor at serving customers, even though it was not always true. The 'Three No's Behaviour' policy has been widely communicated both internally and externally.

In addition to the introduction of these behavioural guidelines, Bank Mandiri has also run a series of corporate advertising campaigns extolling the virtues of its new cultural values, including integrity, professionalism, customer focus and a commitment to service excellence. These campaigns have helped strengthen the brand image with customers and other external stakeholders, but importantly also influenced employees and strengthened the internal culture around these values.

QUESTIONS FOR REFLECTION

1   Describe the steps taken by management to change the culture within Bank Mandiri following the merger of the four constituent banks. Was this successful? What else could they have done?
2   Taking this case as an example, what role does leadership and communication play in the transformation of an organizational culture?

Source: Information for this case was sourced from www.bankmandiri.co.id, and from discussions with Bank Mandiri employees; quotes in the case are taken from Lassere, P. (2004) Bank Mandiri: a case in Strategic transformation, INSEAD case study. Fontainebleau, France: INSEAD.

COMMUNICATING DURING A CHANGE

12.3 An important area of corporate communication involves communicating to employees during and after a change. Large organizations are prone to initiate and implement many organizational changes, ranging from, for example, a restructuring, a new performance initiative, the adoption of new technology or new way of working, or the laying-off of parts of the workforce. All of these changes affect employees in one way or another and their successful implementation often crucially depends on communication. Poorly managed change communication may result in rumours and resistance to change.

Communication and change are related in a number of different ways. Communication is central to how a change is formulated, announced and explained to employees, and also contributes to a successful implementation and institutionalization of the change. Kurt Lewin highlighted the importance of communication in his simple model of the change process.[4] Lewin likened the change process to the process of water freezing. When snow melts as a result of heat from the sun and then refreezes again when the temperature drops, it takes on a different texture (e.g., it becomes more icy). Lewin argued that change in an organization is a very similar process, involving an alteration of the organization (water) in terms of its structure or function (in the form of snow or ice) over time. Based on this metaphor, he argued that change involves four phases: (1) recognizing the need for change (unfreezing); (2) developing a change plan (vision); (3) implementing the new change (moving); and (4) routinizing the change (refreezing). All of these phases (identification of the need for change, formulation of a change initiative, implementation of the change, and institutionalization of the change) require communication between managers and employees.

Depending on the focus and nature of the change, an organization will have to identify an effective way of communicating the change to employees. Obviously, when a change is radical or substitutive and involves the entire organization, managers would have to engage in many conversations with employees across all levels of the organization, to initiate the desired overhaul in thinking. Alternatively, when the change is more additive and involves, for example, an updating of technology (e.g., the introduction of a new intranet system) communication may consist of informing employees about the new technology and training them in how to use it. The management scholar Phillip Clampitt and his colleagues observed five different communication strategies that managers use to communicate a change to employees.[5]

1 *'Spray and pray'*: The first strategy, labelled 'spray and pray', involves managers showering ('spray') employees with all kinds of information about the change. The idea with this strategy is that information is simply passed on to employees who, it is hoped ('pray'), will then themselves sort out the significant from insignificant details and work out what the change means for their day-to-day job. While this strategy may seem admirable, it is rarely effective. More information does not necessarily equate to better communication when it is not sufficiently focused and tailored to the needs of employees.

2 *'Tell and sell'*: A second strategy, labelled 'tell and sell', involves managers communicating a more limited set of messages that they believe address the core issues about the change. In this strategy, managers first tell employees about the key issues and then try to sell employees a particular approach. It is a top-down strategy; employees are not engaged in a dialogue, but simply informed of a change. The danger with this strategy is that employees feel that they are not listened to and become sceptical, if not cynical, about the change.

3 *'Underscore and explore'*: The third strategy is labelled 'underscore and explore' because it involves managers focusing on the fundamental issues most clearly linked to the organizational change, while allowing employees

the creative freedom to explore the implications of the change in a disciplined way. When managers use this strategy, they often assume that communication is not complete and effective until they know how employees react to the core ideas behind the change. In other words, managers are concerned not only with developing a few core messages, but also with listening to employees in order to identify potential misunderstandings and unrecognized obstacles to the change.

4 *'Identify and reply'*: The fourth strategy, labelled 'identify and reply', is different from the first three because it starts with the concerns of employees. The strategy involves employees setting the agenda, to which managers reply. The assumption behind the strategy is that employees are in the best position to know the critical issues and the feasibility of a change. However, the danger is that employees do not have the wider picture of the entire organization and that managers use this strategy as a defensive posture in which they are seen to attend to employee concerns without actually using that feedback.

5 *'Withhold and uphold'*: The final strategy, labelled 'withhold and uphold', consists of managers withholding information until they can no longer do so because of rumours or employee revolt. When confronted by rumours or revolt, managers simply uphold the party line. Managers who use this strategy often assume that information is power, that employees are not sophisticated enough to grasp the big picture or simply do not need to know the rationale for a change.

Managers may use one or a combination of these five strategies. The underlying differences between these strategies involve the degree to which employees are provided with relevant information, are given guidance on the change, and feel involved and consulted in the change process. As demonstrated in Figure 12.1, the communication strategies towards the middle of the figure tend to offer employees more guidance by prioritizing communication and by providing relevant and focused information on the change. These strategies are also more sensitive to employee concerns and needs, although of course they make different assumptions

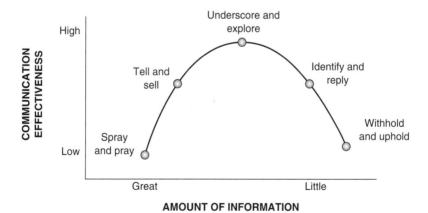

FIGURE 12.1 Change communication strategies

about the importance and nature of those concerns and needs. The 'underscore and explore' strategy, in particular, maximizes the likelihood of effective change by creatively synthesizing managers' change initiatives and employee concerns.

The 'underscore and explore' strategy is in line with what other research on organizational change has supported: organizational change is more successful when employees in non-management positions are able to exert influence over the change process by providing feedback on the change and its implementation. Managers may be tempted to impose changes on employees. However, joint involvement and collaboration between managers and employees in identifying the need for change and in formulating and implementing change programmes lead to greater employee commitment to a change. In a general sense, then, bottom-up involvement in change is generally more effective than a top-down or programmed implementation of change.

At the same time, many organizations do not or cannot always involve all of their employees in the formative stages of a change. Particularly in large, multinational corporations, top-down approaches are still common for practical reasons because it is impossible to involve all, if not most, of their employees in the development of a change initiative. British Airways (see Case Study 12.2 at the end of this chapter), for example, has often opted for top-down implementation of changes using a combination of 'tell and sell' and 'identify and reply' strategies. Issues in customer service, for example, have been 'sold' to all front-line staff through training programmes after they had been 'identified' by employees.

The choice of either a top-down or bottom-up approach to communicating change is coupled with the use of certain media.[6] When organizations opt for a top-down approach, they may involve employees only to a limited extent in the routinization of the change. Managers will not consult employees in the identification of the need for change and the formulation of a change initiative; instead, they will meet each other in management meetings and will consult external sources (e.g., management consultants), periodicals and formal documents. Once a change initiative is formulated, it will then be rolled out to employees through organization-wide media such as the intranet, announcement meetings and one-way audio or video messages. On the other hand, in a bottom-up approach, employees are involved to a greater degree in the entire change process. Managers speak to employees face-to-face and through emails and over the phone in the identification stage, will meet them in meetings and electronic conferences in the formulation stage, and will engage with all employees through interactive meetings and technologies (video-conference, email, etc.) during the implementation and routinization stage.

The communication consultants Larkin and Larkin argue that for top-down change initiatives to be successful, they need to be communicated to employees in plain English and largely through face-to-face communication.[7] They argue that managers should only communicate the facts and essential information to employees, and not refer to management speak. Face-to-face communication is also more successful, they argue, than videos and newsletters because of the involvement of the employee and because it allows employees to ask questions and talk back (see Chapter 3). Ideally, employees prefer the news about the change to be given to them by their direct supervisors rather than more senior managers. Employees are more likely to trust their immediate supervisors, increasing the likelihood of the change being understood and accepted and decreasing the likelihood of resistance.[8] Face-to-face communication is also associated with an 'open' communication climate. Communication climate refers to the possibilities within an organization for employees to respond and to ask questions about the change. A more 'open' climate influences employees' trust, commitment and the willingness to change.[9]

Managing change thus involves encouraging participation from as many employees as possible, addressing their concerns in the change programme and ensuring that managers act as role models for the changes.[10] However, as mentioned, managers cannot always involve all employees in the entire change process from formulation to routinization. In some change initiatives, the need for communication efficiency is higher than in others. Communication efficiency is defined as the accomplishment of change communication with a minimum expenditure of time, effort and resources.[11]

The need for communication efficiency is high in organizations where (1) it is physically impossible to communicate in a face-to-face or interactive manner with all employees; (2) when resources devoted to change communication are scarce; and (3) when there is an urgent need to progress through the change process and thus little time for interaction about it. Besides deciding how efficient the communication process should be, managers also need to decide how important a consensus with employees is for the success of the change.

Consensus-building is defined as the effort in change communication to achieve commitment to a course of action as a result of joint decision-making. The need for consensus-building is high in organizations (1) when changes are perceived to be radical and/or controversial; (2) when there is a history of resistance to similar change; (3) when critical resources (e.g., expertise, approval) are controlled by employees; and (4) when ongoing support and cooperation are needed to maintain the change. When these two dimensions of the change situation are combined, managers are provided with four different communication strategies. These communication strategies provide an element of depth to the 'underscore and explore' strategy discussed above by highlighting the differential treatment of different groups of employees and the practical considerations of communication efficiency and consensus-building that will go into the decision for a change communication strategy. Figure 12.2 shows the matrix of factors affecting the choice of communication strategies.

High need for communication efficiency	Need to know strategy	Quid pro quo strategy
Low need for communication efficiency	Equal dissemination strategy	Equal participation strategy
	Low need for consensus building	**High need for consensus building**

FIGURE 12.2 Factors affecting the choice of communication strategies

1 *Need to know strategy*: With this strategy, managers keep quiet about planned change except to those employees who really need to know or who explicitly express a desire for the information. This is done in part out of an efficiency motivation, in part to avoid giving rise to potential objections from some employees, and in part to avoid overburdening employees with large amounts of information for which they have little time or use. The strategy's exclusive focus on a select group of employees may be useful when the change is more convergent or additive than radical or substitutive and when employees of the organization are themselves selective about which of the organization's activities are of interest to them.

2 *Quid pro quo strategy*: In this strategy, as the name implies, managers give more communicative attention to those employees who have something valuable (e.g., expertise, approval power, resources) for the change process. A franchise organization, for example, may only communicate to its franchisees and not to other hired staff about a change in governance. These employees are crucial to the change and thus need to be consulted and communicated with. The strategy combines a focus on consensus-building with efficiency as only certain groups of employees are communicated with. Because of cost considerations, managers focus their time and energy on the employees who are most crucial to the change's success. However, the risk of using this strategy is that they may anger other employees who feel left out of the change process.

3 *Equal dissemination strategy*: This strategy focuses on disseminating information to employees across the entire organization, early, often and, most importantly, on an equal basis. The strategy is one of blanket dissemination of information through newsletters, general meetings, listserve postings, individual meetings, phone calls, posters and banners. The purpose of this strategy is not to involve all employees in the change, but simply to give everyone fair notice of the change and to keep them informed of what is happening in the organization. The strategy is also often used to prevent the complaint by employees unfriendly to the proposed change that they were not told early enough or given enough details. The strategy is common in large organizations where communication channels are abundant and where extensive information dissemination thus adds little further costs.

4 *Equal participation strategy*: This strategy involves two-way communication (i.e., both disseminating information and soliciting input) between managers and employees. This participative strategy is used when employees are crucial to the success of the change. However, the strategy is quite costly and may become overly political when opinions, support and advice from all sectors of the workforce are sought. This strategy is common in small and public sector organizations that embrace participative and democratic values and that have sufficient time, resources and communication channels available.

Organizational changes often present challenges to employees. Employees usually do not resist the change itself, but rather the uncertainty associated with the change:

uncertainty about job security, the fear of losing status and power within the organi-zation, and the uncertainty about whether they will fit in with the changed organiza-tion.[12] Uncertainty and fear may lead to stress, to a lack of trust between employees and managers and to low levels of commitment. It may even encourage people to leave the organization.[13] Effective change communication recognizes these uncer-tainties and as far as is possible (based on the need for communication efficiency) tries to inform employees of the change and tries to engage with them to facilitate the implementation and routinization of the change.

EFFECTIVE LEADERSHIP COMMUNICATION

12.4 Given the significance of organizational changes, managers, in their leadership roles, need to use communication to help employees under-stand and implement the change. Successful management communication can make a massive difference in realizing changes, and requires that managers, as leaders, reflect upon how they communicate with others and how they frame the changes to others to gain their support. A first attribute of successful management or leadership communication involves authenticity or a truthful and passionate commitment to a clear, inspiring change idea. Given the personal nature of leadership communication, it is important that communicating leaders are themselves committed to what they are saying. They know their commitments and convictions beyond the change idea, stay true to them in their advocacy and can communicate consistently in line with those commitments in order to drum up support. Authenticity gives a level of consis-tency and personal touch that is more likely to garner success. It also brings a per-sonal passion that is more likely to win people over. A good example of authenticity in leadership communication involves Al Gore before and after the 2000 US presi-dential elections. In the televised presidential debates, Gore mentioned a number of government initiatives, but neither he nor his advisers had thought about a clear positioning of Gore as a candidate and person. In the end, he set out to project a persona of a competent statesman who would sustain the economy and would bring about greater social democracy. But his delivery lacked passion, as it was largely focused on manufacturing an image, rather than being driven from within his own person. Yet in 2006, Gore toured the world and was able to sell out stadia and movie theatres with people wanting to hear his message about climate change. This time, as shown in his movie *An Inconvenient Truth*, he conveyed a real and personal passion for a subject he cares deeply about. He does not speak any more in terms of political abstractions or technical language, but speaks from his own experiences and delivers the message with his own style and convictions. Such authenticity assumes that man-agers or leaders are sufficiently reflective on their own commitments and of the ways in which they communicate.

Successful leadership communication often involves narratives and stories that present the rationale for the change, the steps needed to realize it, and the overall beneficial outcomes as a result of it. Crudely speaking, narratives and stories present a sequence of actions and events leading towards a particular outcome (the plot). The outcome, in turn, rationalizes any conscious actions taken by individuals to get

there. Given that changes are uncertain and always about a future state, such narratives or stories provide a coherent structure and understanding of what the change
may ultimately lead to. Skilful managers and leaders are mindful of the words that
they use, the narrative patterns they form, and about how they use such narrative
patterns in their day-to-day communication with others around them. The Vice-
Chancellor of the University of Leeds, for example, initiated a strategic change when
he arrived in 2004. He set an ambitious vision for the university of securing a place
among the top 50 universities in the world by 2015. The narrative that he has communicated since is one that highlights the targeted outcome, but with additional elements around core values, collaboration, internationalization and excellence in
research. These elements form the narrative patterns leading up to the desired outcome, and in turn rationalize the performance expectations and commitments that
are required of staff in the university.

Besides an overall narrative or story to frame and rationalize a change, managers
or leaders also need conversational skills to tap into ongoing conversations about the
change across the organization. If leaders are to succeed in inspiring enduring enthusiasm for changes, they need to set aside any idea of imposing their will or moving
their listeners to a predetermined position. The aim is rather one of mobilizing conversations at the interpersonal level to enable others in the organization to see possibilities that they have hitherto missed. It means relating to the language of others in
conversational settings so that they themselves can view the organization and their
relations with others in a new light.

The very concept of conversation implies a dialogue in which two parties can
relate to and elaborate on each other's points, rather than being a straight monologue
or negotiation. Successful leaders and managers are able to have open conversations.
They are willing to say where they stand and what they think, at least provisionally,
while showing themselves to being open to entertaining alternative viewpoints. They
listen carefully to what others say, trying to make sense of their points and explore
the implications. These conversations may also trigger a reformulation in the definition or implementation of a change. Barge and Oliver comment on the importance
of these conversations as follows:

> Historically, managerial communication skills have been associated with encoding and decoding
> skills – a model of communication that is based on an approach to language in which it is assumed
> that meaning is fixed and that the point of communication is to clearly convey one's point to another.
> … Viewing conversation as sites where various discourses intersect and meaning is continually
> unfolding requires managers to develop the ability to pick up the flow of conversation and to
> develop a sensibility for when and where to shape the conversation in new directions.[14]

The importance of conversations and conversational skills emphasizes that a
straightforward leadership presentation about change that is broadcasted across the
organization may not be sufficient. At most, it is simply a beginning. In order to continue and accelerate the enthusiasm for, and implementation of, a change requires
that managers or leaders have regular, ongoing conversations with the people they
are leading, about the things going on in their context, and about how they can
address any emerging issues. It is these detailed conversations that often matter the
most and may be the deciding factor as to whether individuals in organizations are
supportive of or resistant towards a particular change. A good example of these

principles of leadership communication is presented in the following case study of British Airways.

CASE STUDY 12.2

BRITISH AIRWAYS: CHANGE AND LEADERSHIP COMMUNICATION AT THE WORLD'S FAVOURITE AIRLINE

British Airways (BA) has made concerted efforts to become not just a global player, but effectively a global company. Senior executives of BA took the view that the airline industry was undergoing consolidation, and that in future the industry would consist of a very small number of very large international airlines. Emphasis was therefore placed on globalizing the business, primarily through establishing alliances and partnerships in the USA, Australia and Europe, to overcome gaps in BA's coverage of routes as well as to access the lucrative but highly protected US domestic market.

Coupled with the effort to globalize the company's operations, BA also constantly tries to upgrade its product by improving flights and services at an internationally competitive rate. The company also felt that in order to become a truly global airline it had to adapt its corporate identity. The current corporate identity of BA follows from the company's vision: 'To become the undisputed leader in world travel by ensuring that BA is the customer's first choice through the delivery of an unbeatable travel experience.' The identity of the BA brand is based on a blend of Britishness, cosmopolitanism, innovation and service. The strap-line or motto associated with this identity is the well-known 'The world's favourite airline', which is carried through in all of the design, livery, and communication of BA.

To give this corporate identity shape, BA unveiled a striking new visual identity in June 1997. Fifty ethnic designs were commissioned from artists around the world to adorn the tailfins of BA's entire fleet, as well as ticket jackets, cabin crew scarves and business cards. The launch of the new corporate identity coincided with two trade union ballots on possible strike action, which promoted criticism from the unions that the airline should attend to its employees rather than its image. One dispute over the sale of the company's catering division was quickly resolved, with management proposing a new deal. The other dispute concerned the cabin crews and turned out to be more delicate.

One cabin staff union, BASSA (British Airlines Stewards and Stewardesses Association), felt that some of its staff would lose out under the proposed new salary scheme. BA accepted that a minority of staff might lose money, but guaranteed that existing cabin crew would not suffer financially and offered loyalty bonuses and employee travel entitlements. Unsatisfied with this response, the largely female cabin staff voted for a 72-hour strike. When the strike deadline approached and talks broke down, BA warned those considering taking part in the strike that they risked being sacked or even sued for damages. BA argued that the strike ballot was procedurally flawed, making the strike illegal. Only a small fraction of staff eventually went on strike, but 1,500 called in sick, disrupting BA's schedule for days. BA followed a tough approach in asking staff who reported sick to produce a doctor's note. This approach was widely criticized by the British press and by ten Labour MPs, who criticized the tactics of intimidation pursued by the airline.

(Continued)

(Continued)

Looking after employees

In September 1997, BA issued a press release in which the company announced the settlement of the cabin crew dispute that had provoked the strike. BASSA had agreed to the pay package on the table and BA lifted sanctions against the 300 cabin crew who had gone on strike. As Ayling commented at the time:

> Today's agreement signals a genuinely new beginning for relations and a spirit of cooperation within the company. It safeguards our plans for growth and will help the airline at the forefront of what is now a ferociously competitive global industry, in the interests of all our customers, employees and shareholders.

Building on the settlement, BA started an intensive programme of activities to lift staff morale under the heading 'Winning hearts and minds'. Those cabin staff who had called in sick at the time of the strike were interviewed to try to understand what had motivated them to action. Ayling also pledged to staff that he would be more 'caring'. He said that people were back at the top of his agenda and that the company would try to re-engage with everyone inside the business.

BA set up a task force (entitled the *Way Forward*), which was designed to learn lessons from the dispute and to produce a new spirit of cooperation. The mandate of the task force was to look at how morale and motivation could be rebuilt, to find ways to improve customer relationships and to repair the damage to BA's reputation. The task force specifically focused on significant declines in morale in some areas of the business and on improving communication between management and employees. Informed by the findings of the task force, BA launched a series of initiatives, such as a *Good People Management* framework, which was based on interviews with 100 employees about what good managers actually do. The framework set down some simple guidelines on management communication and was also used to simplify the performance management system by introducing more observable behavioural criteria as well as certain mandatory tasks, including two proper performance reviews per year and at least one career development discussion. Another initiative, called *In Touch*, involved placing employees who were normally not in direct contact with customers for one day in the front-line to experience how it felt.

Cutting costs and employee morale

While employee morale improved somewhat as a result of these initiatives, it was quickly under pressure again as a result of the company having to cut costs and make staff redundant. In 1999, BA suffered as a result of the economic crisis in Asia and reported significant losses. The company initiated cost-reduction and efficiency programmes, which had an impact on staff morale. An internal survey showed that many employees doubted management's ability to manage costs effectively without sacrificing quality, their desire to communicate openly and honestly, and the extent to which they cared about employees. Informed by the survey findings, BA initiated a motivational programme for staff entitled *Putting People First*, which was meant to train staff in customer service and to increase a sense of belonging.

(Continued)

(Continued)

In 2000, Rodd Eddington took over as the CEO of BA and faced the challenge of further cutting costs by downsizing while sustaining an acceptable level of employee morale. When he took over, Eddington said:

It is my job to empower the organization to be able to [compete]. People are the lifeblood of any airline and it is the people of British Airways, both as individuals and as a team, who will deliver its future success. I look forward to meeting as many as possible over the coming weeks and months and listening to what they have to tell me about how we can further improve our products and services.

In 2001, BA laid off 5,200 employees and saved £37 million. In 2002, BA launched its *Future Size and Shape* programme, which was designed to save costs by £650 million per annum. As part of the programme, 5,800 job cuts were announced at the head office. A year later, the airline introduced an electronic swiping card system in order to monitor employee absenteeism. BA wanted to reduce absenteeism from an average of 17 days per employee to 10 days within a year and save £30 million as a result. Because of these cost-cutting exercises and the ongoing pressures on staff to become more efficient in their work practices, BA recognized that it needed to look after employee morale. In late 2003, the company started the *Industrial Relations Change* programme, a joint initiative with the trade unions which was designed to develop better working relationships between BA and its trade unions. BA also announced an Employee Reward Plan, which provides employees with rewards when profit margins of the airline move towards 10 per cent.

Rodd Eddington stepped down as CEO in September 2005 and was succeeded by Willie Walsh. Walsh had attracted the nickname of 'Slasher' at his previous employer, Aer Lingus, where he was responsible for cutting a third of the workforce. In December 2005, as a result of high fuel costs and lower ticket prices, Walsh announced plans to cut a further 600 management jobs at BA but he insisted that the airline had long-term scope to grow. The job cuts involved a 50 per cent reduction in senior managers, from 414 jobs to 207, and a 30 per cent reduction in middle managers, from 1,301 jobs to 911 jobs. Walsh rationalized the job cuts as follows: 'We are restructuring the airline to remove duplication, simplify our core business and provide clearer accountability. Managers will have greater accountability for making decisions, delivering results and leading the business.'

On top of the cuts in management jobs, Walsh warned staff in March 2006 to brace themselves for a fresh wave of further job losses as BA attempted to cut £450 million of costs. 'We're going to target every single aspect of the cost base', Walsh explained, 'Employee costs are an element of that but they're not the only part. We will continue to introduce new work practices and efficiencies, which will allow us to run the business with fewer people.' BA's cost-cutting target in 2006 was for £225 million of savings and the same in 2007. The airline has put a squeeze on suppliers and has told every internal department to produce monthly reports on progress towards cuts.

In recent years, Walsh has faced turmoil with the chaotic opening of Terminal 5 at Heathrow Airport as well as further industrial relations problems as he struggles to modernize the airline's labour agreements. The opening of Heathrow's fifth terminal for BA in 2008 was meant to bring further efficiencies, with more self-service

(Continued)

(Continued)

check-in kiosks and automated baggage handling. But a catalogue of IT errors with the new automated system and a lack of staff training meant that the first few days of Terminal's were a fiasco, with around 20,000 bags lost or stranded in the system and flights delayed or cancelled. Whereas it was meant to have been an opportunity for BA to demonstrate its new facilities, it led to a crisis for BA and for the British Airports Authority (BAA), the operator of Heathrow airport. Alistair Carmichael, a Member of Parliament in the UK, criticized the lack of communication response from BA or BAA: 'It's a national disgrace, a national humiliation. Where is the leadership? There is a ferocious amount of buck-passing between BA and BAA. No one is prepared to take responsibility.' Eventually, a full day after the fiasco, Willie Walsh appeared in front of the cameras and admitted that the opening was 'Not our finest hour'. He offered a 'promise to do better'.

In 2010, relations with trade unions culminated in proposed plans for a strike in March of that year. A strike by BA cabin crew looked certain to go ahead after Walsh refused to guarantee that they would not sack union officials of BASSA, the Unite trade union cabin crew branch at the heart of the industrial action. BA had also started disciplinary proceedings against 38 members of the trade union. Walsh appeared to harden his stance in subsequent communications with the union, a move that was criticized by employment analysts and academics as a blatant attempt to break the union's influence over cabin crew, and effectively over the company.

As part of its communications offensive to explain its stance, BA launched a viral social media campaign, with a video of Willie Walsh talking of his disappointment over the forthcoming strike action and the negative consequences for customers. In the video, Walsh talks about how he is staking his own personal reputation on ensuring that the company does everything it can to limit the inconvenience to customers. Philip Allport, from the BA corporate communications team, explained the use of the video: 'This is the first time we've used *YouTube* to support our crisis communications' he said. 'We recognise how important social media is as a way to communicate directly to our customers.' The release of the video coincided with the start of industrial strike action and with a number of news stories backing British Airways. The Transport Minister Lord Adonis told the BBC: 'I absolutely deplore the strike. It is not only the damage it is going to do passengers and the inconvenience it's going to cause – which is quite disproportionate to the issues at stake – but also the threat it poses to the future of one of our great companies in this country.' Prime Minister Gordon Brown equally intervened and criticized the strike action as 'deplorable'.

QUESTIONS FOR REFLECTION

1   Reflect upon management and leadership communication within BA from the perspective of employees. What, in general, can you say about the approach to communication with staff?

2   Identify the change communication strategy that BA used to communicate the cost reductions and job cuts. Was this the right strategy for the company or should another strategy have been used?

(Continued)

(Continued)

Source: This case study is in part based on Clark, A. (2006), 'British Airways warns staff of further job cuts', *The Guardian*, 10 March 2006 and INSEAD (2002), *Flying into a Storm: British Airways (1996–2000)*.

CHAPTER SUMMARY

12.5 The chapter started by defining the importance of leadership and leadership communication in the context of organizational changes. One crucial message in the chapter has been the role of managers, as leaders, communicating with employees in such a way that they feel valued, listened to and involved in organizational changes. This requires that managers are not only aware of and constantly reflect upon their communication style, but also use a range of tried-and-tested interactive strategies to inspire employees to commit to the change and to make the change happen.

DISCUSSION QUESTIONS

1   What defines successful communication around an organizational change? Use examples from cases that you know or from your own experience to motivate your answer.

2   Think about a manager or leader of an organization that you are familiar with or have worked for in the past. How successful was this manager or leader as a communicator? What in your view determined her or his degree (or lack) of success?

KEY TERMS

Additive change

Authenticity

Conversations

Equal dissemination strategy

Equal participation strategy

Identify and reply strategy

Leadership

Leadership communication

Need to know strategy

Organizational change

Quid pro quo strategy

Storytelling

Substitutive change

Tell and sell strategy

Underscore and explore strategy

Withhold and uphold strategy

 FURTHER READING

Barrett, Deborah (2006), *Leadership Communication* (3rd edn). New York: McGraw-Hill.

Fairhurst, Gail (2007), *Discursive Leadership – In Conversation with Leadership Psychology*. London: Sage.

Quirke, Bill (2008), *Making the Connections: Using Internal Communication to Turn Strategy into Action* (2nd edn). Aldershot: Gower.

NOTES

1 Rousseau, Denise M. (1998) 'Why workers still identify with organizations', *Journal of Organizational Behavior*, 19: 211–233.

2 Greenwood, R. and Hinings, C. (1996), 'Understanding radical organizational change: bringing together the old and the new institutionalism', *Academy of Management Review*, 21: 1022–1054.

3 See, for example, Corley, Kevin G. and Gioia, Dennis A. (2004), 'Identity ambiguity and change in the wake of a corporate spin-off', *Administrative Science Quarterly*, 49 (2): 173–208.

4 Lewin, K. (1947), 'Frontiers in group dynamics 1', *Human Relations*, 1: 5–41.

5 Clampitt, P., DeKoch, R. and Cashman, T. (2000), 'A strategy for communicating about uncertainty', *Academy of Management Executive*, 14: 41–57.

6 Timmerman, C.E. (2003), 'Media selection during the implementation of planned organizational change', *Management Communication Quarterly*, 16: 301–340.

7 Larkin, T.J. and Larkin, S. (1994), *Communicating Change: Winning Employee Support for New Business Goals*. New York: McGraw-Hill.

8 See also Llewellyn, N. and Harrison, A. (2006), 'Resisting corporate communications: insights into folk linguistics', *Human Relations*, 59: 567–596.

9 See, for example, Poole, M.S. and McPhee, R.D. (1983), 'A structurational analysis of organizational climate', in Putnam, L.L. and Pacanowksy, M.E. (eds), *Communication and Organization: An Interpretive Approach*. Beverly Hills, CA: Sage; Smidts, A., Pruyn, A.T.H. and Van Riel, C.B.M. (2001), 'The impact of employee communication and perceived external prestige on organizational identification', *Academy of Management Journal*, 44: 1051–1062.

10 Heracleous, L. (2002), 'The contribution of discourse in understanding and managing organizational change', *Strategic Change*, 11: 253–261.

11 Lewis, L.K., Hamel, S.A. and Richardson, B.K. (2001), 'Communicating change to nonprofit stakeholders', *Management Communication Quarterly*, 15: 5–41.

12 Dent, E.B. and Goldberg, S.G. (1999), 'Challenging a "resistance to change"', *Journal of Applied Behavioral Science*, 35: 25–41.

13 Schweiger, D. and Denisi, A. (1991), 'Communication with employees following a merger: a longitudinal experiment', *Academy of Management Journal*, 34: 110–135.

14 Barge, J.K. and Oliver, C. (2003), 'Working with appreciation in managerial practice', *Academy of Management Review*, 28 (1): 124–142, quote on p. 138.

CORPORATE SOCIAL RESPONSIBILITY AND COMMUNITY RELATIONS

13

Chapter Overview

The resident employees, citizens and community groups that populate an organization's geographic operating area are essential to its operations. Corporate social responsibility (CSR) and community relations have emerged as core business functions. Their role is to communicate with local communities and business partners, with the overall aim of building strong and lasting relationships with the communities in which the company operates. The chapter discusses the concepts of corporate citizenship, CSR and community relations, ranging from charitable donations to partnerships that address pressing community issues.

INTRODUCTION

13.1 In other chapters of the book, we have discussed how stakeholder expectations towards corporate and public organizations have changed, and how this affects how organizations operate. Traditionally, organizations were expected to behave as economic entities that were destined to make profits and be accountable to themselves and their shareholders. The shift towards issues of corporate social responsibility and corporate citizenship recast traditional thinking and suggests instead that organizations are expected to demonstrate a level of accountability towards the whole of society. Their licence to operate is not based on profit or dividends, but on institutional legitimacy granted by each of the stakeholders with whom it interacts. BP is a good example of this principle. The corporation has for years been one of the most profitable in the world and admired for its bold attempts to combine an environmental agenda with its commercial operations. However, its social legitimacy has increasingly been questioned given BP's retreat from investments in alternative energies and the massive oil spill in the Gulf of Mexico in 2010, which has done excessive damage to the environment and affected local communities in the Gulf region. The company initially played down the size of the spill and its own role in the initial explosion that caused it, but because of the intervention of the US government it was forced to set up a fund of $20 billion to help compensate those living in the region, whose livelihoods were directly affected. Organizations like BP, which do not align community relations, as an area of corporate communication, with their business operations, are likely to find their licence to operate questioned and possibly challenged by stakeholders, including local and national government officials.

At the same time, of course, these changed expectations also present significant opportunities for organizations. Those organizations that enjoy positive relationships with the communities in which they operate are treated differently and respectfully. It leads to general goodwill and local support from the community and from local and national governments. A successful organization, in other words, is often one which has worked out the best ways of developing and nurturing community relations, responding to community expectations and taking advantage of such expectations in community involvement programmes that mutually support the community and the organization's business goals.

In this chapter, we discuss the wider social remit of organizations and their corporate social responsibility (CSR) towards stakeholders, including the communities in which an organization operates. We outline various ways in which that social responsibility can be realized in stakeholder engagement programmes and how organizations can best communicate about their CSR programmes. The chapter concludes with a closer look at community relations, an area of corporate communication that is closely aligned with the organization's CSR objectives and programmes. Good community relations can improve the community, but can also add to a company's goals and reputation.

DEFINING CORPORATE SOCIAL RESPONSIBILITY

13.2 In previous chapters, we have described how an organization is increasingly seen as being part of a larger social system that includes commercial parties as well as communities, NGOs and government agencies in society, and as being dependent upon that system's support for its continued existence. Organizational goals and activities in this sense must be found to be legitimate and valued by all individuals and groups in the larger social system of society. This society-based model has drastic implications for organizations, both public and private. Even private organizations that do not necessarily protect a public good in society have realized that they need to listen to and communicate with a whole range of stakeholder groups for their own as well as for society's sake.

In a fully developed stakeholder model, a manager's key objective is to coordinate the conflicting interests and values of stakeholders rather than to control them. The aim is not to contain stakeholder interests, but to try to accomplish them through corporate activity. Management should work with all stakeholders, seeking the most creative ways of working for the benefit of all stakeholders. Versions of such a model have been developed in quasi-public enterprises and in several countries. In Germany, for example, trade union involvement at the level of corporate boards (the famous practice of *Mitbestimmung*, or 'co-determination') is seen by many Germans, including chancellor Angela Merkel, as 'an essential part of Germany's economy'. Stakeholder participation and inclusion in such a strong model is not meant to balance or trade off social and economic interests, but is essential for the process of creative decision-making that can advance both. As we know from collaborative decision-making contexts, creativity and mutual satisfaction are based on a commitment to a co-determinative or democratic process rather than just arguing out self-interests.

These democratic models of representation and participation in society also form the foundation for recent ideas on 'corporate citizenship'. Organizations are 'legal entities with rights and duties, in effect, 'citizens' of states within which they operate'.[1] 'Corporate citizenship' refers to the portfolio of activities that organizations undertake to fulfil perceived duties as members of society. The underlying idea is that individual citizens have certain rights and responsibilities in society. Equally, when organizations are granted the legal and political rights of individual citizens through incorporation, they are also ascribed, explicitly and implicitly, a set of rights and responsibilities. Examples of corporate citizenship include *pro bono* activities, corporate volunteerism, charitable contributions, support for community education and healthcare initiatives, and environmental programmes – few of which are legally mandated, but many of which have come to be expected as corporate citizen responsibilities. The World Economic Forum defines corporate citizenship as:

> the contribution a company makes to society through its core business activities, its social investment and philanthropy programmes, and its engagement in public policy. The manner in which a company manages its economic, social and environmental relationships, as well as those with different stakeholders, in particular shareholders, employees, customers, business partners, governments and communities determines its impact.[2]

The idea of corporate citizenship rests on a long and respected tradition of thinking on citizenship in political theory. Corporate citizenship, however, differs in a crucial respect from individual citizenship in society. State-based citizenship is typically conceived as being, more or less, symmetrical. There is a symmetry or balance in the exchange between a government that grants and administers certain fundamental rights, on the one hand, and the citizens who enjoy them, on the other, with taxes and political responsibilities (e.g., voting in elections) serving as the currency of the exchange. This symmetry between rights and obligations in the exchange between governments and citizens is central to citizenship; the advantages that an individual derives from citizenship are mirrored by at least an obligation to contribute whatever is necessary to realize the same for others in the cooperative venture of the state. The citizenship of organizations often seems less symmetrical in this sense. Organizations tend to focus on making positive contributions towards their stakeholders as opposed to, as 'citizens', being locked into a mutually beneficial exchange that protects fundamental human rights and responsibilities. The asymmetry is clear in the numerous instances where big corporations, besides their charitable donations and community initiatives, still negatively affect the health and well-being of certain communities by paying below 'living' wages or through environmentally damaging production or supply chain practices.

The drive for a sense of corporate social responsibility (CSR) came with the appeal to business organizations to deliver wider societal value beyond shareholder and market value alone. The term CSR can be broadly defined as 'the continuing commitment by business to contribute to economic development while improving the quality of life of the workforce and their families as well as of the community and society at large'.[3] Strictly speaking, it implies the adoption by an organization of 'the responsibilities for actions which do not have purely financial implications and which are demanded of an organization under some (implicit or explicit) identifiable contract' with stakeholders in society.[4] This contract is largely a moral 'contract' in the sense that it is expected to meet the social and environmental expectations of stakeholders, as a good corporate citizen, which not only creates goodwill but also provides a licence to operate.

In recent years, CSR has become more pertinent through expectations voiced by the international community, NGOs, and pressure groups. At the European Summit in Lisbon in March 2000, the European Council made a special appeal to companies' sense of responsibility and linked CSR closely to the Lisbon 2010 strategic goal for a knowledge-based and highly competitive, as well as socially inclusive, Europe. Internationally, the UN World Summit for Sustainable Development in Johannesburg in 2002 voiced the need for businesses to contribute to the building of equitable and sustainable societies, wherever they work.

On top of the momentum that has gathered around CSR in the international community and public policy arenas, organizations often also consider CSR in an effort to boost their reputations. With the media constantly reporting on their affairs, and because of the greater product homogeneity and competition in many markets, many organizations have realized that doing business in a responsible and just manner offers strategic and reputational advantages. As with stakeholder management, CSR initiatives may, in the first instance, be started for either moral or instrumental reputational reasons. However, the actual reasons for CSR are often difficult to separate given the 'significant difficulties in distinguishing whether business behavior is truly moral conduct or instrumental adoption of an appearance of moral conduct as reputational strategy'.[5] However, regardless of the underlying motives, CSR initiatives, including community outreach and charity donations, often appear to be of a direct instrumental value to an organization. Research has found that these initiatives are related to reputational returns and an overall better financial performance.[6]

CSR is also often defined in terms of the notion of a 'triple bottom line' that includes people, planet, and profits.[7] John Elkington introduced the term and suggested that CSR can be broken into activities that include social ('people') and ecological ('planet') initiatives alongside the generation of profits and healthy financial accounts ('profit'). 'People' stands for all social and labour issues both inside and outside the organization, including employee support and compensation, gender and ethnic balance of the workforce, reduction of corruption and fraud in business transactions and health and safety codes. 'Planet' refers to the responsibility of organizations to integrate environmental care into its business operations, such as the reduction of harmful waste and residues and the development of environmentally-friendly production processes. 'Profit' involves the conventional bottom-line of manufacturing and selling products so as to generate financial returns for the organization and its shareholders. This latter category of responsibilities ('profit') is often considered as a baseline or requisite before an organization can even start considering meeting its social ('people') and ecological ('planet') responsibilities. That is, these other responsibilities cannot be achieved in the absence of economic performance (i.e., goods and services, jobs, profitability) – a bankrupt organization will cease to operate.[8]

COMMUNICATING ABOUT CORPORATE SOCIAL RESPONSIBILITY

13.3 Most managers' approach to communicating with stakeholders tends to be one that is based on a model of strategic persuasion rather than 'democratic' communication or 'dialogue' (see Figure 3.6). Managers are often hesitant to include stakeholders in crucial decisions by disclosing information, sharing power or granting autonomy. They often also lack the right model and skills of democratic communication necessary for coordinating divergent interests. Stanley Deetz, a communication scholar, has argued that most models of 'dialogue' are borrowed from liberal-democratic communication models used in state processes of governance.[9] These models stress commitment to representation and consensus, which contrasts with participatory models committed to diversity, conflict and creativity. Deetz also argues that the widespread use of these models in corporate organizations may partly account for the poor regard people have for processes of corporate decision-making and the cynicism towards the use of terms such as 'stakeholder dialogue' and 'participation'. Instead, other models of communication, drawn from models of participatory democracy, may better meet the challenge of a 'democratic' and actual stakeholder dialogue. These models specify minimal conditions for stakeholder involvement in corporate decision-making discussions. These conditions include, for example:

- reciprocity of opportunity for expression;
- equality in skills for expression;
- the setting aside of authority relations, organizational positions, and other external sources of power;
- the open investigation of stakeholders' positions to more freely ascertain their interests;
- the open sharing of information and transparency of decision processes;
- the testing of alternative claims in the discussion.

Many of these conditions are directly applicable to corporate organizations. However, it is often difficult for managers (as it is for politicians) to meet these conditions, giving up some of their own power and influence in the process.

These difficulties are reflected in how most organizations communicate about CSR to their stakeholders. Many organizations, for example, put out glossy social and environmental reports that are more about style than substance, according to Sustainability, the consultancy that evaluates CSR reporting of organizations worldwide. A recent report from the think-tank Demos suggests that many companies view social responsibility as a PR exercise instead of a refocusing and reshuffling of their business operations. A survey by McKinsey in 2006 reported that organizations often simply focus on the media and on public relations tactics to manage their CSR initiatives without considering other ways to embed CSR within their organizations.[10] What these examples indicate is that organizations may find it difficult to engage in a real dialogue about CSR with stakeholders. This would require that they are fully and openly responsive to stakeholder expectations. Instead, many organizations approach the subject from a largely instrumental and linear perspective, communicating about CSR for image and reputation-building purposes.

The CSR experts Morsing and Schultz refer, in this respect, to three standard communication strategies for CSR.[11] The first strategy, labelled the *stakeholder information strategy*, is a one-way information flow where information about the company's CSR is made available to stakeholders. With this strategy, there is not necessarily a persuasive intent, but companies instead aim to inform the public as objectively as possible about its CSR activities. Companies produce information and news for the media, as well as a variety of brochures, societal reports, pamphlets, magazines, facts, numbers and figures to inform the general public.

The second strategy is the *stakeholder response strategy*, where stakeholders are asked for feedback on CSR activities, or more generally in response to organizational decisions and actions. The communication model with this strategy is 'two-way' in that stakeholders are asked about their opinions and expectations, but it is the company which decides what the focus of CSR activities should be, and engages with stakeholders to promote these activities. As such, the stakeholder response strategy may turn out to be pretty one-sided, with companies putting out glossy society reports or running campaigns that are intended to convince stakeholders of their CSR credentials. The implication may be that CSR is purely seen as a marketing or PR ploy, rather than as a steadfast commitment to stakeholders and society.

The third and preferred strategy is the *stakeholder involvement strategy*, where there is a real mutual dialogue between a company and its stakeholders. Stakeholders have a say in the CSR commitments of a company, with the company trying to meet, if not exceed, the expectations of various stakeholder groups. Companies not only influence but also seek to be influenced by stakeholders, and therefore change in their CSR commitments when necessary. By engaging in a dialogue, a company ensures that it keeps abreast not only of its stakeholders' expectations, and any shifts in expectations, but also of its potential influence on those expectations, as well as letting those expectations influence and change the company itself. This strategy assumes that companies not only publish reports or issue CSR campaigns but set up public consultation forums with their stakeholders and conduct ongoing surveys on stakeholder opinions. It also implies a strong commitment in the very identity of the organization to its stakeholders and their opinions. This involvement also ensures that CSR activities are seen as authentic and as meeting a voiced, and therefore public, expectation of stakeholders. On balance, companies may be better off involving stakeholders in their CSR policies versus setting their own targets and then trying to convince stakeholders of their efforts. It may also mean that companies would engage less in self-promotion through advertising and press releases (think BP) and instead use 'subtle' CSR communication such as social reports and websites. Case Study 13.1 examines CSR reporting.

CASE STUDY 13.1

CORPORATE SOCIAL RESPONSIBILITY REPORTING

The founders of Ben & Jerry's, the funky ice-cream manufacturers now part of the Unilever group, believe that business should give something back to the community that supports it. But what makes Ben & Jerry's unique and, from a CSR perspective, interesting is that the company was one of the first organizations to acknowledge its shortcomings publicly, going so far as to print them as part of the social assessment in its annual report to shareholders. A growing number of organizations have since followed suit, and are among the elite that now publish rather frank society or social reports that appear alongside financial reports and in which they systematically report upon their social and ecological performance over the past year.[12]

Nowadays, many of the largest and most visible corporations routinely publish CSR reports. For example, more than 90 per cent of the FTSE 100 largest listed corporations in the UK issue such reports, although the percentage quickly decreases in the FTSE 350. But many large organizations around the world still report little, if anything, about their impact upon society. KPMG, in their most recent survey of CSR reporting, report some positive signs in that CSR reporting now includes more hard data on performance on health and safety and climate change issues than before. At the same time, many of the reporting is still patchy or not fully transparent. For example, although 92 per cent of the largest 250 companies worldwide disclose a code of governance or ethics, only 59 per cent report on incidents of compliance with the code. Similarly, nearly all large corporations have a supply chain code of conduct, but only half disclose the details of how it is implemented and monitored. Approximately half of the largest corporations worldwide disclose some level of information about climate risks, but roughly the same number report very little, if anything.

This mixed record may be due to the fact that CSR reporting constantly evolves and that transparent standards and benchmarks of what constitutes social and ecological performance are lacking. As a result, many organizations develop and report on CSR in line with their own operations, and many reports may thus reflect biases and omissions stemming from the company's own perspective. However, in a

(Continued)

(Continued)

recent article in *The Financial Times*, Schrage, an expert on social auditing, warned that these days may soon be over. On a worldwide scale, the public is demanding ever greater scrutiny and more evidence of CSR activities. Governments are also toughening their stance on what they endorse as good CSR reporting. Schrage writes: 'The message to multinational business – and to global regulators – is that social accountability demands the same kind of independent scrutiny as financial auditing.'

Nevertheless, there are difficulties with setting clear, unequivocal standards and with enforcing them because (transnational) authorities and institutions that would develop and guard such standards have not come forward yet. This of course plays into the hands of current CSR malpractice and the 'anything goes' strategy. Schrage acknowledges these difficulties, yet advocates that 'just as the Securities and Exchange Commission and Financial Accounting Standards Board establish a framework in the US for public accountants to evaluate corporate financial performance, a new reporting system is needed for independent review of corporate social performance'. Such a system, when governments and industries are ready for it, will need clear social standards (in such areas as labour conditions, environmental performance and the promotion of human rights), a professional corps of social auditors (independent of corporate control and accountable to the public), and safe harbours that limit legal liability (so as to encourage companies to open their businesses to social audits).

Recent years have already seen some improvements in terms of the development of standards and assurance by third parties. Increasingly, standard tools, such as the Global Reporting Initiative and the Global Compact, are used on a worldwide scale, which increases levels of transparency and comparability between companies. Formal, third-party assurance of CSR reports has also jumped in recent years with greater use being made of major accountancy firms, as auditors, and third-party stakeholder voices and expert statements.

Besides using a standard tool such as the Global Reporting Initiative, companies that are known for their CSR reporting generally appear to adhere to the following guidelines:

1 *Set clear objectives*: A company needs to show that it is serious about CSR by setting clear objectives for social and ecological performance annually, and by systematically reporting on the results achieved afterwards.
2 *Set progressive objectives*: Objectives need to be progressive in bringing new aspirations and standards to bear upon business operations instead of a regurgitating of existing practices that may be seen as socially and ecologically viable.
3 *Involve stakeholders*: Objectives and targets should include issues that are relevant to stakeholders; and should be linked to benchmarks and standards (at the industry and policy levels) wherever possible.
4 *Report transparently*: Reporting needs to be an honest, transparent and full-scale self-assessment instead of a polishing of performance data.
5 *Accountability*: Performance data need to be rigorously assessed and verified by credible auditors (accountants or consultants) wherever possible.

(Continued)

(Continued)

QUESTIONS FOR REFLECTION

1   Collect a sample of the social and environmental reports of companies in a selected industry. What are the differences in objectives and reporting practices displayed by each report?
2   To what extent do these reports meet the five guidelines listed above? What characterizes the best report in this industry?

Source: This case study is based upon Lager, F. (1994), *The Inside Scoop*, New York: Crown publishers Schrage, E.J. (2001), 'A new model for social auditing', *The Financial Times*, 27 May 2010; Maitland, A. (2006), 'The frustrated will to act for the public good', *The Financial Times*, 26 January; KPMG (2008), *KPMG International Survey of Corporate Responsibility Reporting*. London: KPMG.

COMMUNITY INVOLVEMENT PROGRAMMES

13.4 Many large corporations have in recent years encountered activism in the form of protests and boycotts that have directly affected their operations. Wal-Mart, for example, is a company that has grown from very humble beginnings and has excelled in a very effective market expansion and low-cost growth strategy. However, the company has received much more criticism than before for its strategy and for the way in which it engages with, and cares for, important stakeholder groups such as employees and members of the local communities in which the company operates. The State of Maryland, for example, passed the so-called 'Wal-Mart healthcare bill' early in 2006, introducing a law that would fine big companies, and particularly Wal-Mart, for not picking up their fair share of employee healthcare coverage. Wal-Mart's plan to open a store in New York City has also continued to draw organized opposition from a broad coalition of labour, small business, local government and community groups.

Wal-Mart is not the only target of such opposition; large corporations such as Disney, Shell, BP and Monsanto have been similarly affected. Why has this been the case? One reason, as social movement scholars have argued, is that anti-corporate activism has increased in scope and frequency because of the fact that corporations themselves have become larger and more powerful and have increased their hold over individuals.[12] Through mergers and acquisitions, corporations have grown in size and now control a higher share of the overall assets in an economy than they used to do. This concentration of assets means that relatively few large corporations control many aspects of our individual lives. This control ranges from economic power in influencing what products are available to political power in lobbying governments and shaping legislation. A second reason is the so-called psychological contract between companies and communities in society. This refers to the implicit expectations that community members have of companies. People want to live in communities that are clean, environmentally safe, friendly and socially cohesive. Within communities, individuals, including local councilors, shopkeepers and social services, work together to achieve those ends that are shared in common. Similarly, when a company enters a community, different individuals and groups may appreciate its economic and competitive objectives but will also expect a fair and supportive contribution towards the community. It is this implicit 'psychological contract'[13] that defines the expectations between companies and communities, a feat that often influences how community support and involvement programmes are given shape (by companies) and evaluated (by communities). Such support and involvement programmes may meet, exceed or fall short of community expectations.

For companies, it is important to gauge such expectations at the level of each community affected by the company's operations as well as how such expectations may change over time. For example, in the past many communities expected companies to provide lifetime employment to residents, to support important community projects, to be involved in civic and business organizations and support the community's values and way of life. Presently, many communities expect employment opportunities (but not necessarily for life anymore) and that companies are generally more responsive to the concerns and issues within a community. This may involve partnering in improving public education, being environmentally responsible and correcting past mistakes and problems. In other words, companies are now more than ever assumed to act as responsible and proactive 'citizens'. In fact, such changing attitudes, expectations and behaviours towards companies impacts on a company's licence to operate. The freedom that companies once had for making business decisions has become constrained and challenged by local communities which expect ever greater forms of socially responsible behaviour and community involvement. As such, community involvement needs to be managed by companies, as part of its corporate communication. If not, companies may see a further challenge to their licence to operate, and no longer may have the support of the community that it needs for survival.

Prior to the 1980s, the contribution of many companies towards communities consisted of charitable donations, often to high-profile charities. The community relations expert Edmund Burke refers to this as the 'balloon and T-shirts era' to make the point that community relations in those days consisted of giving freebies to non-controversial non-profit organizations such as hospitals, museums and community centres.[14] The relationship was often one of purely making donations, rather than taking an active part in community issues or causes. The decision-making around those donations was often also *ad hoc*, triggered by approaches from community leaders or by senior executives' networks and family ties. The overall objective with such donations was to create some goodwill on the part of the community towards the company.

The 1980s saw a marked change in community relations programmes. One change involved the greater emphasis on employee volunteer programmes. Because of the harsher economic climate, many governments had introduced drastic cuts in social welfare programmes. There was a real and pressing need for such programmes to continue, and many governments called upon business organizations for their contributions. In the USA, for example, Reagan called upon businesses to double their charitable donations and to become involved in alleviating social problems. It is essentially in this era, with the growing pressures from governments and charities placed upon business organizations, that community relations emerged as an important subfield of corporate communication. As a result of this development, companies themselves also started to redefine their expectations for the community. They were looking for a motivated workforce, backed up by a strong and thriving community that would essentially help businesses secure a competitive edge. At the same time, employees themselves were looking for companies that had a strong reputation in the communities in which they operated.

The third and final stage of community relations started from the 1990s onwards. It suggests a further shift beyond a company's charitable donations and employee volunteer programmes. It encompasses more broadly how a company acts, as a citizen, and what it does for the community, besides any charitable donations. This 'citizenship' approach is driven by the wider expectations and the rise of community stakeholders. A company, it is argued, needs to behave in ways that promote and build trust between it and the community, and that provide it with legitimacy to operate in that community. Legitimacy refers to some kind of social acceptance resulting from the adherence of a company to regulations but also to community norms and expectations. In contrast, goodwill and reputation refer to an evaluation of an organization and its ability to deliver a particular good. Reputation does not necessarily capture the same normative dimension of civic and morally sound behaviour that communities, as well as many other stakeholders, now expect of businesses.

Of course this shift implies that organizations are pressured into building sustainable and ongoing relationships in a community in order to gain trust and legitimacy. The development of trust depends on respectful relationships which are hard earned over time. Such trusting relationships are, however, helpful to companies to keep track of changing expectations in the psychological contract with communities. The social acceptance that it implies also means that when things go wrong, companies are more likely to be given the benefit of the doubt.

TABLE 13.1 Characteristics of the 'old' and 'new' approaches to community relations

	Charitable donations (prior to 1980)	Community involvement (1980–1990)	Corporate citizenship (1990–present)
Objectives	Goodwill (with local community leaders and resident employees)	Reputation as employer of choice (with resident employees)	Trust and legitimacy (across stakeholders in the community)
Scope of community programmes	Charitable donations to local charities and causes	Employee volunteer programmes, growing involvement in social welfare programmes	Partnerships with local public institutions in bettering the community and increasing welfare
General approach	Idiosyncratic implementation dependent on requests from community leaders or managers' personal networks	Specific approach of fostering productive workplaces, linked to competitive goals	Wide-ranging approach driven by mission, values and wider range of stakeholders

FIGURE 13.1 Elements of a community relations programme

The overall changes in how companies have approached community relations are summarized in Table 13.1. These approaches also suggest a number of different community relations programmes. Ronald Speed, when he was Vice President for public affairs at the Honeywell Corporation, defined three different programme elements: philanthropy, volunteers and partnerships.[15] Figure 13.1 demonstrates how these elements can be combined to improve levels of commitment and support. Case Study 13.2 below illustrates the use (or lack of use) of these elements as part of a community involvement programme in the case of Kraft's takeover of Cadbury in 2010.

1 *Philanthropy*: At the bottom of Figure 13.1 are the company's charitable donations, or philanthropy. These are cash or in-kind contributions to local community causes or charities. While they may be seen as indicating a minor involvement in community affairs, they do provide a strong symbolic signal that the company cares about the community.

2 *Volunteers*: At the intermediate level are employee volunteering programmes. Employee volunteers are the most important resource of a company; they can help build relationships with local communities. When employees are working on local causes or public programmes, they act as ambassadors for the company, enhancing its reputation. Toyota, for example, has contributed to communities in the form of financial grants and the volunteer time of Toyota associates. In 2001, for instance, Toyota initiated a reforestation project in China's Hebei Province, where the environment had undergone considerable degradation over the years. Toyota employees volunteered to plant 500 hectares of land with poplar, pine and wild apricot trees. Another 'Toyota Teach Primary School Project' has been serving 140 schools in the areas of Umlazi and Umbumbulu in South Africa. Toyota South Africa Manufacturing, based in Prospecton, has been sourcing most of its employees from these areas. The project has been aiming to swell the number of students with mathematics and science competencies who may later pursue technology-related careers, and may thus ultimately choose to work for Toyota.

3 *Partnerships*: The final element, partnerships, assumes an even higher level of commitment and community involvement. Here, companies engage in partnerships with community agencies, and may form alliances with other organizations, to address public or community issues around education, infrastructure and welfare. Doing so may allow a company to not only help address pressing community needs, but may also mean that it can leverage and enhance the entire community relations programme. For example, Toyota partnered with the Japan Alliance for Humanitarian De-mining

Support (JAHDS) in Thailand and Cambodia to provide landmine detection technologies and backup systems to international NGOs. In Britain, Toyota has joined with the British Red Cross to hold interactive roadshows to raise awareness regarding road accidents involving children. In both cases, Toyota makes its expertise and technology available to address issues that affect local communities. Similarly, FedEx provides transportation and logistics support for emergency and disaster relief. The company has partnerships with several relief agencies, including American Red Cross, United Way International and Heart to Heart International, to help ensure that aid reaches people quickly and efficiently in such crises. In these examples, the partnerships not only link up with the expertise or the technology of these companies, but also with the larger causes or issues (road accidents, logistics for disaster relief) in the name of community support.

As suggested in Figure 13.1, partnerships imply a greater involvement with community causes. Companies that are known for good community relations intimately connect and internalize such programmes with the values of the company. The point, then, is to align external commitments with the internal values and responsibilities of a company. Companies that have not aligned these programme elements risk losing their reputation or goodwill in the community. Shell, for example, has not partnered with local community leaders and movements in the Niger Delta to address the environmental problems in the region. While the company has increased its charitable donations, it has not involved itself in making real changes to the welfare of the community. Nnimmo Bassey, from Environmental Rights Action in Nigeria, for example, has said: 'Despite Shell's public commitment to CSR and specific promise it has made to communities, life on the fence line can too often be likened to hell. From Nigeria to Ireland, the Philippines to South Africa, Shell still too often fails to respect the environment or the needs of local communities.'[16] Shell's poor environmental record in Nigeria is perhaps an indication of its lack of community involvement, failing to compensate communities such as the people living in the Niger Delta and helping them in addressing sanitary and health issues arising from the degradation of the land.

CASE STUDY 13.2

KRAFT'S TAKE-OVER OF CADBURY: FORGETTING THE COMMUNITY?

Kraft Foods, the second largest food company in the world, managed to take over Cadbury, a strong player in the confectionery market, in January 2010. The key motivation for Kraft was to expand its global presence and to gain a foothold in emerging markets such as India, where Cadbury had a strong presence. The acquisition would also bring certain brand portfolio and cross-selling opportunities with it, as it brought many famous brands, such as Kraft's Oreo cookies and Cadbury's chocolate bars under one roof. For Kraft, the idea was that the acquisition would expand its market reach and that it would also increase the margin potential of the combined business. Kraft believed that the acquisition would provide meaningful synergies and at the

(Continued)

(Continued)

same time yield pre-tax cost savings of at least US$625 million annually to boost its growth targets. The bidding process started in August 2009. Before the final deal was announced, Kraft Foods had repeatedly approached Cadbury. Initial offers were rejected and Kraft was pressured to increase the offer value a number of times. The background to this drawn-out process was that Cadbury was a very profitable and successful company in its own right, with a market share of 70 per cent in the Indian chocolate market and with 1.2 million retail outlets in that country. Cadbury occupied a leadership position in 20 of the world's top 50 emerging confectionery markets. In 2008, with a market share of 10.5 per cent, Cadbury was also effectively ranked in the number two position in confectionery worldwide.

Cadbury and the community

The history of the Cadbury company dates back to 1824, when John Cadbury opened a grocery business in the city of Birmingham. His most popular products were at that time cocoa drinks and chocolate. In 1831, he expanded and began manufacturing his own cocoa products. A few years later his brother joined the business, and together they concentrated on manufacturing and wholesale distribution, spinning off the retailing part of their business to a nephew in the family. John left this business to his two sons (George and Richard), who struggled for a few years, but then developed a new process for pressing cacoa butter, which provided the basis for better quality chocolate drinks and products. In 1868, Cadbury Brothers, as the firm was known at that time, began marketing its own lines of chocolate candy. The company revived its fortunes and expanded operations in the UK and in a number of key sites and markets around the world, including India and Australia.

This expansion went hand in hand with a commitment to the communities in which manufacturing facilities were set up and Cadbury products were sold. A good example of this commitment was the development of the Bournville manufacturing site. In 1893 George had bought some land around Birmingham where he planned a model village which would 'alleviate the evils of modern more cramped living conditions'. Cottages and houses were built for workers. The houses had large gardens and modern interiors. The Cadbury brothers were particularly concerned about the health and fitness of their workforce, creating park and recreation areas, and stimulating their workers to take up sports or other leisurely exercise. Playing fields were created, as well as several bowling greens, a fishing lake and indoor and outdoor swimming pools. Workers and their families could use these facilities free of charge. The Cadbury brothers cared deeply about their employees; they believed in the social rights of workers. After his brother died, George established two works committees (one for men and one for women) which discussed proposals for improving the company. He also advanced other ideas, such as an annuity, a deposit account and education facilities for every employee.

Although the company expanded greatly over the years, it remained a family business. Members of the Cadbury family occupied management positions in the company and the vast majority of its stock belonged to family members or trusts. In line with its social and family values, Cadbury also maintained a strong commitment

(Continued)

(Continued)

to local communities. The company has, for example, been credited with good community relations in India. Cadbury established partnerships with farmers in Kerala to cultivate cacoa and has transparently reported on its efforts to reduce excess packaging, and to cut water and energy use. In addition, when the company was confronted with two crisis scenarios – the first when worms were discovered in Cadbury products and the second about an ill-judged advertisement about Kashmir – they responded directly by improving the retailing and distribution set-up and by apologizing publicly. Regardless of whether the worms contaminated the product at the manufacturing stage or within a retailing setting, Cadbury addressed the crisis head-on and consumers judged it to be a one-off incident rather than a breach of trust or a reflection of the brand equity that Cadbury had built up.

Controversy around the take-over

Even as Kraft was making its bids for Cadbury, the senior management of Cadbury was seriously concerned about the take-over and what it would imply for the Cadbury business and workers. Cadbury repeatedly insisted that their offers were far too low. Roger Carr, Chairman of Cadbury, urged shareholders not to sell themselves short: 'Kraft is trying to buy Cadbury on the cheap to provide much needed growth to their unattractive low-growth conglomerate business model. Don't let Kraft steal your company with its derisory offer.' Politicians and union officials also weighed in, protesting against the take-over. The trade union Unite estimated that a take-over by Kraft would saddle the company with £22 billion worth of debt and could put some 30,000 jobs at risk, including around 7,000 jobs at Cadbury. Gordon Brown, the then Prime Minister of the UK, sought assurances from Kraft that 'Cadbury workers – the 5,500 – can retain their jobs and make sure that new investment goes into a product that is distinctly British and is sold throughout the world'.

Carr also criticized the role of shareholders in the take-over bidding, many of whom secured some profits by selling Cadbury shares, a process known as 'top-slicing'. These shares were snapped up by short-term investors such as hedge funds, which gambled that Kraft or another bidder would prevail. 'At the end of the day, there were simply not enough shareholders prepared to take a long-term view of Cadbury and prepared to forgo short-term gain for longer-term prosperity', Carr said. Felicity Loudon, George Cadbury's great-granddaughter, said her ancestors would be 'turning in their graves' knowing that Cadbury had been sold to a company that 'makes cheese to go on hamburgers'. Peter Cadbury, a great-grandson, said: 'It is regrettable that a company which took 186 years to build up has had its future decided by investors whose aims are short term'.

Promises to communities

In the bidding process, Kraft had assured the British government that UK jobs would be protected. However, on 9 February 2010, Kraft announced that they were planning to close the Somerdale factory with the loss of 400 jobs. Kraft had initially promised to keep the factory open, but then decided that plans to move production to Poland were already too advanced to be realistically reversed. Employees from

(Continued)

(Continued)

the factory felt betrayed and demoralized. The government's Business Secretary, Lord Mandelson, had met with Kraft chief executive Irene Rosenfeld, who had given no hint of the closure. Mandelson expressed his frustration and said:

> When I met the chief executive of Kraft last week, I made it clear that she had not given me any specific commitment or reassurance about any plant in Britain. What I do think, however, is that a week ago, she would have known what announcement was going to be made, barely six days later, and I think it would have been more honest, more straightforward and straight-dealing with the company and its workforce, and also with the Government, if she had told me what their intentions were.

Shadow Business Secretary Kenneth Clarke was similarly dismayed: 'Kraft gave me reassurances last week that they expected to be able to keep the factory open, despite Cadbury's announcement in 2007 that it would have to close.' The local Cadbury management team at the facility has since been partnering with regional development and job agencies to minimize the impact of the closure on the workforce and local economy.

Kraft was initially reluctant to engage with any local communities of Cadbury, but has since gone on the PR offensive. In March 2010, a community group in Bournville approached Kraft for a constructive meeting to demonstrate its commitment to the new company and to ensure that 'support for the local community is maintained or further enhanced; and to maximize the chances of Kraft seeing their investment in Bournville in its widest context and thereby maximizing the chances of securing local jobs into the long term'. Kraft has since agreed to meet with the community group.

QUESTIONS FOR REFLECTION

1 Describe and evaluate the approach to community relations within Cadbury, before and after the take-over by Kraft.
2 What, in your own view, should be the approach to community relations within Kraft, as part of its wider stakeholder management?

Source: This case study is based on BBC news (2010) 'Clegg attacks Brown over RBS funding for Cadbury bid', 20 January 2010 (see http://news.bbc.co.uk/1/hi/8470776.stm); Skapinker, M. (2010) 'Staff ownership can save a company's soul', *Financial Times*, 8 February 2010; Dixon, L. (2010) 'Mandelson attacks Kraft on Cadbury job losses', *The Times*, 10 February 2010; 'Rock-bottom morale putting Cadbury production at risk', *The Daily Mail*, 10 February 2010.

CHAPTER SUMMARY

13.5 Community relations is the practice of communicating and building relationships with the community. Effective community relations is nowadays about being a good corporate citizen. As a new emerging discipline within corporate communication, the area of community relations is, however, not often documented in standard texts on the subject or in training and educational programmes. This chapter has therefore discussed the basic concepts of corporate citizenship, corporate social responsibility and community relations, and has documented principles and approaches to how companies can communicate about their CSR and engage with communities in different ways and with varying degrees of commitment.

 ## DISCUSSION QUESTIONS

1 What is the difference between corporate citizenship and corporate social responsibility?
2 Describe in your own words the idea of a triple bottom line.
3 What would be the important objectives for an organization when engaging in community relations?

 ## KEY TERMS

Anti-corporate activism

Charitable donations

Community relations

Corporate citizenship

Corporate social responsibility

Democracy

Partnerships

Philanthropy

Social reporting

Transparency

Triple bottom line

Volunteering

 ## FURTHER READING

Burke, Edmund M. (1999), *Corporate Community Relations: The Principle of the Neighbour of Choice*. London: Praeger.

May, Steven K., Cheney, George and Roper, Juliet (2007), *The Debate over Corporate Social Responsibility*. Oxford: Oxford University Press.

Soule, Sarah A. (2009), *Contention and Corporate Social Responsibility*. Cambridge: Cambridge University Press.

NOTES

1 Marsden, C. (2000), 'The new corporate citizenship of big business: part of the solution to sustainability', *Business and Society Review*, 105: 9–25, quote on p. 11.

2 World Economic Forum (2003), *Global Competitiveness Reports*. Davos, Switzerland: World Economic Forum, p. 4.

3 Holme, R. and Watts, P. (2000) *Corporate Social Responsibility: Making Good Business Sense*. World Business Council for Sustainable Development, p. 8.

4 Gray, R., Owen, D. and Maunders, K. (1987), *Corporate Social Reporting: Accounting and Accountability*. Hemel Hempstead: Prentice-Hall, quote on p. 4.

5 Windsor, D. (2001), 'The future of corporate social responsibility', *The International Journal of Organizational Analysis*, 9 (3): 225–256, quote on p. 226; see also Pavelin, S., Brammer, S.J. and Porter, L.A. (2009), 'Corporate charitable giving, multinational companies and countries of concern', *Journal of Management Studies*, 46: 575–596.

6 See, for example, Margolis, J.D. and Walsh, J.P. (2003), 'Misery loves companies: rethinking social initiatives by business', *Administrative Science Quarterly*, 48: 268–305; and Orlitzky, M. Schmidt, F.L. and Rynes, S.L. (2003), 'Corporate social and financial performance: a meta-analysis', *Organization Studies*, 24: 403–441.

7 Elkington, J. (1997), *Cannibals with Forks: The Triple Bottom Line of the 21st Century Business*. London: Capstone Publishing Limited.

8 Carroll, A.B. (1991), 'The pyramid of corporate social responsibility: toward the moral management of organizational stakeholders', *Business Horizons*, 34 (4): 39–48.

9 Deetz, S. (2007), 'Corporate governance, corporate social responsibility, and communication', in May, S., Cheney, G. and Roper, J. (eds), *The Debate over Corporate Social Responsibility*. Oxford: Oxford University Press, pp. 267–278.

10 McKinsey (2006) 'Global survey of business executives', *The Mckinsey Quarterly*, 1 (1), pp. 1–10.

11 Morsing, M. and Schultz, M. (2006), 'Corporate social responsibility communication: stakeholder information, response and involvement strategies', *Business Ethics: A European Review*, 15: 323–338.

12 Soule, Sarah A. (2009), *Contention and Corporate Social Responsibility*. Cambridge: Cambridge University Press.

13 See, for example, Rousseau, D.M. (1995), *Psychological Contract in Organizations: Understanding Written and Unwritten Agreements*. London: Sage.

14 Burke, Edmund M. (1999), *Corporate Community Relations: The Principle of the Neighbour of Choice*. London: Praeger, p. 15.

15 Burke (1999), pp. 130–133.

16 MacAllister, Terry (2007), Campaigners urge Shell to put profits into clean-up', The Guardian, 31st of January 2007.

GLOSSARY OF CORPORATE COMMUNICATION AND OTHER COMMUNICATION TERMS

4 Ps Product, Price, Promotion (marketing communications) and Place (distribution)

Above the line All media that remunerate agencies on the basis of commission (e.g., advertising)

Acceptance strategy Organizational claim accepting responsibility or culpability for a crisis

Accidents A damaging incident that may be harmful to an organization or individual persons; includes product defects, employee injuries and natural disasters

Accommodative strategy Organizational claim accepting responsibility for a crisis and preventing it from happening again

Account management The process by which a communications (PR, advertising) or marketing agency or supplier manages the needs of a client (corporation)

Accountability An evaluation of the contribution of functions or activities against their costs

Active issue An active point or matter of discussion, debate, or dispute between an organization and one or more of its stakeholder groups

Added value The increase in worth of an organization's product or services as a result of a particular activity. In the context of communications, the activity might be effective stakeholder dialogue

Additive change A change that is an incremental addition to the existing strategies, routines and procedures within an organization (*see also* Substitutive change)

Advertisement A paid-for dedicated space or time in which only the advertiser is represented

Advertising The process of gaining the public's attention through paid media announcements

Advertising agency An agency specializing in advertising and other marketing communications on behalf of a client organization

Advertising campaign A planned use and scheduling of advertising over a defined period of time

Advertising media Paid-for communications channels such as newspaper (print) or television

Advertising value equivalent (AVE) A measure of evaluating press publicity by counting the column inches of press publicity and seconds of air time gained and then multiplying the total by the advertising rate of the media in which the coverage appeared

Advertorial An editorial feature paid for or sponsored by an advertiser

Advocacy An attempt to try to change stakeholder expectations and public opinions on an issue through issue campaigns and lobbying

Advocacy advertising Advocacy advertising expresses a viewpoint on a given issue, often on behalf of an institution or organization

Agenda setting Media reporting on organizations that primes awareness of an organization and certain content about that organization

Alignment A situation where the projected identity of an organization, as symbolized by its brands, is in line with the way in which the company is actually perceived by stakeholders

Ambient media Originally known as 'fringe media', ambient media are communications platforms that surround us in everyday life, from petrol pump advertising to advertising projected on to buildings to advertising on theatre tickets, cricket pitches or even pay slips

Ansoff matrix Model relating marketing strategy to general strategic direction. It maps product-market strategies – e.g., market penetration, product development, market development and diversification – on a matrix showing new versus existing products along one axis and new versus existing markets along the other

Anti-corporate activism Political activism directed at specific organizations, industry sectors or general issues associated with corporations and capitalism

Association strategy Claim of connecting the organization to things positively valued by stakeholders and publics

Attention The act or faculty of attending, especially by directing the mind to a message or activity

Attitude A learned predisposition towards an object (e.g., organization, product), person or idea

Audience fragmentation The process or trend whereby audience segments become more heterogeneous and divided (and therefore more difficult to reach in one)

Audit *See* Communication audit

Authenticity The quality or condition of communication (e.g., leadership communication) being authentic, trustworthy, or genuine

Awareness Measure of a proportion of target audience who have heard of the organization, product or service

BCG matrix Boston Consulting Group matrix based on market share and market growth rate

Below the line Non-media advertising or promotion when no commission has been paid to the advertising agency. Includes direct mail, point-of-sale displays and giveaways

Benchmark studies Studies comparing organizations in a particular sector or industry, used to create yardstick comparisons for improvement and allowing outsiders to evaluate the relative performance of organizations

Blog A blog (short for weblog) is a personal online journal that is frequently updated and intended for general public consumption

Boundary spanning The role of corporate communication to act as an intermediary between the organization and external stakeholder groups

Brand The set of physical attributes of a product or service, together with the beliefs and expectations surrounding it – a unique combination which the name or logo of the product or service should evoke in the mind of the audience

Brand acceptance The condition wherein an individual, usually a customer, is well disposed towards a brand and will accept credible messages

Brand awareness The condition wherein an individual, usually a customer, is aware of the brand

Brand equity The notion that a respected brand name adds to the value of a product (and therefore generates returns to an organization upon customer purchase)

Brand image The perception of a brand in the eyes of an individual, usually a customer

Brand loyalty Extent to which individuals, usually customers, repurchase (or utilize) a particular branded product or service

Brand management The process by which marketers attempt to optimize the 'marketing mix' for a specific brand

Brand positioning The way in which a brand is communicated to its target market, describing the attributes and values of the brand and its added value/appeal relative to its customers and the competition

Branded identity A structure whereby businesses and product brands of an organization each carry their own name (without endorsement by the parent company) and are seemingly unrelated to each other

Bridging Organizations adapting their activities so that they conform with external expectations and claims of important stakeholder groups

Budgeting The costing of communication activities against a specified amount of money

Buffering Organizations trying to ignore the claims and interests from stakeholders or stop them from interfering with internal operations

Business communication The (vocational) discipline of writing, presenting and communicating in a professional context

Business plan A strategic document showing cash flow, forecasts and direction of a company

Business strategy The means by which a business works towards achieving its stated aims

Business-to-business Relating to the sale of a product for any use other than personal consumption. The buyer may be a manufacturer, a reseller, a government body, a non-profit-making institution, or any organization other than an ultimate consumer

Business-to-consumer Relating to the sale of a product for personal consumption. The buyer may be an individual, family or other group, buying to use the product themselves or for end use by another individual

Buzz Media and public attention given to a company, its products or services

Campaign The use of a mediated form of communication (e.g., mass media advertising) aimed at specific stakeholder audiences at a particular pre-planned point in time

Centralization Bringing tasks and/or activities together as the responsibility of one person or department in an organization

Change communication Communication activities to support the formulation, implementation and routinization of a change (e.g., restructuring) within an organization

Channel noise Confusion caused by too many messages trying to be delivered at one time

Channels The methods and media used by a company to communicate and interact with its stakeholders

Charitable donation A gift made by an individual or an organization to a non-profit organization, charity or private foundation

Clutter The total number of messages competing for attention of the audience; usually mentioned in the context of excessive amounts of communications

Cob-web method A technique whereby individuals rate an organization on a number of selected attributes, which are then visually represented in the form of a wheel or web with eight or more scaled dimensions

Communication audit A systematic survey of members of a target audience (often members of the media or potential customers) to determine awareness of or reaction to a message about a product, service or company

Communication climate The ease with which information flows freely between managers and employees through an organization's formal and informal networks

Communication effects The impact of communication programmes or campaigns on the awareness, opinions, reputations and behaviours of stakeholder groups

Communication efficiency The accomplishment of communication with a minimum expenditure of time, effort and resources

Communication facilitator Role in which practitioners act as liaisons, interpreters, information brokers and mediators between the organization and its stakeholders

Communication programme A set of communication activities and campaigns put in place to address ongoing needs for reputation building, as laid down in the overall communication strategy. A programme is reviewed periodically to determine whether its objectives have been met

Communication strategy The general set of communication objectives and related communication programmes or tactics chosen by an organization in order to support the corporate strategy of the organization

Community of practice A group of people who share a common interest in a particular domain or area, and is often created specifically with the goal of gaining knowledge and advancing ideas and technologies related to their field

Community relations The various forms of activity and communications companies use to establish and maintain a mutually beneficial relationship with the communities in which they operate

Competence Knowledge of a certain (professional) area that is difficult to emulate. A domain of knowledge or specific expertise that an individual needs to properly perform a specific job

Competitive advantage The product, proposition or benefit that puts a company ahead of its competitors

Competitors Companies that sell products or services in the same marketplace as one another

Consumer Individual who buys and uses a product or service

Consumer behaviour The buying habits and patterns of consumers in the acquisition and usage of goods and services

Consumer research Research into the characteristics, changes, usage and attitudes of consumers

Continuous research Research conducted constantly to pick up trends, issues, market fluctuations, etc.

Conversations Informal discussions; often used in the context of leadership and management to emphasize the importance of leaders or managers engaging in ongoing conversations with employees about the organization including any possible changes

Copy The written words (storyline, formatting, etc.) to appear in a communications medium (press release, commercial, etc.)

Copy date The date by which a publication or medium requires copy

Copy testing Research into reactions and responses to written copy

Copywriting Creative process by which written content is prepared for communication material

Corporate advertising Advertising by a firm where the corporate entity, rather than solely its products or services, is emphasized

Corporate brand *See* Monolithic identity

Corporate citizenship Expressions of involvement of an organization in matters concerning society as a whole

Corporate communication The function and process of managing communications between an organization and important stakeholder groups (including markets and publics) in its environment

Corporate frame The way in which an organization frames a decision or action when is briefing the media or the general public

Corporate identity The profile and values communicated by an organization.

The character a company seeks to establish for itself in the mind of its stakeholders, reinforced by consistent use of logos, colours, typefaces, etc.

Corporate image The way a company is perceived, based on a certain message and at a certain point in time. The immediate set of meanings inferred by an individual in confrontation or response to one or more signals from or about a particular organization at a single point in time

Corporate information and communication systems Technologies (e.g., intranet) used to disseminate information about the organization to employees across all ranks and functions within the organization in order to keep them informed on corporate matters

Corporate personality The core values of an organization, as shared by its members (*see also* Organizational identity)

Corporate public relations Public relations activities towards 'corporate' stakeholders, which excludes customers and prospects in a market. Includes issues management, community relations, investor relations, media relations, internal communication and public affairs

Corporate reputation An individual's collective representation of past images of an organization (induced through either communication or past experiences) established over time

Corporate social responsibility (CSR) Actions which do not have purely financial implications and which are demanded or expected of an organization by the society at large, often concerning ecological and social issues

Corporate strategy The general direction taken by a company with regard to its choice of businesses and markets and approach of its stakeholder groups

Council meeting A formal executive or advisory forum in which communication professionals and senior managers participate, for example in discussion brand and communication related issues and strategy

Coverage Percentage of target audience who have the opportunity to be confronted with the communications message at least once

Crisis A point of great difficulty or danger to the organization, possibly threatening its existence and continuity, and that requires decisive change

Crisis communication plan A set of pre-programmed activities and lines of communication preparing the organization for probable crisis scenarios

Crisis management The reactive response to a crisis in order to pre-empt or limit damage to the organization's reputation

Culture The general values and beliefs held and shared by members of an organization

Customer A person or company who purchases goods or services (not necessarily the end consumer)

DAGMAR Defining Advertising Goals for Measured Advertising Response – a model for planning advertising in such a way that its success can be quantitatively monitored

Database A collection of information about relevant data, e.g., information about past, current and potential customers

Database marketing Whereby customer information, stored in an electronic database, is utilized for targeting marketing activities. Information can be a mixture of what is gleaned from previous interactions with the customer and what is available from outside sources

Decoding Process where the receiver converts the symbolic forms transmitted by the sender

Democracy Form of government, also used as a term to indicate models of stakeholder participation and dialogue with organizations

Demographics Information describing and segmenting a population in terms of age, sex, income etc., which can be used to target communication campaigns

Departmental arrangement The administrative act of grouping or arranging disciplines, activities and people into departments

Depth interview An interview, usually one-to-one, exploring deeper motivations and beliefs

Design The visual design of an organization including its brand logos and visual house style (on letters, memos, reports, etc.)

Desk research Using publicly available and previous data (e.g., on certain issues, markets)

DESTEP Demographic, Economic, Social, Technological, Ecological, and Political analysis. A broad analysis of macro factors that may impinge upon an organization's business and operations

Dialogue strategy A process of communication in which both parties (organizations and stakeholders) mutually engage in an exchange of ideas and opinions

Differentiation (competitive strategy) A competitive strategy whereby the unique and added value of a product or service is emphasized (which then warrants a premium price)

Direct mail Delivery of an advertising or promotional message to customers or potential customers by mail

Direct marketing All activities which make it possible to offer goods or services or to transmit other messages to a segment of the population by post, telephone, email or other direct means

Direct response Communications (e.g., advertising) incorporating a contact method such as a phone number, address and enquiry form, website identifier or email address, with the intention of encouraging the recipient to respond directly to the advertiser by requesting more information, placing an order, etc.

Distance strategy Claim of distancing the organization from direct responsibility for the crisis

Distribution channels The process and ways of getting the goods from the manufacturer or supplier to the user

Dominant coalition The group of people, usually the executive or senior management team, within an organization making the important decisions (concerning the direction and focus of the firm, etc.)

Downward communication Electronic and verbal methods of informing employees about their organization, its performance, and their own performance in terms they can comprehend

Economic/market stake Where the interest of an individual or group in an organization is strictly financial or utilitarian (e.g., receiving a good quality product for paying money)

Elaboration likelihood model A theoretical model of how attitudes are formed and changed based on an 'elaboration continuum', which ranges from low elaboration (low involvement and attention) to high elaboration (high involvement and attention)

Emotional message style Attempts to provoke involvement and positive reactions through a reference to positive (or negative) emotions

Employee participation A general situation or specific communication mechanisms (e.g., on-line forum, feedback meetings) allowing employees to participate in the decision-making and operations of an organization

Employee voice A state in which employees are able to speak up, express opinions and are listened to by managers

Encoding The process of putting information into a symbolic form of words, pictures or images

Endorsed identity A structure whereby businesses and product brands of an organization are endorsed or badged in communications with the parent company name

Environmental scanning The process whereby the environment of an organization is continuously scanned for issues and trends, usually in relation to important stakeholder groups

Equal dissemination strategy A process of communication in which managers disseminate information to all stakeholders early, often and, most importantly, on an equal basis

Equal participation strategy Two-way communication (i.e., both disseminating information and soliciting input) between managers and stakeholders

Equity stakes Where the interest of an individual or group involves holding an equity stake (share) within the organization in question

Evaluation An assessment of the effects of a communication programme or campaign

Exchange The process by which two or more parties give up a desired resource to one another

Execution The act of carrying something out (usually a set of planned for communications programmes)

Executive team The senior management team of an organization, typically led by the Chief Executive Officer, responsible for the overall management and strategic direction of the firm

Expert prescriber A role in which a communication practitioner acts as a specialist on communication problems but largely independently of senior management

Exposure The condition of being exposed to a company-related message or activity

External analysis Study of the external environment of an organization, including factors such as customers, competition and social change

Faux pas A claim made by an external agent (e.g., NGO) that the organization violates accepted, although unwritten, social rules and expectations

FMCG Fast Moving Consumer Goods, such as packaged food, beverages, toiletries and tobacco

Focus groups A tool for market, communications and opinion research where small groups of people are invited to participate in guided discussions on the topic being researched

Forecasting Calculation of future events and performance

Formal research techniques *See* Informal research techniques

Formative evaluation A type of evaluation which has the purpose of improving communication programmes or campaigns

Frame alignment A situation where an organization's explanation of a decision, issue or event coincides with the way in which journalists think about the same decision, issue or event

Frame conflict Situation where journalists frame a corporate decision or action in a different way from how organizations explain it, or have previously framed these decisions or actions

Frame contest The negotiation between communication practitioners and journalists about the preferred angle to a story about an organization

Frame negotiation The process of communication professionals and journalists discussing the framing of a particular corporate issue or decision

Framing Presenting a story about an organization from a particular angle

Frequency Average number of times the target audience will have the opportunity to be confronted with (see) a certain communications message

Full service agency An agency that specializes in a whole range of communications disciplines and can assist the client in the full process of communications planning and execution

Gatekeeping research An analysis of the characteristics of a press release or video news release that allow them to 'pass through the gate' and appear in a news medium

Generic message style Straight claim about industry or cause with no assertion of superiority

Geodemographics A method of analysis combining geographic and demographic variables

Global brand A brand which has worldwide recognition (e.g., Coca-Cola)

Goal The primary and direct result a company is attempting to achieve through its communications efforts

Grass-roots campaigning People or society at a local level (e.g., citizens) rather than at the centre of major political activity who campaign on political or corporate issues

Hierarchy of effects The sequence of effects that audiences may go through from exposure to a message to, ultimately, behavioural change

Horizontal structure The informal and formal coordination mechanisms that can be used in organizations to coordinate the work done by communication professionals across departments and divisions within the organization

Image An individual's perceptions of an organization, product or service at a certain point in time

Identify and reply strategy Change communication strategy where managers or leaders respond to issues or change initiatives identified by employees at lower levels in the organization

Ideology Conventional ideas about society, for example as in the case of pre-set views of journalists or media organizations

Industrial goods Products or resources required by industrial companies

Industry coalition A collation of corporate organizations and interests representing a corporate voice to government and politicians

Influencer stake Where the interest or influence of an individual or group on an organization is one associated with

raising public awareness or influencing public opinion on the organization's decisions and actions

Infomercials An advertising commercial that provides extensive information

(In)formal research techniques Standardized methods for collecting and analysing data on stakeholder opinions, markets and industries.

Informational strategy A process of making information available a bout the organization to its stakeholders

Integration (integrated communication) The act of coordinating all communications so that the corporate identity is effectively and consistently communicated to internal and external groups

Intense issue Situation where an already active issue for debate (see active issue) has become a real challenge to an organization in terms of its reputation and ongoing operations

Intentional communications Message that an organization intends to convey

Intermediary Any individual or company in the distribution channel between the supplier and the final consumer

Internal analysis The study of a company's internal resources in order to assess opportunities, strengths or weaknesses

Internal communication All methods (internal newsletter, intranet) used by a firm to communicate with its employees

Interviews Part of media relations where journalists formally interview an official spokespersons or the CEO or other senior executives of an organization

Issue An unsettled matter (which is ready for a decision) or a point of conflict between an organization and one or more publics

Issues management The proactive attempt to identify and control issues in order to pre-empt or limit damage to the organization's reputation

Journalist A person engaged in journalism; especially a writer or editor for a news medium

Kelly grids *See* Repertory grids

Laddering A research technique whereby people's opinions are represented as a means–end chain. It is used to infer the basic values and motivations that drive people

Latent issue A development or trend in the public arena that can be detected and monitored, and which in time may result in an active issue that becomes associated in the public mind with an organization or industry sector

Leadership The skill and activity of leading others within an organization

Leadership communication The general skills of a leader in communicating to employees in an organizations; including visionary and transformational abilities to inspire and motivate employees as well as skills to initiate and maintain conversations

Legitimacy The assessment of an organization against the norms, values and expectations of its stakeholders in terms of what those stakeholders deem is acceptable and is favoured of the organization

Licensing The act of formally accrediting an agency or professional, often done by a professional association or legal body

Life cycle Stages through which a product or brand develops (*see* PLC)

Lifestyle Research classification based on shared values, attitude and personality

Likert scale Research scale which uses statements to indicate agreement or disagreement

Line extension Extending existing brands to other products in the same product category

Line function An organizational function that is directly involved in the core and operational business process (i.e., the 'line') of producing products and bringing them to market (e.g., marketing)

Lobbying A form of corporate advocacy with the intention of influencing decisions made by legislators and officials in the government

Logo A graphic, usually consisting of a symbol and/or group of letters, that identifies a company or brand

Low-cost (competitive strategy) Competitive strategy where the lower cost of a product or service is emphasized

Macro environment The external factors which affect a company's planning and performance, and are beyond its control, e.g., socio-economic, legal and technological change

Management communication Communication between managers and employees; restricted to dyads and small groups

Manager (communications manager) Practitioner who makes strategy or programme decisions concerning communications and is held accountable for programme success or failure and who engages in research, strategic planning and management of communications

Market A defined group for whom a product is or may be in demand (and for whom an organization creates and maintains products and service offerings)

Market development The process of growing sales by offering existing products (or new versions of them) to new customer groups (as opposed to simply attempting to increase the company's share of current markets)

Market orientation Steadfast adherence to the marketing concept: an approach in which customer needs and wants are the underlying determinants of an organization's direction and its marketing programmes

Market penetration The attempt to grow one's business by obtaining a larger market share in an existing market

Market research The gathering and analysis of data relating to marketplaces or customers; any research which leads to more market knowledge and better-informed decision-making

Market segmentation The division of the marketplace into distinct subgroups or segments, each characterized by particular tastes and requiring a specific marketing mix

Market share A company's sales of a given product or set of products to a given set of customers, expressed as a percentage of total sales of all such products to such customers

Market structure The character of an industry, based on the number of firms, barriers to entry, extent of product differentiation, control over price, and the importance of non-price competition

Marketing The management process responsible for identifying, anticipating and satisfying customer requirements profitably

Marketing audit A comprehensive and systematic review and appraisal of every aspect of a firm's marketing programme, its organization, activities, strategies and people

Marketing communications All methods (advertising, direct marketing, sales promotion, personal selling, and marketing public relations) used by a firm to communicate with its customers and prospective customers

Marketing concept The process by which the marketer responds to the needs and wants of the consumer

Marketing mix The combination of marketing inputs that affect customer motivation and behaviour. These inputs traditionally encompass four controllable variables, 'the 4 Ps': Product, Price, Promotion and Place

Marketing objective A market target to be achieved reflecting corporate strategy

Marketing public relations The use of what are traditionally seen as public relations tools (media, free publicity) within

marketing programmes that are used to reach marketing objectives

Marketing strategy The set of objectives which an organization allocates to its marketing function in order to support the overall corporate strategy, together with the broad methods chosen to achieve these objectives

Matrix structure A structure where a professional has a dual reporting relationship. This structure aims to foster both functional expertise and coordination at the same time

Media 1. Members or tools for disseminating the news; unbiased third parties (press representatives) 2. Communication channels for a certain campaign

Media coverage Mention in the media of a company, its products or services

Media favourability Positive news coverage of an organization in which the organization is praised for its actions or is associated with activities that should raise its reputation

Media monitoring Research that aims to survey coverage of companies in the media

Media plan Recommendation for a media schedule including dates, publications, TV regions, etc.

Media relations The function or process of gaining positive media attention and coverage

Media richness The ability of a medium to allow for immediate feedback between the two parties and for expressing and articulating the message in different ways

Media schedule Records of campaign bookings made or a proposal (with dates, costs, etc.) for a campaign

Merchandising Traditionally, in-store promotion and displays

Message style The way in which a message is given form and delivered to a target audience

Micro environment The immediate context of a company's operations, including such elements as suppliers, customers and competitors

MIIS Management Intelligence and Information System – system of collecting and examining environmental and/or market data

Mission A company's overriding purpose in line with the values or expectations of stakeholders

Mission statement A company's summary of its business philosophy and direction

Monolithic identity A structure whereby businesses and product brands of an organization all carry the same corporate name

Multinational A corporation whose operational and marketing activities cover multiple countries over the world

Need to know strategy A process of communication in which managers keep quiet about decisions or changes except to those stakeholders who really need to know or who explicitly express a desire for the information

Neo-classical economic theory Theory where firms operate as strict economic agents and are positioned at the centre of the economy. Their decisions and behaviour is largely motivated by financial gains and rational decision making to increase profits

News desk The department or section of a newspaper, television, or other news organizations that writes, edits, or releases news. Desks are often divided around specific topical content or subject angles

News frame The way in which journalists frame a news item associated with an organization

News routines The way in which news is produced in a particular media organization, starting with the journalist consulting sources and ending with the editor making the final decisions about an article or feature

Niche marketing The marketing of a product to a small and well-defined segment of the marketplace

Noise *See* Channel noise

Non-existence strategy Claim made by an organization denying an issue or crisis

Non-verbal communications Transmission of a message without the use of words or language

Objective A company's defined and measurable aims for a given period

One-time studies Studies focused on measuring the effects at a single instant in time, e.g., after a corporate advertising campaign

Online newsroom An online facility, often on the corporate website, archiving press releases, video materials and company reports

Organizational change Initiative of changing the organization, for example in terms of its structure, identity and culture, products and services or general ways of working

Organizational identification The perception of oneness with or belongingness to an organization, where the individual defines him or herself in terms of the organization(s) of which he or she is a member

Organizational identity The set of values shared by members of an organization (*see also* Corporate personality)

Organizational silence A state in which employees refrain from speaking up and withhold information about potential problems or issues

OTH Opportunities to Hear – the number of opportunities a target consumer has of hearing an advertisement

OTS Opportunities to See – the number of opportunities a target consumer has of seeing an advertisement

Output analysis A measurement of the amount of exposure or attention that the organization receives in the media; often achieved by collecting press clippings (copies of stories or articles in the press) and by recording the degree of exposure in terms of column inches in print media, the number of minutes of air time in the electronic media or the number of cites on the web

Partnership promotion Joint promotions aiming to achieve additional exposure

Partnerships Relationship between an organization and local public institutions in bettering the community and increasing welfare

Perception The way a corporation, product, event or stimulus is received and evaluated by an individual

Personal selling One-to-one communication between the seller and prospective purchaser

Persuasion A means by which a person or organization tries to influence and convince another person to believe something or do something, using reasoning and coaxing in a compelling and convincing way

Persuasive strategy A process of communication in which an organization, through campaigns, meetings and discussions with stakeholders, tries to change and tune the knowledge, attitude, and behaviours of stakeholders in a way that is favourable to the organization

Philanthropy The act and effort of increasing the well-being and welfare of communities through charitable aid or donations

Pitch A prepared sales presentation by an agency to a client organization, usually on a one-on-one basis

Planning Setting communication activities and campaigns on the basis of communication objectives and against a time-line

PLC Product life cycle. The supposed stages of a product, e.g., birth, growth, maturity and decline

Political action committee A committee formed by business, labour or other special-interest groups to raise money and make contributions to the campaigns of political candidates whom they support

Porter's five forces An analytic model developed by Michael E. Porter. The five forces, in terms of which the model analyses businesses and industries, are: Buyers, Suppliers, Substitutes, New Entrants and Rivals

Portfolio (and portfolio analysis) The set of products or services which a company decides to develop and market. Portfolio analysis is the process of comparing the contents of the portfolio to see which products or services are the most promising and deserving of further investment, and which should be discontinued

POS Point-Of-Sale. The location, usually within a retail outlet, where the customer decides whether to make a purchase

Position–importance matrix A tool to categorize stakeholders and publics according to their position on a particular issue and according to their importance to the organization

Positioning The creation of an image for a company, product or service in the minds of stakeholders, both specifically to that entity and in relation to competitive organizations and offerings

Power–interest matrix A tool to categorize stakeholders on the basis of the power that they have and the extent to which they are likely to have or show an interest in the organization's activities

PR *See* Public relations

Pre-emptive message style A generic claim about an organization with a suggestion of superiority

Press agentry The use of press agents, promoters and publicists to promote and publicize an organization and its products or services through the media; often used to describe communications during the early decades of the twentieth century

Press conference An organized gathering or event where an organization announces decisions or fiscal results to journalists

Press kit Several press deliverables combined in one package (usually a folder)

Press release A paper or electronic document submitted to the media with the intent of gaining media coverage

Prestige The level of respect or status associated with an organization and which may reflect upon its members

Problem-solving process facilitator Role in which communication practitioners collaborate with other managers to define and solve organizational problems

Process documentation A way of coordinating the tasks and activities of communication professionals by mapping and documenting their work processes (typically through flow-charts)

Process effects Evaluation of the cost-effective manner in which a communication programme or campaign has been planned and executed

Projective technique Qualitative research technique by which an individual is asked to respond to ambiguous stimuli such as vague statements or objects; designed to measure feelings, opinions, attitudes and motivations

Proposition The message that the advertiser wants the customer to focus upon

Psychographics A base for segmentation derived from attitude and behavioural variables

Public People who mobilize themselves against the organization on the basis of some common issue or concern to them

Public affairs The public policy aspect of corporate communication

Public information The use of writers and publicists to inform and reassure the general public of corporate practices; often used to describe communications before the Second World War

Public relations The function or activity that aims to establish and protect the reputation of a company or brand, and to create mutual understanding between the organization and the segments of the public with whom it needs to communicate

Publicity Media coverage

Publicly syndicated rankings Public measurement and ranking of large and visible firms often within a country or industry sector

Pull strategy Pull communications, in contrast to push communications, address customers directly with a view to getting them to demand the product, and hence 'pull' it down through the distribution chain. It focuses on advertising and above-the-line activities

Push strategy Push communications relies on the next link in the distribution chain – e.g., a wholesaler or retailer – to 'push' out products to the customer. It revolves around sales promotions, such as price reductions and point-of-sale displays, and other below-the-line activities

Q-sort Type of reputation research where each respondent is asked to rate and rank statements about the organization written on cards (qualitative and quantitative research methods mentioned in list)

Qualitative methods see qualitative research

Quantitative methods see quantitative research

Qualitative research Research that does not use numerical data but relies on interviews, 'focus groups', 'repertory grid', and the like, usually resulting in findings which are more detailed but also more subjective than those of 'quantitative research'

Quantitative research Research that concentrates on statistics and other numerical data, gathered through opinion polls, customer satisfaction surveys, etc.

***Quid pro quo* strategy** A process of communication in which managers give more communicative attention to those stakeholders who have something valuable (e.g., expertise, approval power, resources) for a decision or change process

Rational message style A superiority claim based upon actual accomplishments or delivered benefits by the organization

Reach The percentage or number of people exposed to a media vehicle at least once

Recall Used by researchers to establish how memorable a certain communications message was

Receiver In communications theory, the party receiving the message

Repertory grid A technique for representing the attitudes and perceptions of individuals, also called Personal Construct Technique. The technique can be useful in developing market research (and other) questionnaires

Reputation *See* Corporate reputation

Return on investment (ROI) The value that an organization derives from investing in a project

Sales promotion A range of techniques used to engage the purchaser. These may include discounting, coupons, guarantees, free gifts, competitions, vouchers, demonstrations, bonus commission and sponsorship

Sampling The use of a statistically representative subset as a proxy for an entire population, e.g., in order to facilitate quantitative market research

Secondary research *See* Desk research

Segmentation *See* Market segmentation

Selective attention Where receivers only notice some of the message presented

Selective distortion To see and hear differently from the message presented

Selective exposure Idea that individuals only expose themselves to certain messages

Selective perception The process of screening out information that is not of interest and retaining information of use

Sender In communications theory, the party sending the message

Share of voice Calculation of a brand's share of media expenditure in a particular category

Shareholder value The worth of a company from the point of view of its shareholders

Skill (communication skills) The ability to produce or craft something (e.g., a written document by way of writing skills) or perform a certain task

Slogan Frequently repeated phrases that provide continuity in messages and campaigns of a certain corporation, its products or services

SMART objectives Objectives that are Specific, Measurable, Achievable, Realistic and Timely

SME Small to Medium Enterprise. Variously defined. According one EU definition, it must employ under 250 people, have either a turnover of less than £40 million or net balance sheet assets of less than £27 million, and not be more than 25 per cent owned by a larger company

Social media Media that are enable social interaction, using web-based technologies that turn communication into interactive and often instant dialogues

Socio-economic theory Theory where firms act at least in part as moral agents, balancing economic interests against social or normative imperatives to attend to social and environmental issues and societal groups such as local communities

Social reporting The social and environmental issues and achievements declared by an organization and as assessed and written down in a formal report

Spin The attempt to manipulate the depiction of news or events in the media through artful public relations; often used with derogatory connotations

Spokesblogger An official spokesperson for an organization who, while publishing an independent blog, often does not speak only for him or herself, but also on behalf of his/her employer or the organization that he/she represents

Spokesperson An official representative of the organization who deals with journalists and the media

Sponsorship A specialized form of sales promotion where a company will help fund an event or support a business venture in return for publicity

Staff function An organizational function (e.g., communications) carrying no direct executive power over the primary operational process or responsibility for it, but fulfils an advisory role to other functions within the organization

Stakeholder Any group or individual who can affect or is affected by the achievement of the organization's objectives

Stakeholder audit A systematic survey of stakeholders to determine the nature of the relationship, issues and possible reactions to corporate actions

Stakeholder collaboration A situation where an organization builds long-term relationships through working together with stakeholders on issues of common concern

Stakeholder mapping An analytical tool whereby stakeholder groups are identified and their relationship to the organization becomes visually represented in a map

Stakeholder salience The visibility or importance of a stakeholder based on their possession of one or more of three attributes: power, legitimacy, and urgency

Storytelling The act of telling stories or narratives in an organization to persuade employees or other stakeholders into certain ways of thinking about an organization

Strategic intent The general direction of an organization, often articulated in objectives, together the general patterns of actions that will be taken to achieve these objectives

Strategy General broad patterns of actions to accomplish corporate, market and/or communications objectives

Substitutive change A drastic change within an organization that changes the very *status quo* and previous ways of working

Suffering strategy Claim that the organization suffers from the crisis or a public policy decision

Supportive behaviour Behaviours of stakeholders that are positive and supportive towards the organization (e.g., investing in shares, buying products and services, etc.), often in a way that is desired by the organization

SWOT A method of analysis which examines a company's Strengths, Weaknesses, Opportunities and Threats;

often used as part of the development process for a corporate or marketing plan

Symbolic association message style Claim of associating the organization with general (culturally shared and recognized) moral values, symbols and sentiments

Symbolism All of the design parameters of an organization that may convey or symbolize an image of the organization; including its office buildings, dress code and visual lay-out of its facilities and day-to-day operations

Tactics Specific action items to support strategies and objectives

Target audience The key groups or individuals that a company wants to receive with its communications messages

Target market The segment of a market at which marketing efforts are directed

Targeting The use of market segmentation to select and address a key group of potential purchasers

Team A group of professionals, possibly from different departments and divisions, who work together on a pre-defined task or project (e.g., the launch of a new product or communicating during a crisis)

Technician (communication technician) A practitioner who in his/her day-to-day work focuses primarily on programmatic and tactical communication activities such as writing, editing, producing brochures, etc.; a technician thus tactically implements decisions made by others

Telemarketing The marketing of a product or service over the telephone

Tell and sell strategy Change communication strategy where managers or leaders tell employees of a proposed change initiative and then try to sell it to them in order to gain their buy-in and support in realising the change

Terrorist attacks The calculated use of violence (or the threat of violence) against civilians or organizations in order to attain goals that are political or ideological in nature; this is done through intimidation or coercion or instilling fear

Themed message Messages that are identified as central to the organization's reputation and that are designed to change or reinforce perceptions in line with the vision of how the organization wants to be known

Through the line Mixture of below- and above-the-line communications

Tracking Surveying attitudes and perceptions (images and reputations) of individuals to an organization, products or services on a continuous basis

Trademark Sign or device, often with distinctive lettering, that symbolizes a brand

Transgression An intentional act taken by an organization that knowingly places stakeholders or publics at risk of harm

Transparency The state where the image or reputation of an organization held by stakeholder groups is similar to the actual and/or projected identity of an organization

Triple bottom line The idea that organizations have social ('people') and ecological ('planet') responsibilities besides their economic imperative of generating of profits and healthy financial accounts

Underscore and explore strategy Change communication strategy where managers or leaders set the agenda for a change but then allow employees to work out the implications and suggest ways in which the change can best be realised

Unintentional communication A message that an organization does not intend to convey

Upward communication Information from employees that is cast upwards towards managers within the organization; involves information about the employee him/herself, information about co-workers, information about organizational practices and policies, and information about what needs to be done and how it can be done

USP Unique Selling Proposition. The benefit that a product or service can deliver to customers that is not offered by any competitor; one of the fundamentals of effective marketing and business

Vertical structure the way in which tasks and activities (and the disciplines that they represent) are divided and arranged into departments (defined as the departmental arrangement) and located in the hierarchy of authority within an organization. The solid vertical lines that connect the boxes on an organization chart depict this vertical structure and the authority relationships involved.

Vision The long-term aims and aspirations of the company for itself

Volunteering The act of people working on behalf of others or a particular cause without payment for their time and services

Web 2.0 Web applications that facilitate interactive information sharing, interoperability, user-centred design and collaboration on the World Wide Web

Withhold and uphold strategy Change communication strategy where managers or leaders do not tell employees about an anticipated or planned change initiative and uphold the party-line when they are being challenged or quizzed by employees

Word-of-mouth The spreading of information through human interaction alone

Zero-based media planning A review of media options during communications planning based on research, analysis and insight, not habit and preference

INDEX

Page numbers in *italics* indicate figures and tables
Page numbers in **bold** indicate case studies and examples